INSIDE THE WARREN COURT

Inside
the Warren Court

BERNARD SCHWARTZ

with STEPHAN LESHER

1983
Doubleday & Company, Inc.
Garden City, New York

Library of Congress Cataloging in Publication Data
Schwartz, Bernard, 1923–
Inside the Warren court, 1953–1969.
1. United States. Supreme Court—History.
I. Lesher, Stephan. II. Title.
KF8742.S33   1983   347.73′26′09
347.3073509
ISBN 0-385-18326-7
Library of Congress Catalog Card Number 83-1980

*For Aileen
and to the memory of Lila and Murray Lesher*

CONTENTS

INTRODUCTORY NOTE

This account of what went on behind the scenes in the Warren Court is based on material never before published. It was amassed by Bernard Schwartz from the conference notes and docket books of five justices, and the correspondence, notes, diaries, memoranda, and draft opinions of seven justices.

Schwartz also interviewed the living members of the Warren Court (except for Thurgood Marshall), Chief Justice Warren E. Burger, Judge Earl Warren, Jr., Governor Edmund G. (Pat) Brown, some thirty former law clerks of Chief Justice Warren, and others, and undertook further extensive research on the Court and the cases discussed. A more scholarly book on Chief Justice Warren and his Court was written by Schwartz and is being published by New York University Press.

Stephan Lesher then researched and developed additional material concerning the contemporaneous events surrounding the Warren Court's deliberations, most of the historic settings in which the Court's operations unfold, and did most of the writing for this version. Acknowledgments and documentation are contained in the N.Y.U. Press book.

In the main, this book avoids making value judgments on the relative strengths and contributions of the various justices. Their actions and words, especially those which had never been known before, should be allowed to speak for themselves.

The goal was to provide a full and fair portrait of how the United States Supreme Court and its members manage to function.

INSIDE THE WARREN COURT

Midwife to Change

JUST AFTER FIVE O'CLOCK on a hot July day in 1974, William J. Brennan, Jr., left his chambers in the nation's ornate marble temple to justice that one predecessor, Harlan F. Stone, had called "bombastically pretentious," and climbed into his red VW square-back sedan.

Driving from the Supreme Court, he turned west on Constitution Avenue and headed to Georgetown University Hospital, where his old comrade-in-the-law Earl Warren was being treated for a heart attack—his third that year—that had felled him a week earlier.

Brennan found Warren, then eighty-three, surprisingly alert and in good spirits. The man whom Brennan fondly called "Super Chief," and who had avidly followed politics and the course of jurisprudence since his retirement from the bench five years before, was eager to hear the latest on the celebrated Nixon tapes case.

Brennan had a lot to confide. At three o'clock that afternoon, Tuesday, July 9, the Supreme Court justices had concluded their conference on whether President Nixon must surrender his potentially incriminating Watergate tapes to the United States district court.

Those tapes, it was widely believed, contained the "smoking

gun" evidence sought by the Special Prosecutor and by congressional investigators of Richard Nixon's participation in a felonious "cover-up" of illegal acts committed on behalf of his administration. The President had maneuvered politically and had fought legally to maintain possession of the tapes—and the primacy of executive privilege. He even had threatened obliquely that, if a less than overwhelming majority of the Supreme Court ordered him to give them up, he might refuse.

The eight justices participating in the conference, Brennan told Warren, had decided unanimously that Nixon must turn over the crucial tapes to the court. It was a decision that, one month later, despite Nixon's pugnacity, would force the removal from office of a President for the first time in the nation's history.

The case had provoked a "lively discussion" at the conference, Brennan said. "It was very quickly apparent," he told Warren, "that the President would be treated like any other person."

Central to their unanimity was the reaffirmation of the key assertion of *Marbury* v. *Madison,* handed down one hundred and seventy-one years earlier by Chief Justice John Marshall, that "it is, emphatically, the province and duty of the judicial department, to say what the law is."

Brennan had suggested to Warren's successor, Chief Justice Warren Burger, that the Court might deliver a joint opinion, as it had done only once before, in its decision ordering prompt integration in the schools of Little Rock, Arkansas. Brennan believed the action would dramatically reinforce the justices' unanimity.

Burger disagreed. Chosen by Nixon to replace Warren because, Nixon explained, "I happen to believe that the Constitution should be strictly interpreted," Burger said simply, "The responsibility is on my shoulders."

When Brennan told Warren the news, the old Chief lifted himself from the pillows.

"Thank God, thank God, thank God!" Warren declared fervently. "If you don't do it this way, Bill, it's the end of the country as we have known it."

Earl Warren sank back on the bed. The judiciary had again wielded ultimate political power in the United States. It had issued a final judgment that not even a President, facing disgrace and, possibly, prison, dared resist.

And, this time, the Supreme Court had not bested just *any* President, but the man hated by Earl Warren as "a cheat, a liar, and a crook."

Less than three hours later, with what must have been a sweet sense of victory flickering through his mind during his final moments, Earl Warren was dead. The institution he served for sixteen years, from 1953 to 1969, lived on. It was a period in which the Supreme Court furiously generated precedent after legal precedent that would touch more American lives, then and later, more directly than any other institution or series of events in the twentieth century save the Great Depression.

That sixteen-year period would be known to history as the Warren Court. Its special nature was recognized by Warren's colleagues when, in an unprecedented action, they requested that his flag-draped casket and his custom-made judicial chair be placed in the Supreme Court's Great Hall. As mourners and admirers filed past Warren's bier, the opinion sealing the fate of Burger's political sponsor was being circulated among the justices.

For most of its existence, the Supreme Court, when it chose to test its authority, had overwhelmed Presidents, overruled Congress, had given life and freedom to uncounted thousands with the mercy of Hosea's God—and had taken those gifts away from thousands more with the harsh justice of Amos's.

The years of the Warren Court, however, spanned—and, perhaps, spawned—the greatest American social and political revolutions since the War Between the States.

When Warren became Chief Justice of the United States, most black Americans were so invisible they were forbidden to drink from the same public water fountains as whites; rural America held the reins of government—and, through it, wielded disproportionate influence on the course of education, health, welfare, transportation, commerce, and communications; Senator Joseph McCarthy had reached his pinnacle of terror; apathy characterized the intelligentsia and the poor alike.

By the time Warren stepped down, white patrimony had

yielded to black power; political dominance had been transplanted whole to the cities, where the majority could decide the nation's fate; national paranoia had shifted from Communists to criminals; civil disorder—ignited by poverty at home and warfare abroad—rocked areas as disparate as urban cores and college campuses.

America had changed irrevocably—and the Warren Court had been midwife to that change, if not its sire.

Yet, whether deciding the fates of nations, Presidents, plutocrats, or paupers, the Warren Court invariably acted with roughly equal dollops of law, precedent, politics, personality, pettiness, flashes of intuition, occasional genius, pure chance, and plain patriotism.

That it was obeyed, however controversial its decisions, is a tribute to the instinctive understanding by a free people (the members of the Supreme Court principally among them) that adherence to the rule of law, however unpopular or wrongheaded that rule may sometimes be, is paramount to all other considerations in a democracy. It is also testimony to the Supreme Court's ultimate reflection of the popular will, despite its insulation from electoral politics, its inherently undemocratic structure, and the almost impenetrable secrecy in which it operates.

In expanding civil liberties, broadening political freedom, extending the franchise, reinforcing freedoms of speech, assembly, and religion, limiting the power of the politicians in smoke-filled rooms, defining the limits of police power, the Warren Court had no equal in American history.

The same Warren Court, however, shaded its own landmark rulings in Warren's last years. Warren himself supported a stop-and-frisk law, objected to liberalizing state residency requirements for welfare applicants, and refused to classify pornography as free speech. The fabled champion of the Bill of Rights, Hugo Black, sharply opposed overturning the arrests of blacks for sit-ins—the technique of defying color barriers at segregated restaurants and other quasi-public facilities.

The legendary traditionalism of Felix Frankfurter faded when, almost single-handedly, he prevented the Supreme Court from voting precipitously—and fractiously—in the school segregation cases. And the supposed studied civility among justices of the Supreme Court frequently came unglued in the face of deep-seated animosities that erupted among several of the prima donnas of the Warren Court. Robert Jackson was convinced that Black's dislike for him had prevented the appointment of Jackson as Chief Justice; Black believed that Frankfurter intervened to stop Black's appointment as Chief Justice. Warren forbade his clerks from "leaking" information to Frankfurter; Frankfurter sometimes thought Warren's far-reaching opinions bordered on ignorance.

Black resented public acclaim of Warren for legal principles Black maintained he had formulated before Warren's appointment to the Bench. Warren explained away Black's late-career anti-civil rights positions by suggesting, cattily, that his southern colleague "wants to be buried in Alabama."

And justice often was achieved in unexpected ways.

A casual comment by Tom Clark in an elevator resulted in adoption of the extraordinarily influential exclusionary rule in state cases—the prohibition against securing a state conviction by using evidence gathered by illegal means. Clark once privately requested information from J. Edgar Hoover concerning a pending case on whether accused Communists could examine evidence against them.

To accommodate an objection by Justice Potter Stewart in a draft dissent, a majority tempered an opinion that would have prohibited the presence of television news cameras in court-rooms.

President Eisenhower dispatched his Solicitor General to bring pressure on Warren to uphold the government in a case involving the jurisdiction of a foreign court over an American serviceman. Attorney General John Mitchell sent an aide to persuade the Court to modify a ruling that Mitchell feared would lead to disclosure that the government was tapping the telephone lines of forty-six foreign embassies in Washington.

Some of the Court's most important opinions were drafted and written largely by clerks barely out of law school; other insertions by clerks—such as the famous reference in the school segregation opinion to Gunnar Myrdal's sociological study of racism—were debated extensively by the public but had been of little interest to the justices.

Some justices, such as Charles Whittaker, were bewildered by the law's complexities; once, feeling wholly at sea after a peroration by Frankfurter, Whittaker broke into tears. Other justices, such as William O. Douglas, dashed off dissents so fast and so frequently many of their colleagues believed some of them were, from a legal view, useless and meaningless.

Seemingly, the only nexus among the justices in the Warren years (and, by implication, throughout the Court's history) is that, whatever their legal perspectives or personal views, they all cared deeply about the law, about the ultimate authority of the Supreme Court, and about the impact of their decisions on events both great and small.

In arriving at decisions, whether seemingly routine or historically wrenching, the Warren Court frequently defied expectation and challenged orthodoxy.

Indeed, from the moment Earl Warren demanded that President Eisenhower make good his pledge to appoint him to the first vacancy on the Supreme Court—a Court dominated by some of the most memorable and talented justices in America's history—it seemed certain that whatever direction the Warren Court might take, predictability and legal orthodoxy would not be among its principal characteristics.

ONE

A Jap's a Jap

THE WORLD INTO which Earl Warren was born in 1891 was, as it usually is, filled with beauty, promise, ugliness, and danger.

Van Gogh, Cézanne, Gauguin, and Toulouse-Lautrec were painting what would become masterpieces; Tchaikovsky, Dvořák, and Gilbert and Sullivan were reaching the peak of their musical powers, while Mascagni, Leoncavallo, and Puccini were laying claim to the future; Wilde and Barrie were amusing theatergoers, while Ibsen was raising their consciences; readers were diverted by Whittier, uplifted by Kipling, shocked by Hardy, and challenged by Zola.

Anthropologist Eugène Dubois discovered the bones of *Pithecanthropus erectus*, George Eastman recently had produced roll film for cameras, the Eiffel Tower had been completed two years earlier, construction began on the Trans-Siberian Railroad, the first Laborite was elected to Britain's Parliament, Idaho and Wyoming were admitted to the Union the year before as the forty-third and forty-fourth states, and President Benjamin Harrison signed into law the Sherman Antitrust Act to restrict monopolistic business practices.

Behind the outpouring of art and literature, the explosion of technological ingenuity, and nascent political liberalism, the world was starting to seethe with discontent, its ominous future foreshadowed in 1888 by the murdering rampage of "Jack the Ripper" in London.

Shortly before Warren was born, the United States Senate rejected a bill protecting Negro voting rights, Kaiser Wilhelm II unceremoniously sacked Otto von Bismarck and persuaded Austria and Italy to join Germany in the Triple Alliance, Italy unsuccessfully claimed Ethiopia as a protectorate, civil war erupted in Chile and revolution struck Brazil, Frenchmen were scandalized by revelations of corruption in the financing of the Panama Canal, and famine began sweeping across Russia.

Evil and vulgarity dominated Warren's own world as he grew up in the lawless, frontier-style milieu of Bakersfield in Southern California. The population was 7,000 (of which 500 were prostitutes), gambling houses were open twenty-four hours a day, latter-day cowboys rode their horses into the saloons, and outlaws gunned down the sheriff and the city marshal (who were the father and uncle of a golden-voiced boy named Lawrence Tibbett). Nearly a half century later, when Warren was district attorney two hundred and thirty miles to the north in Alameda County, he endured an ugly reminder of his past. Warren's father, who had been a Southern Pacific Railroad worker, was brutally murdered in Bakersfield.

For better or worse, Warren retained the memories of Bakersfield throughout his life. He recalled "conditions in many of the homes where the breadwinner had lost his earnings at the gaming tables." He said he "witnessed crime and vice of all kinds countenanced by corrupt government."

His summer jobs as a "call boy" for the Southern Pacific, rounding up train crews from bars, casinos, and whorehouses, gave him firsthand knowledge of the "effect on the people of a community" of rampant vice.

Warren also acquired his town's xenophobic dislike of Orientals. The red-light district was called "Jap Alley." Chinese imported as cheap labor by the railroad did not rate having their names listed in the telephone directory; the word "Oriental" was followed by the street address and telephone number.

Warren escaped from Bakersfield, geographically speaking, after high school. He earned his undergraduate and law degrees from the University of California at Berkeley, served in the Army during World War I, worked briefly as a legislative aide, and, in 1920, became a deputy on the staff of Alameda County's district attorney. In three years, Warren became chief deputy, and two years after that, when the district attorney resigned, Warren succeeded him—and stayed in the job for thirteen years.

Alameda was California's third-largest county. Its population of a half million was diversified in industry, commerce, and agriculture. Warren's law practice as the county's prosecutor was diversified, too—running the gamut of crime: bootlegging, gambling, dope peddling, protection rackets, gang warfare, government corruption, crimes of passion, assaults, robbery, murder.

Warren had been instrumental in obtaining a public defender for Alameda County, but "he was a tough prosecutor—hard as nails," California governor Pat Brown remembered. "He would really go after people." His reputation for balancing toughness with fairness extended to his refusal to allow police to eavesdrop electronically on a suspect in the murder of his father in Bakersfield. The murder remained unsolved.

In a 1931 survey of district attorneys, Raymond Moley, who would become part of FDR's Brain Trust, concluded "without hesitation that Warren was the best district attorney in the United States."

He allowed his deputies to participate in politics in their spare time for the candidates of their choice. In 1928, Warren led the Alameda County campaign for Herbert Hoover while one of his deputies plumped for Al Smith.

Warren's politics were unabashedly Republican. He viewed the National Industrial Recovery Act as "the first major effort to change by stealth the greatest free government of all time into a totalitarian state wherein men are but the pawns of a dictator." He denounced Upton Sinclair's "reform" program for California as "a foreign philosophy of government, half Socialistic and half Communistic . . . It means chaos to California."

When, in February 1935, the Supreme Court upheld President Roosevelt's action lowering the gold content of the dollar, Warren was incensed by the "extreme radicalism" of the time. He burst into his office flushed with indignation. Noticing that one of his deputies was surrounded by open law books while working on a brief, Warren stalked to the aide's desk and slammed the books shut. "Throw them away," he hissed. "Forget them. They're no good now. Contracts don't mean anything anymore."

In 1938, Warren ran for state attorney general and exhibited his deep concern for civil rights. At a luncheon meeting, a leading California Democrat, Robert W. Kenney (who would vainly oppose Warren for governor eight years later), wanted to hear the district attorney's views on the issue. The majority, Warren said, was obligated to defend the civil rights of minorities "no matter how violently they disagree with their views. I believe that the American concept of civil rights should include not only an observance of our Constitutional Bill of Rights but also the absence of arbitrary action by government in every field and the existence of a spirit of fair play on the part of public officials toward all."

At the time, the Bill of Rights was characterized by scholars as "a certain number of amendments on comparatively unimportant points"—and the Supreme Court held that its provisions were not binding on the states, a circumstance that would be altered in due time by the Warren Court.

Warren brought his prosecutor's zeal and essential sense of fairness to his term as attorney general and his years as governor. His never-ending hostility to gambling, illicit sex, and political corruption was reinforced by his devotion to his home and family—his Swedish-born wife, Nina, and their six children.

The foundations of his values, as Justice Potter Stewart would observe, were "those eternal, rather bromidic platitudes in which he sincerely believed. They were a great source of strength—having these foundations on which his thinking rested—regardless of whether you agreed with him."

Warren's instinctive evenhanded application of justice detoured abruptly near the end of his term as attorney general; Warren became the central figure in the euphemistically styled "Japanese evacuation" in World War II. In fact, Warren, on the eve of his first campaign for governor, played a key role in imprisoning Japanese-Americans in concentration camps—and he acted with the unapologetic fervor of a super-patriot.

Warren's antipathy toward Orientals was ingrained deeply. His political idol, the liberal crusader Hiram Johnson, had signed, as governor, California's 1913 Alien Land Law, barring Japanese from owning land in the state. For years, Warren had been an active member of the Native Sons of the Golden West, an organization which, among its overt racist positions, urged excluding people of Japanese ancestry from American citizenship. Shortly before the Japanese attack on Pearl Harbor, he affirmed that in times of national peril "we most need loyal and patriotic organizations like the Native Sons. This is your order and mine."

A few weeks after the United States entered the war, Warren declared that "the Japanese situation as it exists in this state today may well be the Achilles' heel of the entire civilian defense effort."

Unverified reports of Japanese spying and sabotage swept through Los Angeles. The mayor, Fletcher Bowron, said, "There were reports they were in touch with the Japanese fleet and we didn't have any way to tell who were loyal and who weren't." Tom C. Clark, sent to the West Coast by the Justice Department to participate in the Japanese "evacuation," said, "I think that you have to live it to understand the feeling Californians had about the people of Japanese descent after Pearl Harbor."

"The sad truth of the matter," *Nation* editor Carey McWilliams said, "is that you could count on the fingers of two hands the number of so-called public personages in California who opposed the mass evacuation of the Japanese."

The venerated commentator Walter Lippmann, who, curiously, had been silent about Adolf Hitler's anti-Semitism, openly supported the "evacuation." Lieutenant General John L. DeWitt, commander of the Western Defense Command, fortified civilian fear and prejudice by declaring, in the classic illogic of bigotry, "A Jap's a Jap. They are a dangerous element, whether loyal or not."

Nonetheless, as McWilliams pointed out, "no one person had more to do with bringing about the removal of the West Coast Japanese during World War II—citizens and aliens alike; men, women, and children—than Mr. Warren."

Mr. Warren pursued the removal of Japanese with uncommon determination. In February 1942, when a congressional committee conducted hearings on the issue in California, Attorney General Warren testified, "We believe that when we are dealing with the Caucasian race, we have methods that will test the loyalty of them. But when we deal with the Japanese, we are in an entirely different field and we cannot form any opinion that we believe to be sound."

More than a year later, Governor Warren asserted at the 1943 Governor's Conference in Columbus, Ohio, "If the Japs are released, no one will be able to tell a saboteur from any other Jap."

Clark, like most participants in the internment of Japanese during the war, regretted his role. "I have made a lot of mistakes in my life," he said in 1966, while a justice of the Supreme Court, "but one that I acknowledge publicly is my part in the evacuation of the Japanese from California in 1942."

While he lived, Warren never issued a similar *mea culpa*. Toward the end of 1944, he convened a meeting of California's Law Enforcement Advisory Committee to discuss the return of the Japanese to the state. The State Coordinator of Law Enforcement, Robert B. Powers, prepared a resolution condemning the evacuation. "No," Warren said. "This won't do, Bob. This sentence that you've got in here—that this was an 'improper thing' to do in the first place. We agree on that now, but none of us raised a voice against it when it happened."

Years later, when Chief Justice Warren was lunching with his law clerks, he twitted one from a southern state about violations of voting rights for blacks in his home area. The clerk bristled indignantly. "Wait a minute," he snapped. "What was the name of that guy in California? The one who put all the Japanese in concentration camps in World War II?"

A hush fell. Two other law clerks at the table stared at their soup spoons awaiting the inevitable, icy rejoinder from the Chief. Warren's unexpected chuckle broke the silence.

"Well, I get your point," he said. "But that was a clear and present danger. We really thought their fleets were going to land in California—and I didn't think I had any choice."

Not until his memoirs were published posthumously did Warren go beyond standard, political reasoning for his actions. "I have since deeply regretted the removal order," Warren wrote, "and my own testimony advocating it, because it was not in keeping with our American concept of freedom and the rights of citizens."

To be sure, most of Warren's actions as governor built and furthered his image as a liberal crusader. "He's a Democrat and he doesn't know it," Harry Truman had chortled in 1948, characterizing Warren. The governor had urged enactment of a comprehensive state health insurance program ("Communist-inspired," the California Medical Association said) and the creation of a Fair Employment Commission. Both proposals died.

Nonetheless, the Warren administration (the first to be elected to office three times in California) modernized the state's hospitals, improved its corrections system, increased old-age pensions and unemployment benefits, and built new highways over the state. Warren balanced the budget and secured significant tax reductions.

Not until he came to the Court, however, did Warren have both the opportunity and the will to restore in significant measure the "American concept of freedom and the rights of citizens" which, once in his earlier career, he had neglected.

TWO

Getting Warren out of California

WARREN WAS ELECTED governor of California by overwhelming majorities in 1942, 1946, and—even after the Dewey-Warren ticket had been defeated in the embarrassing presidential election upset of 1948 (in which Warren failed to carry California for the ticket)—again in 1950. He was the most popular and enduring politician in the history of a state storied for its political fickleness.

He thought he could win the Republican Party's presidential nomination in 1952; to his dying day, he would blame his failure to do so—and his failure to become President—on the political perfidy of his fellow California Republican Senator Richard Nixon.

His ambitions thwarted by the Eisenhower-Nixon victory in 1952, Warren decided to serve out his third term as governor and not to seek a fourth. He hoped he would receive an invitation to serve in Eisenhower's Cabinet. If he did not, it seemed likely his public career, which he had begun thirty-two years earlier as a deputy district attorney in Alameda County, would come to an end.

However, Eisenhower owed Warren a debt, though neither

man ever acknowledged it. At the 1952 Republican National Convention, there was a strong possibility that neither of the front-running favorites, General Dwight Eisenhower and Senator Robert Taft, would succeed in winning a sufficient number of delegate votes for the presidential nomination. Warren was considered the likely dark-horse beneficiary of a deadlock.

The governor, however, blundered politically, either because of high principle or through plain naïveté. A deadlock depended on the seating of contested delegates pledged to Taft. Herbert Brownell, who had masterminded the "Dewey Blitz" overwhelming Taft and Harold Stassen four years earlier, now was Eisenhower's campaign manager. He drafted the ingeniously conceived and brilliantly named "fair-play amendment," which, if adopted by the convention, would prohibit any contested delegate from voting on the question of his own seating. If the pro-Taft contested delegates could not vote on their legitimacy, they would be defeated, pro-Eisenhower delegates would replace them, and the opportunity for an Eisenhower nomination would be enhanced. Adoption of the "fair-play amendment" hinged on California's votes; at Warren's personal direction, all seventy California delegates voted in favor of the pro-Eisenhower rule.

Eisenhower's subsequent lead brought him close to victory—too close for a deadlock to continue for long. Warren could not bring himself to assure the general's nomination by yielding his own votes from California. However, Warren E. Burger, the floor manager for fellow Minnesotan Stassen, recommended a switch of Stassen votes to the leader—and the move put Ike over the top.

A month after the election, Warren's usual early-morning reading in his Executive Mansion bed in Sacramento was interrupted by a seven o'clock telephone call. It was Eisenhower, calling from the East Coast.

"I am back here selecting my Cabinet," he said, "and I wanted to tell you I won't have a place for you on it." Ike said that because of Warren's extensive background as a prosecutor, California attorney general, and governor, he had been considered seriously for Attorney General of the United States. The

President-elect said, however, he had decided to appoint Brownell to that position.

Warren's initial dejection changed quickly, though, when Eisenhower, barely missing a beat, offered him something else.

"I want you to know," he told Warren, "that I intend to offer you the first vacancy on the Supreme Court."

"That is very generous of you," Warren said.

"That is my personal commitment to you," Eisenhower pledged.

Six months later, Warren was asked by Brownell to become Solicitor General. The President, Brownell said, thought that Warren's resumption of active lawyering after nearly eleven years as governor would be a valuable antecedent to his appointment to the Supreme Court. In August, Warren agreed to take the job. On September 3, Warren announced publicly he would not seek a fourth term. He did not disclose his plans to become Solicitor General, which, though he would describe that position later as "the most prestigious one in the practice of law," he clearly considered a stepping-stone to the Supreme Court, as it had been for two of its current members, Robert Jackson and Stanley Reed.

On September 8, Chief Justice Fred Vinson died unexpectedly. Eisenhower was in a quandary. He did not want to appoint Warren Chief Justice, nor did he believe his commitment extended to that special post. He and Brownell discussed elevating Jackson to Chief Justice and naming Warren as the new Associate Justice. Jackson, however, was a Democrat—and this would be the first Supreme Court appointment by a Republican President since Herbert Hoover had named Benjamin Cardozo in 1932. The only Republican on the Court, in fact, was Truman-appointed Harold Burton, who, whether because of his failing health (as Brownell has said tactfully) or because Eisenhower had little confidence in Burton's ability to lead the Court, was not considered seriously for the job.

News reports speculated that Eisenhower was certain to nominate Warren to fill the vacancy created by Vinson's death. One of Warren's closest confidants, Representative William S. Mailliard, told the President during a White House breakfast that Warren wanted to be on the Court.

Eisenhower questioned whether Warren would be happy as a justice.

"Do you think he would really want it?" he asked Mailliard. "After his years as attorney general, governor, and all of this? Wouldn't it be pretty rarefied for him?"

"He'd very likely be bored to death," Mailliard replied, adding quickly, "My answer would be emphatically different if we were talking about the Chief Justiceship. He could run the place."

Warren's enemies were at least as eager to see Warren move out of the state. Vice President Nixon called on Eisenhower to urge Warren's appointment. "You must get Warren out of California," Nixon reportedly told the President. "He has control of the Republican Party machinery and we can't do business with him."

Of *all* people, Warren would not do business with Nixon. The year before, like all California delegates to the Republican National Convention, Senator Nixon signed a pledge to support Governor Warren for President. Nixon quietly worked to develop support in California for Eisenhower. Joining the Warren campaign train in Denver on July 4, 1952, the night before it was due in Chicago for the convention, Nixon and his political allies moved through the cars soliciting support for Ike. Warren, they explained, did not have a chance; California would profit if the delegates jumped on the Eisenhower bandwagon.

Warren, when he learned of Nixon's activities, considered them a "betrayal." He told reporters that "a delegate cannot break his pledge and still be a man of honor." As Governor Pat Brown of California recalled, Nixon's "deal to support Eisenhower" resulted in his being rewarded with the vice presidential nomination. "Warren never forgave him. He thought he double-crossed him." Earl Warren, Jr., said his father "just detested Richard Nixon as an abiding passion." To Warren, Nixon would henceforth be "a crook and a thief," "Tricky Dick," and "an evil man."

Still, Eisenhower was unmoved. He did not like Warren particularly, he did not like being pressed into keeping a commitment he did not think he had made, and he did not relish the idea of appointing someone Chief Justice of the United States to satisfy, of all people, the nominee's political opponents.

Less than three weeks later, Eisenhower ordered Brownell to fly to California in an attempt to persuade Warren that Eisenhower's promise to offer him the first vacancy on the Court referred to an Associate Justiceship. One man who did not hold out much hope for Brownell's success was Arthur T. Vanderbilt, Chief Justice of the New Jersey Supreme Court, whom Eisenhower was considering for Vinson's seat. Vanderbilt told a colleague, "They haven't got a Chinaman's chance of getting him to give up such a commitment."

Brownell tried to telephone Warren but the governor was deer hunting with his sons on a remote coastal island without a telephone. On September 25, Brownell raised Warren through a radio message that asked him to telephone the Attorney General in Washington.

Warren ordered an airplane to return him to the California mainland, where he telephoned Brownell and arranged a meeting two days later at an Air Force base ten miles from Sacramento. Brownell arrived in an Air Force plane at eight o'clock in the morning on September 27. He proceeded to a private room where Warren awaited him.

As Warren later recalled for his son and for a Supreme Court colleague, Brownell made clear that the President was under the impression that his promise to Warren was for an "ordinary" vacancy on the Court; it did not apply to Chief Justice of the United States.

If Warren agreed to "defer the commitment," the President would agree to naming the governor to any cabinet position he fancied. "Name your own," Brownell said.

Warren rejected the offer. He said he was not interested in a cabinet position nor could he afford to take one. Besides, Brownell recalled, "Warren took the position that he was ready to accept the Chief Justiceship that was offered to him by the President, that he did feel he had a commitment for the next vacancy—and this was the next vacancy."

Faced with Warren's implacable insistence, Vanderbilt was

told later, the Attorney General "had to cave in." Brownell had one last card to play, however. The President, he said, wanted his nominee to accept an interim appointment and be in Washington for the start of the new Court term—precisely one week later.

"That is a hell of a way to leave a state administration of eleven years," Warren said acidly. Nonetheless, he had announced he would not seek an additional term and, in fact, he had been planning to resign to accept the appointment as Solicitor General. He would be there, he told Brownell.

The Attorney General returned to Washington and selectively leaked the news of the impending appointment. When, at his September 30 news conference, the President formally announced his nomination of Warren as the nation's fourteenth Chief Justice, he acknowledged that most Americans already knew.

"I could start off, I think," Eisenhower said, "by confirming something that is certainly by no means news anymore."

Despite his political successes in California and his place on the Republican Party's 1948 national ticket as Thomas E. Dewey's vice presidential running mate, Warren was perceived generally as little more than a blandly competent politician and administrator. Even most who believed his innovative achievements as governor and attorney general demonstrated a facility for leadership would not have predicted that, in a generation, the Warren Court would forever change the face of America.

Those who gave the matter any thought probably would have agreed with this estimate made in 1947 by the journalist John Gunther in *Inside U.S.A.*:

> Earl Warren is honest, likable, and clean, [characterized by] decency, stability, sincerity, and lack of genuine intellectual distinction. He will never set the world on fire or even make it smoke.

THREE

Finding God

EVEN AFTER HE named his old political crony Fred M. Vinson Chief Justice of the United States in 1946, Harry Truman continued to rely on him for advice as well as diversion. Together, they discussed legislative strategy, quoted Latin classics, and played poker. In 1948, Truman planned to dispatch the Chief Justice to Moscow "to find some common ground with the Russians." Truman's speech announcing the mission had been written, the radio hookup arranged, and Vinson was actually packing his bags when the President was persuaded the trip would create diplomatic difficulties for his Secretary of State, George C. Marshall.

Vinson once even advised Truman (incorrectly, as it turned out) that the Court would uphold him if he were to nationalize the strike-threatened steel industry in time of national emergency.

In the autumn of 1951, with his popularity rating having dipped below 25 percent, Truman told Vinson he and the nation needed him more than ever. The Chief Justice was invited to the presidential retreat at Key West, where Truman urged Vinson to step down from the Bench in order to seek the Democratic nomination for President the next year. Only Vinson, Truman believed, could head off an almost inevitable Republican victory.

Vinson was cool to the idea. He said he did not think the Court should become a springboard to the White House; more likely, Vinson didn't share Truman's confidence in his ability to reverse the Republican political tide. In any event, he told Truman later that Mrs. Vinson had vetoed the idea with finality.

Had Truman prevailed, it seems unlikely that the outcome of the 1952 presidential election would have been different. The course of judicial history in the United States and America's road to racial equality, however, would have changed drastically.

At about the time the President and the Chief Justice were mulling over the nation's political future while sunning themselves in Florida, a man named Oliver Brown was consumed with a more immediate, personal concern in a courtroom in Topeka, Kansas.

Brown thought it unsafe, inconvenient, and unfair that his eight-year-old daughter, Linda Carol, should be forced to cross railroad yards to board a bus that carried her to an all-black school twenty-one blocks away when, in fact, there was a "whites only" elementary school only five blocks from her home.

Segregated facilities for whites and blacks had been the law and the life style in southern America since the end of Reconstruction. In 1896, the Supreme Court had decided segregation was not unconstitutional—as long as the segregated facilities were equal. That year, Homer Adolph Plessy, one-eighth Negro (an "octoroon" in the racist parlance of the day), had been arrested for refusing to move to a "colored only" coach on a train he had boarded in New Orleans. Louisiana law required railroads "to provide equal but separate accommodations for the white and colored races." (No one, it appears, challenged the authority of the railroad, the train conductor, or the state to make the anthropological determination of Plessy's race in the first place.)

In his ringing dissent from the decision in *Plessy* v. *Ferguson*, the first Justice John M. Harlan set what would become the American standard for racial equality: "Our Constitution is color-blind."

The "separate but equal" rule was applied by the Court in the 1938 *Gaines* case, in which the state of Missouri was ordered to permit a black student to attend the state's only law school. By 1951, the *Gaines* doctrine had been applied in three other graduate-school cases.

Admitting even a handful of blacks to all-white, tax-supported postgraduate institutions of learning was greeted with hostility by a majority of white Southerners. In 1950, two politicians who had found merit in the Court's rulings—Senator Frank Porter Graham in North Carolina and Senator Claude Pepper in Florida—were among those unseated by their opponents' overt appeals to racial discord and fear. Because of the concurrent spread of Communism (the United States had "lost" China to the Communists in 1949), twisted logic of the time decreed that, because Communist doctrine proclaimed racial equality, Americans professing to find the same guarantees in the Constitution and the Bible were either Communists themselves or, at least, Communist dupes.

In reality, the Supreme Court's rulings adhering to *Plessy* strengthened and extended segregation by giving Jim Crow legal justification and support at the most exalted level.

Education and transportation in all their forms were segregated. So were restaurants, parks, water fountains, movie theaters, seating on buses (and, with cruel irony, seating in courts of law)—all aspects of everyday life. Most communities dropped the fiction of equality. Most schools for Negroes were inadequate, even dilapidated, had poorly educated teachers, and lacked even rudimentary facilities and equipment—including textbooks. Few municipalities would admit Negroes to any public parks and pools. Downtown restaurants rarely had sections, separate or otherwise, in which blacks could be seated; "coloreds" got their food at stand-up carry-outs and took their lunch breaks in alleys, at construction sites, or on the stoops of abandoned buildings. Negroes motoring along southern highways were not permitted to use the rest rooms at gas stations. Blacks on extended trips by automobile, whether small children or elderly grandmothers, were forced to relieve themselves in wooded areas along the way.

The complaint of Linda Carol Brown was a battering ram that threatened to smash into the fortress of segregation and, in short order, destroy it and its defenders. Little wonder that when *Brown* reached the Supreme Court, Fred Vinson—genial, jovial, sometimes courtly, but always Kentuckian—demurred.

Opening the discussion on the case at the Court's conference on December 13, 1952, Vinson told his colleagues "there is a whole body of law back of us on 'separate-but-equal.' However we construe it, Congress did not pass a statute deterring and ordering *no* segregation." To the contrary, Vinson argued, Congress, which ruled over the District of Columbia and its numerous Negro citizens, had provided for segregated facilities in the nation's capital. "I don't see how we can get away from the long-established acceptance in the District," he said. "For ninety years, there have been segregated schools in this city."

Underlying Vinson's argument that the Court should follow legal precedent was his prescient fear of the anguished response to a decision that would require wholesale integration of schools. "We can't close our eyes to the seriousness of the problem," he warned. "We face the complete abolition of the public school system in the South."

Concurring in Vinson's arguments, whether on legal or on emotional grounds, were Tom C. Clark, who, like Vinson, was a Southerner appointed by Truman, and Roosevelt-appointed Justices Stanley F. Reed, another Kentuckian, and Robert H. Jackson, the chief American prosecutor at Nuremberg, who, like Reed, had been a Solicitor General arguing for much of FDR's New Deal program before the Bench both now occupied.

Four justices adamantly opposed continued acquiescence by the Supreme Court of the United States in blatant inequality. They were Roosevelt cronies William O. Douglas and Hugo L. Black and Truman appointees Harold H. Burton and Sherman Minton.

It was Shay Minton, not considered among the more articulate jurists of the period, who encapsulated the anti-segregation concept of his colleagues at the December 1952 conference. "Classification by race," he said, "is not reasonable and segregation is, per se, unconstitutional."

The swing vote was added by Felix Frankfurter, the former Harvard don whose personal gregariousness and ebullience con-

trasted with a stern sense of judicial traditionalism. On the issue
of segregation, however, Frankfurter could not hold with a precedent that, in effect, maintained the Constitution could tolerate
different laws for different races.

More than his fellow justices, however, Frankfurter sensed
that a five-to-four vote abolishing racial segregation in public
schools would have an explosive impact on the South and would
risk widespread rejection of and disobedience to an order of the
Supreme Court.

Frankfurter possessed keen political insights which often were
overlooked or ignored because of his professorial air and occasional pomposity at Court conferences. Potter Stewart, after joining the Court, remarked that, at the conferences, "Felix, if he
was really interested in a case, would speak for fifty minutes, no
more or less, because that was the length of the lecture at the
Harvard Law School."

Douglas despised Frankfurter's demeanor. A week after the
Court handed down its *Brown* decision, Douglas sent Frankfurter a curt memorandum. "We all know," Douglas wrote,
"what a great burden your long discourses are. But I do register
a protest at your degradation of the conference and its deliberations."

Douglas could be "absolutely devastating" and "drive Frankfurter crazy . . . after one of those fifty-minute lectures," Stewart
recalled. "When I came into this conference," Douglas said once
after a tedious lecture by Frankfurter, "I agreed with the conclusion that Felix has just announced. But he's just talked me out of
it."

Both men were political activists—a common trait among Supreme Court justices, fully two-thirds of whom, according to political scientist Bruce Allen Murphy, "engaged in some form of
extra-judicial behavior" while serving on the Bench.

Unlike Douglas, however, Frankfurter lobbied tirelessly to win
converts to his judicial views within the Court. "Douglas," according to one law clerk, "was just as happy signing a one-man
dissent as picking up four more votes."

In the school segregation cases, Frankfurter sought more than
a majority; he believed that only a *decisive* majority could avert

a national calamity. A premature decision, Frankfurter said, would have resulted in "four dissenters and, certainly, several opinions for the majority view. That would have been catastrophic."

To prevent—or, at least, delay—catastrophe, Frankfurter reached for the politician's time-tested defensive weapon: buying time.

Following a usual course, the decision and opinions in *Brown* v. *Board of Education* would have been handed down in the spring of 1953. It seemed impossible that a decisive majority could be forged by that time. Vinson was less than sanguine about his chances of pulling the Court together on the issue. "He was distressed," one close associate said, "over the Court's inability to find a strong, unified position on such an important case."

The Chief Justice himself was a cause of the divided Court. For one thing, he could not command the judicial respect of colleagues of the caliber of Frankfurter, Jackson, Black, and Douglas. One justice thought Vinson possessed "a second-class mind." Another said that several members of the Court "openly displayed their contempt for the Chief." Frankfurter recalled that when Vinson presented cases at the Court's conferences, he "blithely hits the obvious points, disposing of each case rather briefly by choosing, as it were, to float merely on the surface of the problems raised by the cases."

Even more important, Vinson opposed striking down segregation—hardly a posture from which he could wield moral suasion over his fellows.

Immediately after the Court's initial conference on the case, Frankfurter set about to find a plausible pretext for a long delay —reargument in the following term that would begin nearly a year later. To win over a majority, Frankfurter had to come up with a reason that would not be viewed as a stalling tactic (which is precisely what it was). None of the justices would support a blatantly delaying action; all feared that a weak and evasive move by the institution would risk its public credibility.

Still, Frankfurter knew his colleagues composed a willing audience. Even though the conference had discussed the case and had established what Justice Burton described as a "trend," the justices declined to take even a tentative vote. "No one on the Court was pushing it," Frankfurter said. Vinson didn't want to force a vote that he would lose, and few in the majority were satisfied with a five-to-four split.

In the spring of 1953, shortly before the Court had to reach its decision, Frankfurter persuaded his colleagues to consider an alternative. "If we can get together some questions for discussion and reargument," he told his law clerk, Alexander Bickel, "the case will be held over."

Together, Frankfurter and Bickel developed five questions which they distributed for a conference scheduled on May 29. The first three were substantive. They asked attorneys to discuss their understanding of the intent of the framers of the Fourteenth Amendment regarding school segregation and the judicial power to abolish it. The other two questions were procedural. They sought discussion of the decrees that would be issued to enforce a theoretical decision that school segregation was unconstitutional.

Opposition to posing the questions emanated from an unexpected quarter. Black and Douglas wanted to get on with the vote—thus effectively assuring a five-to-four outcome.

Frankfurter said in a letter to a friend, the eminent jurist Learned Hand, "that if the 'great libertarians' had had their way, we would have been in the soup."

Black argued that "there are too many reasons for my objections to set them out. In the main, however, asking the questions would bring floods of historical contentions on the specific points we asked about which would dilute the arguments along broader lines. I doubt it would be possible to isolate the framers' views about segregation in the primary schools. . . . I rather doubt the wisdom of submitting any questions."

(Before his death in 1971, Black had ordered his conference notes and private Court papers destroyed. His comments on *Brown* survived as notes written on the back of the memorandum from Frankfurter proposing the questions for reargument. The comments had been crossed out and appeared illegible. When copied by xerography, however, the underlying writing came through.)

Douglas supported Black's desire to move quickly, but the others, preferring to delay a vote, backed Frankfurter. Reargument was scheduled for December 1953. The battle was won— but the ultimate victory would depend on whether several minds could be changed in the intervening months.

Developing an accord on the issue appeared insurmountable— even for someone with the golden tongue of a Cicero. Vinson, no Cicero, had failed to transfer his considerable back-room political skills to the Supreme Court and, besides, he stood in opposition. So did Jackson, perhaps the most gifted and persuasive orator on the Court. Of those supporting *Brown*, neither Black nor Douglas were of a mind to lobby for Frankfurter's position. For his part, Frankfurter knew that "good feeling in the Court, as in a family, is produced by accommodation, not by authority— whether the authority of a parent or a vote." In practice, Frankfurter's penchant for pontification often failed to persuade those who, like Jackson and Clark, might otherwise have followed his lead.

In September 1953, less than three months before *Brown* would be reargued, there appeared to be little movement in the position of the justices. Then, without warning, Vinson, at sixty-three, died of a heart attack.

"This," Frankfurter erupted unkindly on hearing the news, "is the first indication that I have ever had that there is a God."

Meanwhile, Governor Earl Warren of California, who was preparing to announce his resignation to accept a position as Solicitor General of the United States, abruptly altered his plans. Now he expected President Eisenhower to make good on his pledge and appoint Warren to the first vacancy on the Supreme Court.

Although the President tried to evade his commitment, Warren's persistence prevailed—but he would never win over Dwight Eisenhower as a friend or, more important to the country, as a powerful ally in the controversies that lay ahead.

FOUR

What Heaven Must Be Like

To MOST JUSTICES of the Supreme Court, the judicial life proved to be a mixture of splendor and drudgery. It was exquisite agony to those who most keenly recognized the enormous, incalculable impact of the Court's actions on every aspect of life—without the requirement that the justices answer to, or be guided by, public opinion for their decisions.

William Howard Taft preferred the Bench to the White House. After Taft became Chief Justice in 1921—nine years after his political idol, Theodore Roosevelt, betrayed him, depriving him of any chance to retain the presidency for another term—he described the Supreme Court as his idea of what heaven must be like. "The Court," Taft wrote, "next to my wife and children, is the nearest thing to my heart in life."

But Justice Robert Jackson only half humorously depicted the Court as "the black hole of Columbia" and "the Marble Mausoleum." Justice Benjamin Cardozo, longing to return to the "lawyer's courts" he had left behind in New York, complained to Professor Felix Frankfurter "with tears in his eyes" that the Supreme Court "is not a court of law."

The caustic, even bitter, characterization of the Court by some of its most profoundly dedicated members arose from the reality that the Supreme Court reflects politics more frequently than it reflects either law or precedent.

That it is, in fact, a Court of human beings, each, inevitably, influenced by a personal, frequently emotionally charged view of the law and justice and right and wrong, assured Warren of a congenial forum. He was a man more at ease seeking concrete objectives in a political arena than he was dealing in abstruse intellectual principles.

Four years as California attorney general, eleven as governor, and an unsuccessful national campaign for Vice President of the United States constituted a powerful crucible in which to develop the instinct and experience to lead any governmental body.

Nonetheless, Warren opted to tiptoe—or, more precisely, to trip—into the Chief Justiceship.

He realized he had a good deal to learn about the Court when, on his arrival there on the morning of October 5, 1953, the man who commanded a professional entourage numbering in the dozens (not to mention a bureaucracy of many thousands) was, understandably, "shocked" to learn his entire staff comprised a secretary, "two very elderly messengers, and three young law clerks recently out of law school."

As he prepared to enter the ornate courtroom, crowded with dignitaries to witness his induction as Chief Justice (including President and Mrs. Eisenhower, who never before had been inside the Supreme Court), Warren put on an old academic gown. Told the gown was inappropriate, he agreed to put on a spare judicial robe found in the Court's robing room. The robe was too long, and Warren tripped over its hem as he stepped up to take his place in the Chief Justice's seat. "I suppose it could be said that I literally stumbled onto the Bench," he recalled later.

Not long afterward, he and Mrs. Warren were invited to a White House dinner. Not having an official car, Warren decided, despite his wife's insistence on frugality, to hire a limousine; he thought it inappropriate for the Chief Justice to arrive at a state dinner in a taxicab. When the car was delivered, though, it was a station wagon with large decals reading "Washington National Airport." The agency's dispatcher thought Warren was planning a flight and required a large car for luggage. It was too late to make other arrangements, and the Warrens bounced into the grounds of the Executive Mansion in the rented station wagon. Within weeks, Congress provided the Chief Justice with an official car.

Warren recognized, though, that the Court's lack of panoply was more than compensated for by its unchallenged power. Justice Jackson had observed that "were there a super-Supreme Court, a substantial proportion of our reversals of state courts would also be reversed. We are not final because we are infallible, but we are infallible only because we are final."

The supreme power accompanying that finality was recognized by Alexis de Tocqueville. "The Supreme Court," he wrote, "is placed higher than any known tribunal. The peace, the prosperity, and the very existence of the Union are vested in the hands of the . . . Federal judges."

Warren made the most of his political assets in his early days by establishing bonhomie among colleagues, staff, and the lawyers who appeared at the Court. Warren emphasized the importance of the ceremony admitting lawyers to argue before the Court, and "every newly admitted attorney," *Newsweek* reported, "gets a smile." He would stride through the building introducing himself to guards and plumbers. "When he says, 'Good morning,'" one of his colleagues said, "he does it as if he hadn't seen you for a year."

Warren disarmed his guarded colleagues at the first conference he attended. The conferences are the Court's most secret and sacred sessions. Warren, however, ordered notes to be delivered periodically, the contents of which he generously shared with the others; the notes contained developments in the World Series between the Brooklyn Dodgers and the New York Yankees. The Yankees won in six games.

Warren openly—and shrewdly—conceded he needed help in learning the Court's procedures and daily routine. He was not wanting for talented tutors. When Warren arrived, Hugo Black had been an associate justice for sixteen years, Felix Frankfurter and William O. Douglas for fourteen, and Robert Jackson for twelve. He borrowed all Frankfurter's decisions on "due process," which he read assiduously, remarking, "I am still endeavoring to orient myself in that field." He asked Black to lead the first three conferences of the term and to assign opinions to the justices—a privilege (and, sometimes, a power) reserved to the Chief Justice if he is in the majority.

Black's three-week role as a stand-in for Warren generated one of the few compliments Frankfurter ever bestowed on Black. "How admirably you conducted the proceedings," Frankfurter gushed. "You guided the talk as talk should be guided—by a firm but gentle rein."

Before Warren could take hold of the reins himself, he first had to understand how the Court operated. Roughly two-thirds of the cases presented are requests for review of decisions of lower federal courts. Most of the rest are cases from state courts in which the litigants believe federal questions are at issue. The great majority of cases reach the Court when at least four justices agree to issue writs of certiorari (from *certiorari volumus,* "we wish to be informed").

Deciding which cases shall be heard and which shall not is the publicly unseen essence of the dispensation of justice. In Warren's first term of 1953–54 (each term starts in October and continues until the following summer), over 1,200 cases were presented; the Court agreed to hear 170. In the 1968–69 term—Warren's last—the Court heard just over 250 cases of the more than 3,000 presented. Unless at least four of the nine justices agree to hear a case, it is over and the decision of the lower court is left standing.

Despite the size of the work load and the awesome implications of many of the Court's decisions, the work is handled by a small cadre. "Alone among Government agencies," Anthony Lewis wrote in the New York *Times,* "the Court seems to have escaped Parkinson's Law. The work is still done by nine men, assisted by eighteen young law clerks. Nothing is delegated to committees or ghost writers or task forces."

Those few law clerks are responsible, nonetheless, for a substantial part of the Court's work—and, some critics insist, possess far too much influence and power in the decision-making process.

After nearly a quarter century on the Bench, Justice William J.

Brennan said in 1979 that his opinions emanated not from him alone but from "the Brennan chambers"—the judge and "the company of sixty-five law clerks who have been associated with me on the Court."

In 1957, William H. Rehnquist, who had been a clerk of Justice Jackson, wrote in *U.S. News & World Report* that justices were delegating too much authority to clerks who "unconsciously" slanted materials to mesh with their own views.

The "materials" include memoranda on each certiorari petition, summarizing the facts and issues of each case and recommending whether they should be heard. About 90 percent of the cases end without further discussion because fewer than four justices agree to hear the case. Warren rarely disagreed with the recommendations of his clerks. Indeed, sheer volume rendered it difficult, if not impossible, even to wade through the clerical summaries. "I just read your memos," Warren told one clerk, "and I don't think you need twenty pages to convince me that those are cert-worthy cases. I hope you can be more brief in the future, because I have to wade through an awful lot of these memos for each conference."

After the Court voted to hear a case, some justices, Warren among them, would direct a clerk to study briefs from opposing lawyers and prepare a bench memo containing greater detail and analysis of the facts and issues, as well as recommendations for a decision. These were designed to aid the justices during oral argument and conference discussions. In oral arguments, each side typically is granted a half hour. Frequently, the justices interrupt with questions and comments, often challenging contesting lawyers. Douglas complained that he "would often squirm at Frankfurter's seemingly endless questions that took the advocate round and round and round." One day, Frankfurter interrupted as Warren was posing a question. "Let him answer my question," Warren snapped. "He is confused enough as it is." "Confused by Justice Frankfurter, I presume," the former professor replied coolly.

At the conferences, cases are discussed and, often, decided—although justices frequently change their positions when opinions are circulated. Conference deliberations are as secret as any guarded by the Pentagon or the CIA. No outsider enters the room during the conference. The junior Associate Justice (Sherman Minton when Warren joined the Court) acts as doorman and messenger, sending for reference material (or, as Warren did sometimes, World Series scores) and receiving it at the door.

Once a vote is taken, the Chief Justice, if he is in the majority, assigns the opinion to himself or to another justice in the majority; if the Chief is on the losing side, the senior justice in the majority assigns the opinion.

On October 17, 1953, Black, still sitting in as presiding justice at Warren's request, assigned Warren his first opinion—*Voris* v. *Eikel*, a case in which the lower courts had denied compensation to a worker because the employer had not been notified of the injury as required by the statute. Warren reversed because it was sufficient for the worker to notify his immediate supervisor. His opinion stated that the law "must be liberally construed and in a way which avoids harsh and incongruous results."

The brief statement foreshadowed an underlying principle in Warren's judicial temperament. "I often thought to myself," Potter Stewart would say later, "that if the Chief Justice can see some issue that involves widows or orphans or the underprivileged, he's going to come down on that side. Warren's great strength was his simple belief in the things we now laugh at—motherhood, marriage, family, and the flag."

He was often "very stubborn," however, in Stewart's recollection. "Once he had made up his mind, you could not get him to change it. He would stick to it regardless of facts and arguments." If he could not "see something involving these eternal, rather bromidic platitudes," Stewart said, "he would say, 'Look, our duty is to resolve this conflict. I'm not a tax lawyer. I'll go whichever way you want to go on this—with the majority—and get this conflict resolved.'"

It was as if Warren were saving himself for the major conflicts that lay ahead. The nation was consumed with the threat of Communism at home and abroad. President Eisenhower had engineered a truce in Korea, but on terms less offensive to North Korea than those Harry Truman had demanded—an action that discomfited the Old Guard of the Republican Party, which had branded Truman as an appeaser.

The Bricker Amendment to limit the authority of the executive in negotiating foreign treaties was gaining strong support in the Senate, much to the chagrin of Eisenhower and Secretary of State John Foster Dulles; the popularity of the proposed constitutional amendment reflected continuing belief among many conservatives that President Roosevelt had committed the United States secretly at Yalta to further "giveaways" to the Soviet Union.

The Old Guard refused flatly to renounce Senator Joe McCarthy in favor of the President; senators such as Robert Taft, William Knowland, and Everett McKinley Dirksen vigorously supported McCarthy's anti-Communist crusade. The so-called right wing worried even more when Eisenhower steadfastly refused to commit American troops to Vietnam to help the beleaguered French defeat the Viet Minh.

Other than Eisenhower's inability to balance Truman's last budget and his decision to issue Executive Order 10450 (easing the dismissal of government employees who were suspected of treachery, lying, unusual sexual habits, or belonging to nudist colonies), domestic problems were not high among Eisenhower's earliest priorities as President. Except for his Vice President's partisan slip during an interview—Nixon referred to Warren as a "great Republican Chief Justice"—Eisenhower barely was aware of the Court during Warren's first months.

Warren, though, was developing rapidly into a respected leader of the Court. Frankfurter's view of Warren, expressed in a letter less than a month after the new Chief took his seat, was that Warren "brings to his work that largeness of experience and breadth of outlook which may well make him a very good Chief Justice. . . . I like him as a human being. He is agreeable without being a back-slapper; he is informal but has native dignity."

Frankfurter had found what he had written earlier "is most needed in a Chief Justice: *ein Tonangeber*—a tone-giver: one who by his example generates in the others complete dedication to the work of the Court."

Where Vinson, in the view of the more gifted justices, failed to provide direction in conferences, his predecessor, Chief Justice Harlan F. Stone, was burdened by "the habit of carrying on a running debate with any justice who expresses views different from his," Frankfurter recalled.

When he arrived at the Court five years after Warren did, Justice Stewart was told that "Stone's problem was that, at a conference, he himself always insisted upon having the last word, and that's not the way you preside—by always arguing." Conferences, as a result, often became "a free-for-all," Stewart said. "Chief Justice Warren just wasn't that way." Justice Byron White said that Warren "never felt he had to get the last word in."

"He was an instinctive leader whom you respected," Stewart said, "and, as the presiding member of our conference, he was just ideal."

Warren's style was, White remembered, to "state his position—and he usually had his mind made up. He usually had a pretty firm view of the case."

Before long, Warren also took firm hold of the Court. He eliminated Saturday work by persuading the justices to conduct their conferences on cases during the week—but to start their Court sessions at ten o'clock each weekday morning rather than at noon. He ordered that the chamber's sound be enhanced and that a microphone be installed at each justice's place, making the proceedings audible throughout the room for the first time. Gradually, he persuaded the justices to announce decisions when they were ready rather than allowing them to pile up for announcement each Monday.

As a rule, the justices would gather in the Court's conference room awaiting Warren's arrival. They would rise as he entered, formally exchange ritual handshakes all around, and begin deliberations when Warren took his seat at the head of the table and called out cheerfully, "Hey-ho, let's get going."

When conferences were over, justices typically briefed their clerks on what had taken place, which cases were decided, what the outcomes were, which justice was assigned to write which opinions, and which of the clerks would write the opinions that fell to each justice.

It was then that the clerks drafted opinions for the consideration of their justices. It was then, too, that controversy arose over whether it was the clerks, brilliant and fresh out of law school, or the people's highest judges, nominated by the President and confirmed with the advice and consent of the Senate, who made the decisions affecting the lives of millions of Americans.

FIVE

Clerk Power

"A SUSPICION HAS grown at the bar," Justice Robert Jackson wrote, "that the law clerks constitute a kind of junior court which decides the fate of certiorari petitions. This idea of the law clerk's influence gave rise to a lawyer's waggish statement that the Senate no longer need bother about confirmation of justices but ought to confirm the appointment of law clerks."

A few years later, in 1958, the notion lost its waggish quality when Senator John Stennis of Mississippi, an antagonist of the Court, urged Senate confirmation of law clerks because of their rising importance and influence.

Jackson's former law clerk William Rehnquist (who would become a Supreme Court justice in 1971) had promulgated a similar view in his 1957 article. So Justice Felix Frankfurter urged one of his former law clerks, Alexander Bickel, who had become a noted constitutional scholar at Yale University, to counter the growing conception that the clerks had become the real, unacknowledged masters of the Court.

In a 1958 article in the New York *Times,* Bickel contended that "the law clerks are in no respect any kind of a kitchen cabinet." Their job, he wrote, is to "generally assist their respective justices in researching the law books and other sources for materials relevant to the decision of cases before the Court."

Some of Frankfurter's best-known opinions were drafted almost entirely by his clerks, notably his famous dissent in the 1962 case of *Baker* v. *Carr*, in which the Court determined that the judiciary could examine questions of disproportionate legislative representation. Frankfurter's clerk Anthony G. Amsterdam not only prepared drafts which Frankfurter accepted with minor changes, but also produced one of Frankfurter's famous satiric dialogues that he distributed to the justices occasionally to criticize actions with which he disagreed. Once, Frankfurter appended minor corrections to a draft prepared by Amsterdam. On the draft he returned to the law clerk, the justice attached an astonishing comment. "If you approve of my revisions," Frankfurter wrote, "send to printer and duly circulate [among the other justices]."

Frankfurter, perhaps conscious that he sometimes surrendered his prerogatives to his clerks, expressed his own concern with the system when, in connection with a series of decisions that had gone against him in March 1957, he wrote to a fellow justice, "I wonder how many who are reversing out of hand in these cases have read the record and not relied merely on the memoranda of their law clerks. And, since my curiosity is very alert this morning, I wonder how many of the law clerks have read the whole record in these cases."

Most justices use law clerks to screen the ever-mounting number of cert petitions and appeals filed with the Court. The volume had grown to more than 4,600 in 1973—a nearly 50 percent increase in the five years since Warren had left the Court; by 1983, the number of petitions for certiorari had reached 5,300, of which only a fraction—3 percent in all—were heard by the Court.

The clerks divide the petitions among themselves and prepare "cert memos" on all the cases for their respective justices. The brief cert memos summarize the facts and issues, and state whether the clerks think the Court should hear the cases.

In addition to ordinary cert memos, the Chief Justice's clerks (three in all, in Warren's day, bringing the total number to nineteen) are primarily responsible for the Miscellaneous Docket, largely comprising what one law clerk called "that handwritten garbage." He referred to *in forma pauperis* petitions. The IFPs are petitions filed by those too poor to pay the usual $100 filing fee. IFPs constitute nearly 60 percent of the total number of petitions filed with the Court. A large percentage of those come from jailhouse lawyers—often uneducated, sometimes barely literate convicts claiming violations of their constitutional rights. Often handwritten on scraps of paper, frequently illegible and incomprehensible, only a tiny number move beyond the law clerks—and few of those are deemed to have sufficient merit by the Court to be heard. Nonetheless, each is screened by the Chief Justice's law clerks—and screened with care.

"Inasmuch as the IFP petitioners generally do not have counsel," Warren instructed his clerks, "it is necessary for you to be their counsel, in a sense."

Indeed, the petition filed in the famous case of *Gideon* v. *Wainwright,* leading to the 1963 decision affirming the right to court-appointed counsel in criminal cases, was printed with a pencil, schoolboy style, by Clarence Earl Gideon. Gideon had been charged with breaking into a poolroom in Florida. Because he was penniless, he asked the court to appoint counsel. The judge refused. Florida law, he said, provided that lawyers should be appointed to represent indigent defendants only in capital cases. The Court acted on his IFP petition, appointed Washington lawyer Abe Fortas to represent him, and decided Gideon had been denied a fair trial. Gideon became something of a national celebrity when his ordeal was described in Anthony Lewis' book *Gideon's Trumpet,* and his story later was dramatized on television with Henry Fonda playing the title role.

Because only one copy of an IFP petition must be filed rather than the forty ordinarily required, the Chief Justice's clerks act as clerks to the entire Court. Sifting through the material, the clerks write brief memoranda on each, copies of which are sent to each justice. In Warren's tenure, before the Court obtained copying machines, each IFP memo was typed with a sufficient number of carbon copies for each justice and the files—eleven copies in all. They were typed on very thin paper (and, as a result, were called "flimsies") to try to make the carbon copies legible. Often, however, the junior justices, who received the last copies, had difficulty reading them.

If the clerk dealing with a petition thinks it has any merit, he circulates the petition itself among the justices. Any justice can call up any petition at any time, of course—but they rarely do so. In effect, the Chief Justice's clerks—at least, during the Warren years—served as the Supreme Court on most IFP petitions by advising the Court they had no merit, with the Court infrequently questioning their judgment.

To most justices, clerk power is accepted in ordinary cert petitions and appeals as well. The clerks do most of the work in screening and summarizing the vast majority of petitions for certiorari. The justices' knowledge of cases is based almost entirely on cert memos from their clerks, and, for the most part, they vote in accordance with the recommendations in the memoranda. To be sure, discussion during conferences, points made by contending attorneys during oral argument, and examination of opinions once they are circulated will lead some justices to change their minds; Justice Tom Clark, for one, would change his mind and his vote frequently—and, sometimes, crucially—without always explaining what had prompted his switch.

Generally, though, the clerks possess enough discretion in handling cert memos to constitute a Court-within-a-Court when it comes to deciding what will be heard. Because fewer than 10 percent of the cases presented are heard by the Court, clerk power is mighty indeed.

Once the conference has started, however, the influence of the clerks recedes.

No one save a justice of the Supreme Court is permitted in the conference, conducted at ten o'clock on Friday mornings during Warren's stewardship. After the ritual handshakes, the Chief Justice takes his seat at one end of the long, rectangular ebony table, and the senior Associate Justice at the other end. The Chief speaks first, the senior Associate next, and so on in the order of seniority.

When Warren arrived at the Court, his clerks, who had been appointed by Vinson, thought Warren distant and cold. The new Chief Justice "didn't quite know what to make of us," one of Warren's original clerks remembered. Warren didn't even recount the outcome of conference discussions with the clerks, an obvious difficulty for a clerk expected to draft an opinion. "We would go down to Justice Burton's to find out what happened," the clerk recalled. Warren "never told us what happened—even the results—during that year."

Later, after Warren had become more accustomed to his new role, he would chat candidly with his clerks about conference discussions, even to the point of presenting vivid characterizations of his colleagues' behavior.

After a time, Warren developed a close, even paternalistic relationship with many of his clerks during the year each would serve him.

He lunched with his clerks every Saturday, occasionally summoning them into his chambers for a cocktail beforehand. One Saturday, he called them in to "have a drink and unwind a bit before we go out." He produced a bottle of rare, aged cognac that a wealthy friend had given him.

"He got this superb cognac," the clerk said, "and just picked up the water tumblers you have to gargle with. I was drinking what was probably the most valuable cognac I've ever had in my life out of a water tumbler."

The Saturday luncheons usually lasted two to three hours. Warren would discuss the work of the Court and the state of the world, would reminisce about his years in politics, and would rue the consistently lackluster performances of the Washington Senators. Nonetheless, during spring and summer, he often would conclude a luncheon discourse by smacking the table and exclaiming, "Boys, let's go to the ball game."

The Chief and his clerks lunched at the University Club, whose membership roll, at the time, was devoid of blacks. Despite public criticism, Warren maintained his membership there. One of his clerks in 1967, a black man named Tyrone Brown, observed that Warren "particularly enjoyed taking me over there with the group for lunch to desegregate the place."

Starting in 1961, Warren's current and former clerks honored the Chief at an annual black-tie dinner. The first one was at the super-segregated Metropolitan Club and attracted President Kennedy as a pre-dinner guest. (The President soon would resign his own membership there to dramatize his antipathy to its

elitist policies.) Considerations more mundane than the desire to
make a racial statement, however, suggested to the clerks that
they should move their subsequent banquets for Warren from
the Metropolitan Club to the Lawyers Club or one of the better-
appointed hotels.

For one thing, the Metropolitan Club closed at midnight. "We
were so offended that they would kick out the Chief Justice because they were closing," one of the dinner's organizers recalled,
"we decided never to go back there." Another embarrassment
was that when President Kennedy arrived for cocktails, he
wanted a beer—and none was available at the club.

President Kennedy, President Johnson, and others of America's
most influential personages were among the cocktail guests at
later dinners at which the clerks, many of them traveling across
the country to attend, honored Warren. No "outsider," however,
was permitted to remain for the meal—with one exception. Thurgood Marshall, then Solicitor General, apparently unaware that
he had been invited only for cocktails, stayed on when dinner
was served. "We couldn't figure out how to get rid of him," one
of the clerks said plaintively.

The continuing affection and admiration of most clerks for
their justices derives, in large part, from the intimate role they
are permitted to play in the decision-making process.

After discussing with his clerks the outcome of a conference,
Warren would indicate which opinions he had assigned to himself. The clerk who had written the cert memo and the more de-
tailed bench memo on a case would be directed to draft the
opinion. The Chief Justice would outline his understanding of
the key facts and his reasoning in reaching the decision. The
clerk was left with considerable discretion as to the details of the
opinion and, in particular, the supporting legal underpinning for
the decision.

Warren would review the draft with the clerk, discuss at
length any section with which he was dissatisfied, and make
stylistic changes. "He had a penchant," one of his clerks remembered, "for Anglo-Saxon words over Latin words, and he didn't
like foreign phrases thrown in where there was a good American
word that would do."

The research and legal support for decisions may not attract wide public attention but is intrinsic to how they are interpreted by lower courts and even by future Supreme Courts. On more than one occasion, supporting cases cited by Warren in footnotes would prompt learned law review articles—and delighted chuckles among Warren's law clerks, who knew that no one on the Court, least of all the Chief Justice, had paid the slightest attention to the footnotes.

Nonetheless, Warren did not believe his clerks were unguided missiles. He prided himself on keeping an open mind and was viewed as being amenable to persuasion. Once he made a decision, though, he didn't agonize—and he didn't waver. "When he made up his mind," Justice Byron White said, "it was like the sun went down."

In 1972, retired Chief Justice Warren launched a stinging attack on a proposal (developed, ironically, with the help of one of Warren's former clerks) to create a National Court of Appeals. The new court's function would be to screen the bulk of the thousands of certiorari petitions that reach the Supreme Court.

In a letter to the former clerk who had served on the committee which drafted the idea, Warren denounced the proposal as "a scuttling of the Supreme Court. I can think of few things which could throttle the Court to a greater extent in its avowed purpose of establishing 'Equal Justice Under Law.'" Removing from the Court its prerogative to determine which cases it would hear was what angered Warren—and what he believed endangered the Court's future.

Usually the best and brightest in terms of outstanding academic records, clerks are selected annually by each justice, who, in turn, usually leaves the nominations to committees of former clerks or to professors at a few of the nation's more prestigious law schools.

At the beginning of his tenure as Chief Justice, Warren relied heavily on Frankfurter for guidance on procedure as well as on law. He sought the former Harvard professor's help in, among other things, the selection of law clerks. Not surprisingly, of the nine clerks who served Warren during his first three Court terms, six were from Harvard or Yale. After 1957, though, only one of Warren's nearly three dozen clerks was a Harvard graduate.

The early warm relationship between Warren and Frankfurter cooled perceptibly after a few years. Warren began disliking everything about Frankfurter, including his Harvard background. Warren was convinced that Harvard was producing "little Frankfurters." The Chief Justice also feared that appointing Harvardians as law clerks would present him with a security problem. Warren thought it likely that the clerks eventually would discuss the activities in his chambers with their former professors, who, in turn, would disclose them to Frankfurter, their old Harvard colleague.

Warren's successor, Chief Justice Warren Burger, once stressed in a memorandum "the private nature of everything that transpires in the chambers of a justice," warning against the "possibility of unfavorable information being 'leaked' to other justices." Clearly, Burger had taken a page from Warren's book. Warren frequently reminded his clerks that they worked for the Chief Justice, not for the Court, and that the activities in his chambers were not to be disclosed to anyone—including other justices and their clerks.

The prohibition by Warren against divulging information from chambers grew even more stringent where contacts with Frankfurter were concerned. "We were enjoined from falling under [Frankfurter's] sway," one Warren clerk said. "[Warren] as much as said, 'I know you're all quite young fellows from law school, and here's this great professor, but don't let him sell you any beans.' And it took the form of a mild paranoia about contacts between his law clerks and Frankfurter, or even Frankfurter's law clerks."

For his part, Frankfurter avoided the temptation of visiting the sins of the father upon the sons. He included Warren's clerks among the people he invited to his chambers for scholarly conversations. (In 1957, when he invited a Warren clerk in for a chat, the justice hesitated, then added, "unless, of course, I've been quarantined.")

Not all justices relied so heavily on their clerks, most notably Justice Douglas. Douglas was the quintessential loner whose occasional "hello" in the Court corridors was greeted as an occasion by the clerks. Former clerks use the word "cold" most frequently when asked to describe Douglas. His severity toward clerks became legendary; at times, he was even downright mean-spirited.

Once, when a major university wanted to invite Douglas to address its students and faculty, its dean asked one of Warren's clerks to make the necessary approach and to introduce to Douglas the student body president, who would, formally and in person, proffer the invitation.

The clerk arranged an appointment. When he was ushered in, he introduced the class officer, who started to explain to Douglas the purpose of the visit.

Almost immediately, Douglas cut him off. "Why are you bothering me with that?" he snapped. "Talk to my agent. The fee is three thousand dollars—and he'll handle it." With that, the two were dismissed.

The legal research by clerks to buttress decisions often is visible in the footnotes of opinions. And, in one of the most significant Supreme Court decisions of the twentieth century, *Brown* v. *Board of Education*, a footnote stirred up nearly as much controversy as the decision itself.

In his opinion in *Brown*, Warren, speaking for the Court, had asserted that segregation presumed that Negroes were inferior—and that presumption was psychologically harmful to black children.

"Whatever may have been the extent of psychological knowledge at the time of *Plessy* v. *Ferguson*," Warren's opinion maintained, "this finding is amply supported by modern authority." This assertion referred to a footnote—the celebrated and disputed footnote 11—listing seven works by social scientists.

Immediately, national discussion and regional outrage focused on the footnote and its clear implication that the Court had substituted the questionable validity of social science for the certitude of the law.

On May 18, 1954, the morning after the *Brown* decision was announced, columnist James Reston wrote in the New York *Times* that the Court had handed down "a sociological decision." Kenneth B. Clark, whose own work, *Effect of Prejudice and Discrimination on Personality Development,* was the first of the seven listed in footnote 11, wrote that "the Court appeared to rely on the findings of social scientists." (Clark was disappointed that the Court did not point out that his study determined that segregation twisted the psyches of white children, too.)

A plethora of learned commentary followed, analyzing in minute detail the works and the authors cited by the Court. The Court was criticized for omitting other relevant works; the validity of social science was debated vigorously; the reliance on its methodology, findings, and theories in deciding controversial legal issues became a burning question to lawyers, journalists, and legislators.

The fount of most of the indignation among opponents of the decision was the citation in footnote 11 of the massive, two-volume study of segregation entitled *An American Dilemma,* by a Swede, Gunnar Myrdal. The study had been published a decade earlier and its mountain of data, demonstrating the ill effects of segregation on almost every aspect of southern life, had been compiled by a large field staff which included, among others, a youthful Ralph Bunche.

Seventeen years after the decision, in 1971, retired Justice Tom Clark said in an interview, "I questioned the Chief's going with Myrdal in that opinion. I told him—and Hugo Black did, too—that it wouldn't go down well in the South. And he didn't need it."

The commentators on whether the Court should base its decisions on sociological treatises could have saved their breath; Chief Justice Warren and his colleagues were, at best, dimly aware of footnote 11 and even less familiar with the works it cited. As to Justice Clark, time may have played tricks with his memory; Clark had mentioned the footnote to Warren, but in an entirely different context and with an entirely different concern.

The footnote was added by Richard Flynn, one of Warren's clerks. In citing supporting authority for the *Brown* decision, Flynn listed works he considered "obvious." He said there was no method to organizing the footnote. "That's just the way it fell," he said. The Myrdal and Clark works, in particular, were the best known in the field at the time.

No justice, save Clark, made any mention of the footnote to Warren. Clark's objection had nothing to do with Myrdal. Rather, he questioned listing Kenneth Clark by his last name only. The Texan thought that some readers of the opinion might attribute the article to the justice rather than to the sociologist. He asked—and Warren readily agreed—that the citation be changed to read "K. B. Clark." In the final opinion, all the other authors are listed only by their last names.

Excessive clerk power troubled Justice Frankfurter as early as 1954, when, referring to the "flimsies" prepared for the justices by the Chief's clerks, he wrote in a memorandum that "normally that was the only knowledge that the Court had of this growing number of cases and on such knowledge alone, with relatively few exceptions, they were disposed of."

In a 1960 memorandum to Justice Potter Stewart, Frankfurter referred to a particular "flimsy" as "a striking illustration of the slanted way in which . . . over the years, term after term . . . these miscellaneous cases [IFPs] are reported to us," based less on law than on "compassionate feelings and inexperienced predispositions . . . on the strength of which, so predominantly, action is taken by the Court."

In the letter to Stewart, Frankfurter pointed out that "the appraisal and appreciation of a record as a basis for exercising our discretionary jurisdiction is . . . dependent on a seasoned and disciplined professional judgment. I do not believe," Frankfurter concluded, "that lads—most of them fresh out of law school and with their present tendentiousness—should have any routine share in the process of disemboweling a record, however acute and stimulating their power of reasoning may be."

To the present, however, clerks have continued to be the primary determinants of which one of every ten petitions for hearing reaches the Court for decision. Indeed, Justice John Paul Stevens has said he does not read 80 percent of the cert petitions that come before the Court. Almost certainly, the great majority of lower court decisions that are unreviewed by the Supreme Court and, therefore, left standing would have been affirmed if the cases were heard. Still, no one really knows that for sure, just as no one knows how many miscarriages of justice might have resulted from the ignorance or inexperience of some-one gifted or well connected enough to be chosen upon gradua-tion from law school to spend a year as a law clerk to a Supreme Court justice.

SIX

Playing the Piano
in a Whorehouse

THE SUPREME COURT that Earl Warren joined in 1953 has been described by Professor Fred Rodell of the Yale Law School as "the most brilliant and able collection of justices who ever graced the high bench together."

The superstars of the Court were the champions of judicial restraint, Felix Frankfurter and Robert Jackson, and the archetypes of judicial activism, Hugo Black and William Douglas. More often than not, the other four justices—Stanley Reed, Harold Burton, Tom Clark, and Sherman Minton—followed the Frankfurter-Jackson lead in the absence of decisive leadership from Chief Justice Vinson. Frankfurter's brilliance and Jackson's incisiveness usually carried the day—and the Court's majority.

The doctrinal differences among the Court's de facto leaders resulted in increasing personal animosity which, in turn, may have solidified their differences as their animus grew progressively bitter. Their disagreements often were petty, their vituperation childish, their prominently displayed egos easily bruised.

The doctrine of judicial restraint is associated most closely with Frankfurter and his judicial godfather, Justice Oliver Wendell Holmes. Two years before he was appointed to the Court, Frankfurter explained judicial restraint this way:

> Self-limitation [by the judiciary] is not abnegation; it is the expression of an energizing philosophy of the distribution of governmental powers. For a court to hold that decision does not belong to it, is merely to recognize that a problem calls for the exercise of initiative and experimentation possessed only by political processes, and should not be subjected to the confined procedure of a lawsuit and the uncreative resources of judicial review.

The case for judicial activism, or a "liberal" construction of the Constitution, was offered in the early nineteenth century by Chief Justice John Marshall in *McCulloch* v. *Maryland:*

> Let the end be legitimate, let it be within the scope of the Constitution, and all means which are appropriate, which are plainly adapted to that end, which are not prohibited, but consist with the letter and spirit of the Constitution, are constitutional.

Before Warren, the principal heir to the Marshall concept was Hugo LaFayette Black, who subscribed to the definition in Bouvier's *Law Dictionary* of a "liberal" construction of the Constitution as "one by which the letter is enlarged or restrained so as more effectually to accomplish the end in view."

The operative word in Marshall's opinion and Bouvier's definition—at least as it applied to Black—is "end." When asked in 1962 whether the Court should defer to congressional judgment on constitutional issues, Black replied in a letter:

> The question just does not make sense to me. This is because if the Court must "defer" to the legislative judgment about whether a statute is constitutional, then the Court must yield its responsibility to another body that does not possess that responsibility. If, as I think, the judiciary is vested with the supreme constitutional power and responsibility to pass on the validity of legislation, then I think it cannot "defer" to the legislative judgment without abdicating its own responsibility.

Ironically, however, Black was as close to the paradigm of the strict constructionist—when it served his ends—as any justice in history. His absolutism was best known in relation to the First

Amendment's prohibition of the passage by Congress of any law respecting the freedoms of speech, press, religion, and assembly.

Black's strict constructionism surfaced in a dissent from a decision that extended the "due process" clause to include a requirement to prove guilt "beyond a reasonable doubt":

> In two places [Black wrote] the Constitution provides for trial by jury, but nowhere in that document is there any statement that conviction of crime requires proof of guilt beyond a reasonable doubt. The Constitution thus goes into some detail to spell out what kind of trial a defendant charged with a crime should have, and I believe the Court has no power to add to or subtract from the procedures set forth by the Founders.

Nonetheless, Black, whose onetime membership in the Ku Klux Klan had caused a furor when President Roosevelt lifted him from the United States Senate in 1937 and appointed him to the Supreme Court, was recognized as the leader of the Court's liberal wing by the time Warren became Chief Justice in 1953.

Of slight build and careful always to maintain impeccable southern manners, Black nonetheless possessed strong physical vitality and was a fierce competitor whether overwhelming opponents on the tennis court or winning intellectual points on the Supreme Court.

"When I was forty, my doctor advised me that a man in his forties shouldn't play tennis," Black was quoted. "I heeded his advice carefully—and could hardly wait until I reached fifty to start again." (That, clearly, is the voice of the strict constructionist as well as that of the competitor.)

In whatever way he was construing the Constitution, Black always was certain that he was right. "You can't disagree with him," Jackson, commenting on Black, told columnist Arthur Krock of the New York *Times*. "You must go to war with him if you disagree."

Jackson, who yearned to become Chief Justice, believed that Black had frustrated that ambition in 1946 after the death of Chief Justice Harlan F. Stone. Black, Jackson thought, had approached President Truman and had threatened to resign from the Court if Jackson was elevated to the Chief Justiceship. Frankfurter wrote a friend, quoting "a most reliable witness," that Truman had planned to name Jackson until the President was "threatened with resignations."

From Nuremberg, where he was chief American prosecutor of Nazi war criminals, Jackson wrote Frankfurter that "Black is now rid of the Chief," alluding to Black's dislike of Stone. "Now if he can have it understood that he has a veto over the promotion of any associate [justice], he would have things about where he wants them."

Black returned Jackson's dislike in full measure. Not long before Jackson's death, Black received a copy of an editorial in the Macon *Telegraph* entitled "Jackson Is an Unmitigated Ass." Writing to a former law clerk, Black mentioned the editorial and, in addition, "an article by John Temple Graves on the same subject. I have nothing but sympathy for John Temple."

About the same time, Jackson wrote Frankfurter that "I simply give up understanding our colleague [Black] and begin to think he is a case for a psychiatrist."

Jackson's acrimony toward Black erupted in a note he sent to Frankfurter when the former professor was unable to attend Court one day. "Congratulations on your absence from today's session," Jackson wrote. "Only if you had been caught playing the piano in a whorehouse can you appreciate today's level of my self-respect."

Frankfurter shared Jackson's disdain for Black because, among other things, Black "represents discontinuity in the law," Frankfurter wrote to Jackson, "and a stick-in-the-mud like me is concerned with decent continuity." Frankfurter railed to Justice Reed about "some untenable notions in Hugo's head," wondering if "any amount of relevant or irrelevant discussion could shake Hugo loose from his conclusion? You might as well ask him to climb a greased telephone pole . . ."

To his diary, Frankfurter confided: "O Democracy, what flapdoodle is delivered in thy name. Not the less so because it was all said in Black's irascible and snarling tone of voice."

Some years later, in a May 19, 1961, note to Justice John M. Harlan, Frankfurter inelegantly, if pithily, characterized a Black opinion by noting, "It makes me puke."

Frankfurter and Jackson were not alone in finding Black difficult. During a conference at which Black, according to Frankfurter, "made one of his inflammatory outbursts," Justice Sherman Minton scrawled a note and pushed it over to Frankfurter. "He is a demagogue," Shay Minton's note said of Black.

Black, like Douglas, was well aware that he riled Frankfurter—and he, too, seemed to relish puncturing the professor's ego. "I thought Felix was going to hit me today, he got so mad," Black said after a heated conference dispute, "but he'll get over it."

Nearly two years after Frankfurter's retirement from the Bench in 1962, Black wrote him that "our differences, which have been many, have rarely been over the ultimate end desired, but rather have related to the means that were most likely to achieve the end we both envisioned."

Black may have forced himself to say a kindly word to Frankfurter. He made no such effort where Jackson was concerned; Black's unsheathed hostility kept Jackson in a state of continual discomfort—and it affected his attitude toward himself and the Court.

Jackson, despite his natural gifts—including an incisive writing style, a natural wit, and an aptitude for phrasemaking matched only by Justice Holmes—never shed his inner insecurity and his sense that he was inferior to his colleagues from the great law schools. Despite the patrician bearing of an upper New York State squire and his elegant Hickory Hill estate in McLean, Virginia (which, years later, would be owned by John and, subsequently, by Robert Kennedy), Jackson came from a poor family; his legal education was limited to one year at what at least one leading professor described as "a second-rate law school." Jackson had made his money from practicing law—and he believed that Black somehow resented, even despised, his plebeian yet financially successful background.

Once, he confided to Frankfurter that he was considering turning down an invitation to sit as a judge in the moot court competition at Harvard Law School. He thought he would be inadequate to the task; besides, he argued, suppose the same parties were to come before the Court sometime in the future?

Frankfurter, recognizing the smoke screen, responded by sending Jackson a mock opinion:

In the Matter of the I.Q. ⎫

Of Robert H. Jackson ⎭

FRANKFURTER, Circuit Justice:

The motion—such it is in effect—to declare Brother JACKSON disqualified to sit in the case [scheduled for moot court at Harvard] boils down to the claim that the skill or learning of undergraduate law students will so undermine the understanding or disinterestedness of Mr. Justice JACKSON's judicial powers that, hereafter, he will not be able to hear with an open mind and judge with impartiality a future proceeding in the jurisdiction of the Supreme Court of the United States between the same parties raising the same issues.

While objectors ought not to be precluded from offering proof as to these moral and intellectual disabilities of the aforesaid JACKSON, I do not feel warranted in taking judicial notice of such disabilities. The motion must therefore be dismissed, without prejudice to an effort to raise them by an appropriate procedure.

So ordered.

Partly, perhaps, to cover his sense of inadequacy, and partly to strike back at Black, Jackson retained a cynical view of the Court, reflected in these quatrains he dashed off "with apology to Kip":

Come you back to Mandalay,
Where the flying judges play;
And the fog comes up like thunder
From the Bench decision day.

Come you back to Mandalay,
And hear what the judges say;
As they talk as brave as thunder—
And then run the other way.

The hostility between Frankfurter and Black appeared rooted more in their judicial and intellectual disagreements than in the

personal animosity that characterized the relationship between
Jackson and Black. That distinction, however, did not minimize
their mutual belligerence.

Frankfurter and Black illustrate the unreliability of using an
individual's past record to indicate how he or she might act as a
Supreme Court justice. Black was a United States senator from
Alabama who had once belonged to the Ku Klux Klan; he became a champion of individual rights for most of his Court career. Frankfurter, when a professor at Harvard, was known for
his interest in progressive causes and he became, from his secure
perch in academia, *l'éminence grise* to FDR's New Deal; on the
Court, he inherited Holmes's mantle as the leading advocate of
judicial restraint.

"One of the things that laymen, even lawyers, do not always
understand," Frankfurter once said, "is indicated by the question
you hear so often: 'Does a man become any different when he
puts on a [judicial] gown?' I say, 'If he is any good, he does.'"

One thing that did not change about Frankfurter—nor about
most men who have been elevated to the Supreme Court—was
his interest and involvement in politics. When Louis D. Brandeis
became a justice of the Supreme Court in 1916, he started paying an annual and secret retainer to Professor Felix Frankfurter
of the Harvard Law School. The purpose was to enable Frankfurter to advance causes that both supported but that Brandeis
could not advocate from the Bench and that Frankfurter could
not afford to pursue on his own.

Even after his appointment to the Court, Frankfurter used former students and law clerks, many of whom became influential
in government, to help shape public policy.

Over the years, justices have taken an active part in presidential elections, have drafted legislation, buttonholed congressmen to get bills passed, and helped write treaties.

It was not Frankfurter's involvement in politics that troubled
Black, himself a seasoned politician; rather, it was what he
viewed as Frankfurter's penchant for hiding behind the judge's
robe to avoid what Black believed was his responsibility as a justice. To Black, Frankfurter's posture was an exercise in hypocrisy
as well as abdication of his judicial duty. As Black had written in

a 1962 letter to a friend, a decision by the Court "does not depend at all, however, upon 'deference' to the Congress, but on the Court's honest judgment as to whether the law was within the competence of the Congress."

Black was hardly alone in believing Frankfurter hid behind his robe to mask his deep-seated conservatism. Perhaps because many liberals of the day had expected something far different from Frankfurter, once the professor had become the justice, former allies tended to turn on him with the special vituperation reserved for traitors.

For Frankfurter, a gregarious man, the loss of old friends—and their respect bordering on hero worship—was difficult. "A policeman's lot is not the only one that's not a happy one," he confided to a federal judge. The conflict between his intense nature and the detachment required by his judicial philosophy was illustrated by a 1940 Frankfurter opinion in which the Court upheld a law making it compulsory to salute the American flag.

Only Justice Stone dissented. Those seeking relief were Jehovah's Witnesses; their refusal to salute the flag touched off a wave of attacks—some violent—against Witnesses around the country. Stone emotionally maintained that the Constitution must preserve "freedom of mind and spirit." Frankfurter felt compelled to explain to him the intrinsic difficulty in a case of that kind:

> Here, also, we have an illustration of what the Greeks thousands of years ago recognized as a tragic issue, namely, the clash of rights, not the clash of wrongs. For resolving such a clash we have no calculus. . . . All my bias and predisposition are in favor of giving the fullest elbow room to every variety of religious, political, and economic view. . . . What weighs with me strongly in this case is my anxiety that, while we lean in the direction of the libertarian aspect, we do not exercise our judicial power unduly, and as though we ourselves were legislators by holding with too tight a rein the organs of popular government.

Not long afterward, Frankfurter was a guest of the President and Mrs. Roosevelt at Hyde Park. Conversation turned to the recent opinion on saluting the flag and Frankfurter tried to explain the dichotomy in his feelings. Eleanor Roosevelt, however, em-

bodied the disappointment with Frankfurter among liberals
when she declared that, regardless of the justice's learning and
legal skills, there was "something wrong with an opinion that
forced little children to salute a flag when such a ceremony was
repugnant to their consciences."

Three years later, the Court flatly overruled its earlier decision, maintaining in an opinion by Justice Jackson that "no
official, high or petty," can prescribe orthodoxy in religion, politics, or nationalism. Frankfurter dissented even more emotionally
than Stone had before, asserting that he was not at leave to follow his "purely personal" view, which would have supported the
majority:

> One who belongs to the most vilified and persecuted minority in
> history is not likely to be insensible to the freedoms guaranteed
> by our Constitution.

Part of Frankfurter's difficulties with his colleagues resulted
from his inability to shed the role of teacher. "I have an incorri-
gibly academic mind," he averred years later to Justice Charles
E. Whittaker. His professorial air was not confined to the long
lectures during the Court's conferences that so disturbed Justice
Douglas and some of the others. He frequently interrupted his
colleagues, including Chief Justice Warren, during their questioning of counsel from the Bench—just as frequently drawing
their rebukes—and he often heckled lawyers during oral arguments. Only once, the story is told, was Frankfurter rendered
speechless. A lawyer from the Midwest, trying to argue his case,
had been interrupted ceaselessly by Frankfurter's rapid-fire
questioning. The lawyer, failing to answer to the justice's satisfaction, exhausted Frankfurter's patience. "Counsel," the justice
demanded testily, "before you go any further, I want to know:
How did you get to this Court?" The lawyer looked up innocently and replied, "I came on the Pennsylvania Railroad."

The message that Frankfurter tried repeatedly to impart to his
fellow justices was, as he wrote to Judge Charles Wyzanski in
1958, that "this Court is an 'undemocratic' element in our democratic society. . . . Judicial nullification of legislation is an 'undemocratic' process." After reading Eugene V. Rostow's assertion

that the process of judicial review possesses a democratic character, Frankfurter wrote Wyzanski, "If you believe that, you'll believe anything."

He tried moving Black to his point of view in a letter of November 13, 1943. It was necessary, Frankfurter wrote,

> . . . to observe the conditions under which judicial review of political authority—that's what judicial review of legislation really amounts to—is ultimately maintainable in a democratic society. [Judges] do not write their private notions of policy into the Constitution [nor] merely translate their private convictions into decisions and call it the law and the Constitution.

Frankfurter described Black as "a Benthamite"—an adherent of the utilitarian ethic that defines the ultimate good as that which brings the greatest happiness to the greatest number; those actions are "right" that contribute to the general happiness. Jeremy Bentham applied that ethic to the law in England in the late eighteenth and early nineteenth centuries.

"As is so often true of a reformer who seeks to get rid of the accumulated abuses of the past," Frankfurter wrote Black on December 15, 1939, "Bentham at times threw out the baby with the bath water." Because "rightness" depended on happy or unhappy consequences that could vary with circumstances, Bentham's utilitarianism could not encompass certain and necessary moral principles because application of these principles could, at times, result in unhappy consequences. Frankfurter maintained that in Bentham's "rigorous and candid desire to rid the law of many far-reaching abuses introduced by judges, he was not unnaturally propelled to the opposite extreme."

In Frankfurter's mind, Black was a Benthamite with a vengeance—a judge acting more like a legislator, a man using the Bench to remake the law in his own image.

In a 1943 case, Black had dissented from an opinion upholding an order of the Interstate Commerce Commission. The opinion stressed that Congress had given the ICC, not the courts, discretion in the kind of case being adjudicated. Frankfurter crystallized his reaction to Black in one of his mock opinions:

SUPREME COURT OF THE UNITED STATES

No. 175—October Term, 1942

The Interstate Commerce Commission, the Baltimore and Ohio Railroad Company, et al.	
Appellants	On Appeal from the District Court of the United States for the Northern District of Ohio
vs.	
Inland Waterways Corporation et al.	

Mr. Justice FRANKFURTER, concurring

I greatly sympathize with the essential purpose of my Brother (former Senator) Black's dissent. His roundabout and turgid legal phraseology is a *cri de coeur.* "Would I were back in the Senate," he means to say, "so that I could put on the statute books what really ought to be there. But here I am, cast by Fate into a den of judges devoid of the habits of legislators, simple fellows who feel that they must enforce the laws as Congress wrote them and not as they really should have been written, that the task that Congress has committed to the Interstate Commerce Commission should be left to that Commission even when it decides, as it did in this case, against the poor farmers of the Middle West."

Frankfurter's concept of the proper judicial role did not allow for Black's opting for morality over law at one end of the spectrum, or for Black's absolutist view of the First Amendment at the other end. Black's absolutist, or strict constructionist, position was enunciated in a widely reproduced 1962 interview:

I learned a long time ago that there are affirmative and negative words. The beginning of the First Amendment is that "Congress shall make no law . . ." I understand that it is rather old-fashioned and shows a slight naïveté to say that "no law" means no law. . . . I took an obligation to support and defend the Constitution as I understand it. And being a rather backward country fellow, I understand it to mean what the words say.

Freedom of speech and of the press, Black believed, was protected from any and all governmental infringements "without deviation, without exception, without any ifs, buts, or whereases."

Just as Frankfurter would bend his doctrines to fit circumstances, as when he found legislated segregation and the judicial principle of separate-but-equal violated the Constitution, so did Black's absolutism on speech break down in cases of speech combined with conduct, as in the sit-in demonstrations. Black denied he was indulging himself in his own "ifs, buts, or whereases," clarifying his position by expounding on Justice Holmes's famous limitation of free speech:

> That is a wonderful aphorism about shouting "fire" in a crowded theater. But you do not have to shout "fire" to get arrested. If a person creates a disorder in a theater, they would get him there not because of *what* he hollered—but because he *hollered*.

To Frankfurter, the only absolute in law was that there were no absolutes. On February 23, 1955, he wrote Justices Reed and Burton that:

> Lincoln for government and Holmes for law have taught me that the absolutists are the enemies of reason—that the fanatics in politics and the dogmatists in law, however sincere, are the mischief-makers.

To Justice Harlan (the Younger), Frankfurter wrote on May 19, 1961, that "Black and Company have gone mad on free speech!"

A year earlier, he circulated a satirical dialogue to drive home his point:

A DIALOGUE

(With Apologies to Gertrude Stein)

Libertarian Lads: Speech is speech is speech.

Frivolous Frankfurter: Crying-fire-in-theater is speech is speech is not "speech."

Libel is speech is speech is not "speech."

Picketing is speech is speech is not "speech."

Pornographic film is speech is speech is not "speech."

Anonymous

Black did not have to face Jackson and Frankfurter without support. Black's judicial alter ego was William O. Douglas. "If any student of the modern Supreme Court took an association test," Black's son wrote, "the word 'Black' would probably evoke the response 'Douglas' and vice versa." In 1958, Black declined an invitation to write an article about Douglas, stating:

> You perhaps know without my stating it that I have the very highest regard for Justice Douglas as a friend and as a member of this Court. In fact, our views are so nearly the same that it would be almost like self-praise for me to write what I feel about his judicial career.

Douglas returned Black's admiration. After Vinson's death, Douglas sent a note to Black. "I wish Eisenhower would make you Chief Justice," Douglas wrote. "It would be the smartest thing he could do politically and the best possible appointment on the merits. But I do not think he's smart enough to do it."

When Chief Justice Hughes had retired in 1941, Douglas hoped that Roosevelt would elevate Black. The appointment, however, went to another sitting justice, the Coolidge-appointed Harlan Stone. Although Roosevelt's decision might have been a bipartisan gesture on the eve of World War II, Douglas was convinced there was a less noble reason. He wrote Black on June 22, 1941, "I am sorry that it did not go to you. I thought you deserved it. And I know it would strengthen the Court greatly if you were the Chief. . . . Felix has done it again, and there is no question in my mind that he was responsible."

Where Douglas was concerned, though, mutual respect rarely translated into warm friendship. He appeared to be the personification of the last frontiersman—a stoic, granite-hewed, close-mouthed, but big-hearted Westerner. As a boy, he had overcome polio and poverty, becoming a sportsman and world-acclaimed mountain climber after he had been told he would never walk again. He rode East on a freight car, enrolled at Co-

lumbia Law School with only six cents left in his pocket, and
went on to become an eminent professor of law, chairman of the
Securities and Exchange Commission, and, finally, a justice of
the Supreme Court at the age of forty.

He was a maverick in his personal life as well as on the Bench.
His second wife confided in Black that "Bill's headstrongness
sometimes cannot be coped with." As a justice, Douglas cared little whether his views carried a majority or whether he stood
alone. He worked harder at publicizing his views than at working to get his position accepted as law. He whipped up opinions
quickly, relying less on his clerks than any other justice—and,
more often than not, the haste and disinterest showed themselves in unpolished work; many of his opinions read like incom-
plete first drafts.

Douglas rarely tried to conceal his lack of interest; indeed, he
seemed to relish the role of the aloof justice. During oral arguments, Douglas often would write letters; every now and then,
he would lift his head, ostentatiously lick the flap of an envelope,
and seal it.

Obviously, Frankfurter viewed Black and Douglas as a brace
of "self-righteous do-gooders," as he put it to Justice Harlan in
April 1957. In 1956, he wrote Judge Learned Hand that Black
and Douglas were worse than the justices who had invalidated
the early New Deal regulatory measures. Those justices, Frankfurter wrote,

> found their economic and social convictions in the Constitution.
> To a very considerable degree that cannot be said of too many of
> their successors. If I gave you a bill of particulars of what I have
> lived through in these nearly twenty years, even you with all
> your knowledge and discernment would realize that you don't
> know nuthin'. I could unto you a tale unfold that would shock
> you, hardened character that you are.

Douglas, like Black, believed that Frankfurter used judicial restraint as a shield. Frankfurter, he wrote, "was a real conservative who embraced old precedents under the guise of bowing
to 'the law,' but who actually chose the old precedents because
he liked them better."

Douglas enjoyed needling Frankfurter, but the professor could get under Douglas' skin, too. After one conference, Douglas sent Frankfurter a bitingly worded memorandum, contending that "I asked you a question [and] an answer was refused rather insolently. This was so far as I recall the first time one member of the conference refused to answer another member on a matter of Court business."

Eventually, the two stopped speaking outside of formal exchanges at conferences or in the courtroom. Once, Fred Rodell of the Yale Law School arrived at the Court to call on Douglas. The justices were in conference, so Rodell sent in a note to inform Douglas that he had arrived and would wait.

After a while, Douglas sent out a note to Rodell; referring to Frankfurter, Douglas wrote: "That little S.O.B. knows you're here—and he's filibustering."

Douglas often grew impatient during the discourses of his colleagues. On June 17, 1963, while the Court was issuing decisions, Justice Clark decided to read every word of a lengthy opinion. Douglas scribbled a note and passed it to Black. "Is he going to read all of it?" the note asked. "He told me he was only going to say a few words. He is on page twenty now; fifty-eight more to go. Perhaps we need an anti-filibuster rule as badly as some say the Senate does."

The remaining four justices included the courtly Southerner Stanley Reed. Douglas wrote that Frankfurter also once pulled strings to block Reed's elevation to Chief Justice; if true, Frankfurter likely rendered a service to the nation.

Reed was a devoted, dependable worker—but his tendency to reduce complex issues to simplistic components negated much of his value as a justice. President Truman's loyalty program of 1947, for instance, presented difficult legal questions to the likes of Frankfurter, among others, but was seen with crystal clarity by Reed.

Responding to growing vigilantism in Congress over the fear of Communist threats to internal security, Truman signed Executive Order 9835 on March 21, 1947, establishing a Federal Employee Loyalty Program. The next day, the FBI began a search for "disloyal and subversive persons" by conducting name checks on the two million federal employees and the half million people who applied for federal jobs every year.

If derogatory information was filed about anyone, the FBI was authorized to conduct a full field investigation. Regional loyalty boards would consider the material, dismiss the charges, or hold a hearing and reach a verdict. Decisions to dismiss an employee could be appealed to a National Loyalty Review Board in Washington; its rulings were final.

Grounds for dismissal included belonging to or, in some cases, knowing someone who belonged to any of the supposedly subversive organizations on a list drawn up by Attorney General Tom Clark. "Reasonable grounds for belief" of subversive activities were sufficient for dismissal; charges could be defined for the accused "specifically and completely" only if "security considerations permit." And the FBI held that the identity of informants could not be disclosed on the ground that future investigations would be jeopardized; therefore, the accused never knew his accuser.

One illuminating example of how it worked involved a forty-one-year-old woman named Dorothy Bailey, a fourteen-year employee of the United States Employment Service who was fired in 1948 on unsupported charges that she had been a Communist and had associated with known Communists. Miss Bailey appealed to the National Loyalty Review Board, which refused to identify her accusers. The Board's chairman, Seth Richardson, said that he couldn't identify them if he wanted to. "I haven't the slightest knowledge as to who they are," he told Paul Porter, Miss Bailey's lawyer, "or how active they have been in anything." Porter insisted "that some identification of this malicious gossip be given [Miss Bailey] or her counsel."

Richardson replied that "if this testimony is true, it is neither gossip nor malicious. We are under the difficulty of not being able to disclose this."

"Is it under oath?" Porter asked.

"I don't think so," Richardson said. A Board member added that the accuser "is a person of known responsibility who had proffered information concerning Communist activity in the District of Columbia."

Miss Bailey's appeal was denied. Richardson reminded her complaining lawyer that government service was "a privilege, not a right."

Justice Reed agreed with Richardson, not Frankfurter. He told his colleague that "we will never agree on loyalty investigations because we are not looking in the same direction. . . . Those who disagree with me, they say that the 'trials' are unfair, therefore unconstitutional, because one is not confronted with his accusers. [But] a negative conclusion [by the Review Board] means nothing more, constitutionally, than a similar inquiry by me of, say, a law clerk." Allowing the Review Board power to decide loyalty cases "on the evidence, including hearsay . . . [is] the only way to conduct affairs."

In the end, however, there were relatively few dismissals of the kind Miss Bailey endured. During the five years of the loyalty program, the FBI reported it screened three million Americans, conducted ten thousand full field investigations, and filed preliminary indictments against nearly all of those. Fewer than three thousand people were arraigned before regional boards and fewer than four hundred were given notice. Summing up his findings for a congressional committee, Richardson said that "not one single case . . . of espionage has been disclosed in the record; not one single syllable of evidence has been found by the FBI indicating that a particular case involves a question of espionage."

As an Associate Justice unmistakably identified with the South, however, Reed's support of judicial decisions to abolish racial injustice helped to persuade important segments of the South's leadership to accept the landmark decisions.

Reed was a Roosevelt appointee like the four incumbent superstars on the Court when Warren arrived. The other three—Harold H. Burton, Tom C. Clark, and Sherman Minton—had been named by Truman.

Burton and Truman became friends in the United States Senate, where Burton was a member of Truman's World War II committee which investigated defense contracts. He had been a leader of his local bar association, a state legislator, mayor of

Cleveland, and a senator from Ohio before Truman appointed him to the Court.

Even his biographer conceded that Burton was "an average justice, not a bright, witty intellectual like a Frankfurter or a Black." He was congenial, however, and fair-minded enough to be nominated by Frankfurter as the judge he would prefer to preside should the former professor be on trial for his life.

Fully appreciative of his modest abilities, Burton was deferential toward Frankfurter. When the Harvard don praised some work Burton had done, the Ohioan sent him a note saying that "I feel as though you have awarded me a mythical grade 'A' in your course on Constitutional Law, of which I may be proud."

Clark had been a prosecutor in Texas and a Department of Justice attorney entrusted with helping to evacuate the Japanese from California in World War II. Despite his Texas pride and his outward flamboyance (he always wore a large, often colorful bow tie, even under his judicial robes), Clark tended to be a follower—first of the generally conservative Vinson and, later, of the judicial progressivism of Earl Warren.

Before his career ended, Clark would play an instrumental role in some of the most far-reaching decisions of the Warren Court. Among other actions, it was at Clark's initiative that the Court adopted the exclusionary rule in state cases, one of the most important and controversial tenets in modern criminal justice. The rule excluded using evidence acquired in an illegal search.

Like Truman and Burton, Shay Minton was a Midwesterner and a United States senator—in Minton's case, from Indiana. Minton, however, had served for eight years as a judge on the U.S. Court of Appeals before being named to the Supreme Court. Where Burton was neat, self-effacing, and delicately built, Minton was square-jawed, had a physique like a heavyweight boxer, and given to salty observations. He is believed to be the last person to use the spittoon provided for each justice behind the Bench—a habit which unfailingly disturbed the fastidious Burton, who sat next to him.

He, too, was influenced strongly by Frankfurter, whose sure political instincts included spending sufficient time and flattery on the likes of Minton and Burton to secure their support and their votes.

Even Minton, however, couldn't resist taking an occasional jab at the learned scholar. In a 1951 case, Frankfurter agonized over a decision to such an extent that he issued a separate opinion bearing the highly unusual label "Mr. Justice Frankfurter, *dubitante.*"

Minton promptly wrote, "My dear Felix: I think you are slipping! I always thought you were a person who sometimes *fortasse errat,* but never *dubitante.*"

It was into this cauldron of brilliance, pettiness, backbiting, extraordinary concern for the law and justice, pulling and tugging over restraint, activism, absolutism, and strict constructionism, that Earl Warren stepped in October 1953.

Years later, Justice Potter Stewart would say that Warren "came to realize very early that this group of prima donnas could not be told to do this or do that in the way the governor of California can tell a subordinate. . . .

"He didn't lead by his intellect and he didn't greatly appeal to the intellects of others. That wasn't his style. He never pretended to be an intellectual. He was an instinctive leader whom you respected and for whom you had affection. As the presiding member of our conference, he was just ideal."

As history would show, he had to be.

SEVEN

Motherhood, Family & Flag

PEOPLE AND INSTITUTIONS change slowly. In 1947, opposing a proposed procedural change at the Supreme Court, Frankfurter urged his colleagues to avoid "breaking with a tradition that is as old as the Court." He argued that "tradition, particularly in this disordered world . . . should be adhered to as one of the great social forces of justice unless change is called for in the interest of the administration of justice. . . . Think twice and thrice," he implored, "before disobeying the injunction 'Remove not the ancient landmarks of thy fathers.'"

When Warren arrived at the Court, the pages—all male and all white—still wore knickers and double-breasted jackets. (Roger Taney was the first Chief Justice to preside over a nine-member Court in 1836, and also was its first member to wear democratic long trousers, not knee breeches, under his judicial robe.) Starting with its very first session on February 1, 1790, with Chief Justice John Jay presiding in New York City's Royal Exchange at Broad and Water Streets, goose-quill pens and pewter inkwells were provided to participating counsel. In 1946, the supply of goose-quill pens, which had been disrupted by World War II, ran out—but Warren replaced them in April 1954, when some could be acquired again.

Frankfurter named the first black law clerk in 1948—but the first black page was appointed in July 1954 and the first female law clerk was appointed by Douglas in 1944—but there wasn't another until Black named the daughter of the well-known lobbyist Tommy Corcoran in 1966. In 1916, Brandeis became the first Jew named to the Court. The appointment of Thurgood Marshall in 1967 broke the color line on the Bench, and in 1982, Sandra Day O'Connor became the first woman to serve as a justice.

Early in 1961, the pens and inkwells gave way to pencils, just as docket entries, entered in script by the Court clerk for more than a century and a half, would appear subsequently in type-written form. In 1963, the Court's pages shed their knickers and replaced them with long gray trousers (or, where appropriate, skirts) and single-breasted dark blue sport coats (styled for women as well as for men).

When, in December 1959, the New York *Times* reported that the Court, "one of the last institutions holding out against the Christmas party, succumbed last week," it did not know that, but for another old tradition—racism—such an event might have occurred twelve years earlier. In 1947, the law clerks decided to throw a Christmas party. They planned to invite all Court employees—including the janitorial staff comprising mostly Negroes.

Chief Justice Vinson thought the notion was novel enough to bring it up at the Court's conference. Justice Reed promptly demurred. If blacks were invited, he said, he would not attend.

One of the justices told Reed that his refusal to attend would place the Court in "a terrible position after all the noble utterances of the Court publicly against racial discrimination."

"This is purely a private matter," Reed replied, "and I can do what I please in regard to private parties."

Frankfurter interjected, "The very fact that we have been sitting here for nearly an hour discussing the right to hold the party makes it difficult to regard it as purely private. The Court is entangled no matter what way you look at it."

The idea for the party was shelved quietly; it may have been more than a coincidence that the following year one of the clerks Frankfurter appointed was black.

Controversy has been a handmaiden to the Court almost from its inception.

Barely three years old, John Jay's Court of six justices ruled in *Chisholm* v. *Georgia* that the state of Georgia could not seize property owned before the Revolutionary War by two South Carolinians who had remained loyal to the Crown. The states were shocked and enraged; paying debts to Tories might lead to their financial ruin. The response was the Eleventh Amendment, prohibiting a federal court from trying a lawsuit against a state by citizens of some other state. The precedent for overruling the Supreme Court, albeit by the laborious process of amending the Constitution, was established early.

The same Court spurned a plea from President Washington when war broke out between Britain and France. Washington worked feverishly to maintain United States neutrality; involvement, he feared, would be disastrous for the new, weak, and financially burdened country. He forwarded to Jay twenty-nine questions on international law and treaties, begging the Court's advice on how to walk the precariously narrow line between his ally, France, and his enemy, Britain. The Court flatly refused to help; constitutionally, it said, it could not participate in executive powers or duties or issue advisory opinions. The Court speaks only on specific cases that come before it for review.

After Thomas Jefferson defeated John Adams in the election of 1800, Adams and the Congress he controlled quickly expanded the judiciary, reduced the Supreme Court to five members (denying Jefferson an early Court appointment), named sixteen new federal judges, forty-two federal officials, and appointed Adams' Secretary of State, John Marshall, as the fourth Chief Justice. Jeffersonian Republicans, upon taking power, repealed the lame-duck Judiciary Act, threatened to impeach some of the justices of the Court, and passed a law suspending the Court's sessions for fourteen months. The Republicans had found repugnant the vigor with which the federal courts had supported the Alien and Sedition Acts of 1798, which provided, among other things, for punishment of "false, scandalous, and malicious writings against the Government, either House of Congress, or the President, if published with intent to defame any of them or to excite against them the hatred of the people . . ."

In the two years in which they were in force, the Acts resulted in the conviction of ten people, all of whom were pardoned by Jefferson.

An immediate Jeffersonian concern with the Court resulted from the haste of Adams' Federalists to leave behind a cadre of supporters after it left office; the Adams government failed to deliver some of the fifty-eight eleventh-hour commissions it had issued, including one naming William Marbury a justice of the peace for the District of Columbia. In December 1801, Marbury asked the Court to issue a writ of mandamus ordering the new Secretary of State, James Madison, to give him his commission. The Court, in a direct challenge to Jefferson, boldly agreed to hear the case—whereupon the Republican Congress suspended the Court's sessions.

When the Court resumed its deliberations in 1803, Chief Justice Marshall faced a dilemma. Jefferson had indicated that if the Court ordered Madison to produce Marbury's commission, he would direct Madison to refuse—and the President would back his Secretary of State to the hilt. Obviously, the judiciary could not enforce its own orders; for that, it depended on the executive. If the Court denied Marbury's petition for a writ of mandamus, Jefferson would claim a Republican victory, which would not only embarrass Marshall, a staunch Federalist, but would imply presidential superiority to the Court.

Marshall found a way out of the quandary—and, in so doing, established the Court's supremacy in constitutional matters. Marbury's suit was grounded in the Judiciary Act of 1789, a portion of which authorized the Court to issue writs of mandamus in cases involving federal officials. That authority gave the Court original jurisdiction in such matters—that is, the authority to hear a case without its having worked its way up through lower courts. The Constitution explicitly gave the Court original jurisdiction in cases "affecting ambassadors . . . and those in which a state shall be a party. In all other cases, the Supreme Court shall have appellate jurisdiction."

Marshall found that portion of the Judiciary Act of 1789 to be

unconstitutional; the Constitution, he declared, "shall be the supreme law of the land" and "it is emphatically the province and
duty of the judicial department to say what the law is." Therefore, although Marshall gratuitously pointed out that Marbury
was entitled to his commission and that a writ of mandamus was
the proper remedy (if the case was started in the proper court),
he ruled that the Court was powerless to issue the writ.

The assertion by Marshall of the power of judicial review, and
the Court's ultimate authority over what the law is, escaped criticism in the storm of protest that followed. The angry response
focused on Marshall's having scolded the President and his Secretary of State for not delivering Marbury's commission. When
the Court soon after restored itself to six members, the howls of
protest turned into cries for impeachment. The Jeffersonians took
aim at Associate Justice Samuel Chase, a staunch Federalist who,
presiding at a circuit court in 1803, denounced the President's
"modern doctrines [of] equal liberty and equal rights," claiming
they would lead to "a mobocracy, the worst of all popular governments." Chase was impeached; Jefferson hinted that if the
Senate found him guilty, Marshall would be next. The Senate acquitted Chase on March 1, 1805; Jefferson called the effort to impeach justices "a farce which will not be tried again." It wasn't,
although one hundred and fifty years later, the most popular
bumper sticker in America read: "Impeach Earl Warren."

A half century passed before the Supreme Court held another
act of Congress to be unconstitutional. In the notorious Dred
Scott decision, a majority of the Court held that Scott, though he
had lived on "free" Missouri soil, remained a slave; Congress
lacked the constitutional authority to limit the expansion of slavery as it had done in the Missouri Compromise.

The 1857 decision stretched popular emotions over slavery,
quite literally, to the breaking point. When Abraham Lincoln
was sworn into the presidency four years later by Chief Justice
Roger Taney, an architect of the Dred Scott decision, the new
President eschewed "any assault on the Court." He warned,
however,

> . . . if the policy of the Government, upon vital questions affect-
> ing the whole people, is to be irrevocably fixed by decisions of

the Supreme Court, the instant they are made, in ordinary litigation, [then] the people will have ceased to be their own rulers.

Lincoln's old antagonist, Stephen A. Douglas, had maintained
that, despite his personal objections to the Dred Scott ruling,
"from that decision there is no appeal this side of heaven." Lincoln's position was that one decision settles only that one case.

The Court, which had grown to seven members in 1807 and to
nine thirty years later, received a tenth member during the war
in 1863. The Reconstructionists, to protect their postwar laws
from a potentially meddlesome judiciary, reduced the Court's
membership to eight (keeping President Andrew Johnson from
appointing justices more in tune with his policies of recon-
ciliation between North and South); after Ulysses S. Grant became President in 1869, Congress added a ninth member to the
Court.

Membership has remained at nine, even though Franklin
Delano Roosevelt, after winning re-election in 1936 by ten million votes, tried to "pack" the Court, whose "nine old men" had
stymied his New Deal program in his first term. The Court had
grown cantankerous before FDR became President; Professor
Felix Frankfurter claimed in 1930 that in the previous decade
"the Court has invalidated more legislation than in fifty years
preceding." When the Court knocked down one New Deal program after another, however, Roosevelt sought power to appoint
an additional justice when one aged seventy did not resign, until
the Court reached a membership of fifteen. At the time, six of
the members already were over seventy.

FDR's plan was denounced scathingly across the country.
However, less than two months later, the Court voted to sustain
Washington State's minimum-wage law; a year earlier, it had
found unconstitutional New York's minimum-wage requirement
for women and children. Two weeks later, the Court upheld the
Wagner Act, the first federal law to regulate disputes between
capital and labor; a year before, the Court ruled that a similar
law was an unconstitutional federal infringement upon state re-
sponsibilities.

No one really knows if the two pro-New Deal decisions were

responsive to FDR's attack on the Court. (There is some evidence that the Court's conference vote in the first case preceded FDR's proposal.) In the wake of the decisions, though, the President quietly allowed his proposal to die. The people, as Lincoln had said in 1861, would decide questions of national policy, whatever the Supreme Court might rule in a specific case. At the same time, the people recoiled at what they perceived to be Roosevelt's "assault upon the Court"; his proposed "reform" would have changed too much, too soon.

Clearly, men, like institutions, change slowly, if at all. Earl Warren was no exception. As attorney general and governor of California, he had participated in activities against the Japanese that suggested racist instincts; at the same time, he was responsible for a range of laws and programs which expanded the rights and welfare of individuals. In his first months on the Bench, an observer remarked that he "had moved directly into Chief Justice Vinson's position of moderate conservatism." Nonetheless, as Potter Stewart recalled, Warren established early a commitment on issues touching "widows or orphans or the underprivileged."

Foreshadowing his commitment to equal rights was Warren's decision in *Hernandez* v. *Texas*, a case in which a Mexican-American appealed his conviction of murder on the ground that persons of Mexican descent systematically were excluded from jury service in Jackson County, Texas. It was the first case in the Court's history which struck down discrimination against a group other than Negroes.

On January 16, 1954, Warren, working from a bench memo prepared by his clerk Richard Flynn, maintained that, while there was no right to proportional representation on juries by various ethnic groups, Texas had disqualified from jury service an entire segment of the populace solely because of its national origin.

Flynn, who had lived on Texas' Gulf coast, remembered that "the record was all one way. It was easy. There were things like [separate] bathrooms in the courthouse being labeled 'Men' and 'Hombres Aquí.'" Flynn's memorandum asserted that "these Mexican-Americans are regarded as a separate 'race' or 'class' and they are excluded from jury service on that basis." He urged Warren to reverse the court below.

Warren won unanimous support, although Justice Clark disagreed at first because he thought Warren's opinion presented an unfair picture of Texas. He persuaded Justice Minton to join him. Clark demurred a few days before the May 3, 1954, delivery of the opinion, stating, "While Shay and I think your facts-as-related set up a 'straw man,' we have decided . . . you have covered the law in the field so well that we go along with you."

On April 12, 1954, Warren demonstrated his immovable opposition to decisions that, in his view, threatened the sanctity of the family. The case was *Alton* v. *Alton,* in which lower courts had invalidated a Virgin Islands law authorizing divorces if the plaintiff had spent six weeks in the territory. Six weeks' residence did not suggest a reasonable intent to be domiciled in the area, a prerequisite to divorce.

As Justice Abe Fortas noted years later, Warren presented cases in terms of ultimate moral values. His conference presentation in *Alton* v. *Alton* came straight to the point:

> The very conception of the place of the family in our civilization, and our constitutional system in placing domestic relations within the control of the states, in effect subjects each state to some regard for the interests of other states in the marital relations of their citizens. No state is free to do what it pleases in dissolving the marriage of citizens of another state. [The law is], in effect, legislation to authorize consensual divorce, because the six-week residence . . . is merely a formality for getting a divorce. My conscience won't permit me to have this Court decide that one of the territories can disregard the interests of all the states by issuing consensual divorces.

Only Frankfurter joined Warren; the husband secured a Connecticut divorce in the meantime, however, and Frankfurter persuaded Warren to see that the case, made moot, was "thrown out by us." Before doing so, though, Warren emphasized in a draft dissent his strong, almost passionate, opposition to any decision approving the divorce law:

> Instinctively [the draft read], I feel this territorial statute constitutes a fraud. . . . It is an attempt to disregard the institution of

> marriage. . . . Marriage is our basic social institution. It is inherent in our civilization . . . and national life. [If] we eventually arrive at [a consensual divorce law] . . . the federal government should not force it on the states through . . . a decision of this Court.

Warren tended to retain some of his prosecutorial instincts in early cases before the Court. The most celebrated of those which, he told attorney Edward Bennett Williams years later, he would change if he could was *Irvine* v. *California*. Authorities secretly had entered the home of a suspected bookmaker, placed microphones in several rooms of his house, including the bedroom, and eavesdropped for over a month until they obtained sufficient evidence to convict him. Justice Jackson appears to have persuaded Warren to uphold the conviction. Referring to the police secreting the microphones in the home, Jackson said, "The fact they kept it for a month is bad—also their breaking in. But is this any worse than other cases we've okayed here?"

The controlling case was the 1949 decision in *Wolf* v. *Colorado,* which held that using illegally obtained evidence to secure a conviction in a state court did not violate the United States Constitution. There were limits, however; in *Rochin* v. *California* in 1952, where police had extracted narcotics a defendant had swallowed by pumping his stomach forcibly, the Court ruled that evidence obtained by methods that "shock the conscience" may not be used in a state criminal trial.

Warren said at the conference that "in cases of this kind we must consider whether the state encourages this kind of conduct. Here, it has slipped in. In California, we do not permit wiretapping at all. The California statute okays dictaphones only when okayed by the police. It does not outrage my sense of decency and I'd affirm."

Jackson cut in. "In some ways, this offends me worse than *Rochin.* I don't want people breaking into my house. But we have said a state may adopt its own rule of evidence, so we must conclude that the state has some latitude." Reed, Clark, and Minton joined Warren and Jackson, to whom Warren assigned the opinion. Frankfurter and Douglas maintained that *Rochin* controlled the case; ultimately, they were joined by Black and Burton.

In writing the opinion, Jackson conceded that "few police measures . . . more flagrantly, deliberately, and persistently violated the fundamental principle declared by the Fourth Amendment." The question was raised whether state officials might not be prosecuted for violating rights guaranteed by the Constitution. Yet the Court refused to declare the evidence inadmissible.

In later years, when Warren rued his vote in *Irvine*, he blamed the doctrine of judicial restraint, an odd position, because Frankfurter, the prophet of judicial restraint, had urged reversal of the conviction on the ground that the evidence was obtained in a manner that shocked the conscience.

Nonetheless, he persuaded himself that it was an example of judicial restraint relegating constitutional protections to paper principles. After he retired as Chief Justice, he told an interviewer that if the Court did not enforce constitutional rights, "we let them go and sweep them under the rug, only to leave them for future generations."

If Warren evinced a certain legal ingenuousness in his first days, he could not be faulted in his efforts to throw himself into the work of the Court. After less than a year on the Bench, Warren's devotion to the Court and its work was noted by retired Justice Owen J. Roberts, who wrote Frankfurter on September 30, 1954, "It looks as if the new Chief Justice is making you fellows work overtime. Do you get one and a half times straight pay?"

Warren was quoted in *Newsweek* as believing his "is the most important job in the world." Columnist James Reston said Warren "is now in love with the Court"; he found, Reston wrote, unexpected satisfaction in the quiet, scholarly life on the Bench.

Judging from the barbed exchanges between Frankfurter and Black, life on the Bench seemed less than quiet and scholarly. In response to an assertion by Frankfurter that he would undertake an extensive inquiry into maritime law in connection with a pending case, Black wrote a sarcastic memorandum to his colleagues on November 17, 1953, expressing "delight" that Frankfurter would be "dissipating all confusion and complexity in that field." Stung, Frankfurter wrote Learned Hand, "Hugo is a self-righteous, self-deluded part fanatic, part demagogue."

Perhaps because Warren was aloof from the growing bitterness among some of his colleagues, not yet molded in a judicial philosophy that would estrange him from one wing of the Court while endearing him to the other, he was able to bring his personal charm and leadership capabilities to bear on his fractious brethren. After serving only a few months as Chief Justice, Warren brought all elements of the Court together—activists, conservatives, Northerners, Southerners—and lighted a beacon that has pointed the way for champions of human justice ever since.

EIGHT

Duck, Pheasant & Justice for All

BY EARLY DECEMBER 1953, when the school segregation cases were reargued before the Court, Warren had gained considerable confidence in his ability to adjust to his new role. He conceded to one biographer that "I am feeling my way, going along with the others" on a number of cases. To another writer, Glendon Schubert, Warren still was "primarily a collectivist with strong authoritarian leanings [and] a trained incapacity to oppose the Government in criminal cases."

The ground under his feet felt firm, however, especially because the *Brown* reargument was primarily a political exercise rather than a legal one.

The previous June, the Court had restored the segregation cases to the docket for reargument on the questions formulated by Frankfurter with the help of his clerk Alexander Bickel. The crucial questions sought historical evidence of what the framers and ratifiers of the Fourteenth Amendment had in mind respecting the amendment's impact on racial segregation in the public schools.

In response to the Court's request, elaborate and voluminous briefs were submitted, setting out exhaustively and meticulously

the background of the Fourteenth Amendment and the intentions of those who drafted, debated, and voted on it in Congress
and in the state legislatures.

From the start, however, the questions posed by the Court
were merely a pretext allowing the justices to delay considering
the issue. Frankfurter had hatched the scheme of conducting a
reargument so that the Court might avert the risk of a constitutional crisis should it divide closely on the segregation cases—a
chilling prospect that Black and Douglas, in their zeal, might
have encouraged.

In fact, before the reargument was conducted, Frankfurter
had circulated among his colleagues the results of assiduous research by Bickel demonstrating the fuzziness of trying to determine if the amendment's framers had meant to abolish segregation.

Before the initial conference on school segregation in December 1952, Frankfurter had wrestled with the painful problem of
whether his philosophy of judicial restraint permitted the Court
to find segregation unconstitutional. Although he confined his
views at that conference to his opposition to segregation in the
District of Columbia, Frankfurter had satisfied himself that the
abolition of segregation was justified by the Fourteenth Amendment in the states as well.

He possessed no qualms about extending consideration of
equality beyond facilities; it was "arbitrary to say that 'equal
rights' means physical things." On the other hand, "we can't say
that the Court has long misread the Constitution. What justifies
us in saying what *was* equal in 1868 is not equal *now?*"

In resolving this question, Frankfurter admonished himself not
to abandon his essential philosophy. "However passionately any
of us may hold egalitarian views," he wrote in a memorandum
while *Brown* was pending, "however fiercely any of us may believe that such a policy of segregation, as undoubtedly expresses
the tenacious conviction of Southern states, is both unjust and
shortsighted, he travels outside his judicial authority if for this
private reason alone he declares unconstitutional the policy of
segregation."

The task Frankfurter set for himself was to find a path paved with legal rather than personal intentions. In handwritten notes headed "Segregation," prepared before the December 1952 conference, he appeared to have found his answer. He wrote that although *stare decisis* "means respect for decisions," it did not prohibit "re-examination of the reasoning and principles on which they were based." Segregation, Frankfurter contended, was a "legacy of history. To what extent is the past perpetuated in the Constitution?"

> Society keeps changing or rots through stagnation. Human needs gradually emerge into consciousness . . . and assert themselves with such impact that they become absorbed into the existing framework of law. . . . The equality of laws enshrined in the Constitution is not a fixed formula defined with finality at a particular time. It does not reflect as a congealed formulation the social arrangement and beliefs of a particular epoch. . . . It is addressed to the changes wrought by time and . . . must respond to transformation of views as well as to that of outward circumstances. The effect of the change in men's feelings of what is right and just is equally relevant in determining whether discrimination denies the equal protection of the laws.

The ultimate decision in *Brown* v. *Board of Education* made clear that the reargument was a spurious exercise. Warren's opinion for the Court dismissed out of hand the value of the data:

> Reargument was largely devoted to the circumstances surrounding the adoption of the Fourteenth Amendment in 1868. It covered exhaustively consideration of the Amendment in Congress, ratification by the states, then-existing practices in racial segregation, and the views of the proponents and opponents of the Amendment. This discussion and our own investigation convince us that, although these sources cast some light, it is not enough to resolve the problem with which we are faced. At best, they are inconclusive. . . . It is not surprising that there should be so little in the history of the Fourteenth Amendment relating to its intended effect on public education.

On December 12, 1953—a day short of a year from the Court's first conference on *Brown*—the justices convened on the issue again, this time under the guidance of its new Chief Justice.

Black, to whom Warren had ceded stewardship of the conferences during the Chief's first weeks at the Court, was attending
his critically ill sister in Alabama. The Chief had no difficulty,
though, in taking the reins firmly.

Warren initially established a ground rule congenial to any experienced politician. He proposed that the justices discuss the
segregation cases informally without taking any votes. "The fact
that we did not polarize ourselves at the beginning," Warren told
an interviewer a year later, "gave us more of an opportunity to
come out unanimously on it than if we had done otherwise." A
decade later, Frankfurter pointed out that *Brown* was the only
case he could recall "in which we postponed a vote after argument for further study. The exception is significant. Who will
deny that this maturing process in the segregation cases fully
vindicated itself?"

Warren laid his cards on the table immediately; whether or
not Frankfurter had shared with the Chief his own thinking on
the unconstitutionality of segregation, Warren followed the same
basic reasoning.

"I can't escape the feeling," he began, "that no matter how
much the Court wants to avoid it, it must now face the issue.
The Court has finally arrived at the place where it must determine whether segregation is allowable in public schools."

To be sure, he understood the legitimate concern that the
Court, if it outlawed segregation, would be reversing older cases
and lines of reasoning accepted for more than sixty years.

"But the more I've read and heard and thought, the more I've
come to conclude that the basis of segregation and 'separate but
equal' rests upon a concept of the inherent inferiority of the
colored race. I don't see how *Plessy* and the cases following it
can be sustained on any other theory. If we are to sustain segregation, we also must do it upon that basis. . . . If the argument
proved anything, it proved that basis was not justified. . . .

"I don't see how, in this day and age, we can set any group
apart from the rest and say that they are not entitled to exactly
the same treatment as all others. To do so would be contrary to
the Thirteenth, Fourteenth, and Fifteenth Amendments. They
were intended to make the slaves equal with all others. Person-

ally, I can't see how today we can justify segregation based solely on race."

Justice Abe Fortas, assessing Warren's leadership years later, said he believed that Warren's presentation of the segregation issues to his colleagues demonstrated his "great gift. . . . He proceeded immediately and very calmly and graciously to the ultimate values involved—the ultimate constitutional values, the ultimate human values. . . . Opposition based on the hemstitching and embroidery of the law appeared petty in terms of Warren's basic-value approach."

Unhesitatingly, Warren had put supporters of *Plessy* on the defensive; subscribing to *Plessy* meant subscribing to racist theory. Reed, who with Jackson, Clark, and the late Chief Justice Vinson had supported *Plessy* a year earlier, felt compelled to explain. "I was not making the argument that the Negro is an inferior race. Of course, there is no inferior race, though they may be handicapped by lack of opportunity."

Warren moved quickly and adroitly into the opening.

"It would be unfortunate," he said soothingly, "if we had to take precipitous action that would inflame more than necessary. The condition in the different states should be carefully considered by the Court."

He said he believed border states like Kansas and Delaware would not have a difficult enforcement problem, because of their smaller black populations. "But it's not the same in the Deep South," he added. "It will take all the wisdom of this Court to dispose of the matter with a minimum of emotion and strife. How we do it is important. . . . My instincts and feelings lead me to say that, in these cases, we should abolish the practice of segregation in the public schools—but in a tolerant way."

Shrewdly, almost magically, Warren had shifted the focus of the conference from *what* the Court would do on segregation to *how* it would be done. Warren and his colleagues knew there was a majority opposing school segregation. The previous year's conference had disclosed there were five votes—Frankfurter, Black, Douglas, Minton, and Burton—leaning toward upsetting the *Plessy* precedent. The replacement of Vinson by Warren provided a sixth vote. Warren's presentation assumed a majority—

but it reached out to shaky supporters as well as to earlier opponents.

Promptly, it appeared as if Warren's tactics had paid off. Clark, who was among those reluctant to overturn segregation a year earlier, indicated willingness to join the majority. "It must be done carefully [and] permit different handling in different places," he said, echoing Warren, ". . . or it will do more harm than good."

Jackson then made it clear his earlier caution was based less on the issue than on the law. Overturning segregation, he said, "was a question of politics. Our problem is to make a judicial decision . . . [and find] a judicial basis for a congenial political conclusion." The operative word was "congenial." Implicitly, if an opinion could be constructed with a firm legal basis for overturning segregation, Jackson would go along. Only Reed was left among those who originally had favored reaffirmation of *Plessy*.

Warren devoted the next month to securing a unanimous opinion by driving home the point that it was unthinkable to support racist theory, and that only a unanimous Court could assure sensitive, sympathetic enforcement. After lunching with Warren on December 17, Burton noted in his diary that "the Chief Justice told me of his plan to try to direct discussion of segregation cases toward the decree as providing . . . the best chance of unanimity."

Warren lunched regularly with his colleagues; a frequent foursome was the Chief, Reed, Burton, and Minton. Warren hoped that the down-to-earth Burton and Minton, former senators from states bordering Reed's native Kentucky, would gently move Reed to agree that a split decision would have a deleterious effect on the Court and the country. He met often with the justices individually; few can withstand for long the magnetism that most successful politicians exude in one-on-one sessions.

Meanwhile, the Chief sought to shore up shaky support. Frankfurter was worried that a majority might try to embroil the Court in enforcement. "The one thing one can feel confidently," Frankfurter asserted in a January 15, 1954, memorandum, "is that this Court cannot do it directly." Jackson continued to chafe at what he perceived was the clear political and social basis of a judicial action. Black, who had returned to Washington from Alabama, was worried deeply about the political impact of the decision in the South.

The second *Brown* conference was scheduled for January 16—and the day before, Warren gathered his colleagues for some conviviality. "The Chief Justice," Burton noted in his diary, "gave the Court (all present) an excellent wild duck or pheasant luncheon. All took duck except Justice Frankfurter, who took pheasant."

The next day, Warren picked up the theme of enforcement—both to appease the Southerners (Reed, Clark, and Black) and to assuage Frankfurter's concerns.

The Court, Warren said, should be "as little involved in administration as we can. We should turn to the district courts for enforcement. But we ought not to turn them loose without guidance of what paths are open to them."

Black demurred. He wanted the Court to stay out of enforcement altogether. "Leave it to the district courts," he said. "Let them work it out."

"Would you give them any framework?" Warren demanded.

"I don't see how you could do it," Black said despairingly. "We should leave it up to the district courts."

Reed agreed in principle, demonstrating that his mind-set was moving closer to accepting the inevitable. Still, he believed the Court "must say a few things." Above all, the Court should ensure that enforcement was "not a rush job. The time they give, the opportunities to adjust—these are the greatest palliatives to an awful thing."

Frankfurter had suggested the appointment of a master to propose decrees. Douglas agreed; it would be difficult for the Court to make specific enforcement decisions. Any decree, he urged, should be flexible and reflect generosity. Burton and Minton agreed in broad terms.

"Our contribution is to decentralize enforcement," Burton said.

"I'm not given to throwing the Court's weight around," Minton added.

"If necessary, let us have seven hundred suits," Black interjected. "Vagueness is not going to hurt. Let it simmer. . . . Let it take time. It can't take too long." In the South, he said, "any man that would come out [in support] would be dead politically forever. In Alabama, most liberals are praying for delay."

Jackson maintained that everyone was missing the point. If the black plaintiffs were entitled to admission to desegregated schools as a matter of right, then they were entitled to admission immediately, as had been claimed, among others, by the National Association for the Advancement of Colored People.

"If what we're doing is to uproot social policy," Jackson asked rhetorically, "what business is it of ours?" Rather than try to resolve the dilemma, Jackson agreed that more time was needed to consider the remedial issue. "Let's have a reargument on the terms of a decree," he proposed.

Clark and Black supported that idea. Ultimately, that is what the Court decided to do. For the time being, Warren was close to achieving his goal. Given flexibility in any enforcement plan, Clark would join the majority and Black would stay part of it. As long as the Court did not directly enter into enforcement, Frankfurter's vote was solid. If a subsequent argument were conducted on the decrees that the Court should issue, Jackson would go along; one note of discord was that Jackson might wish to render a separate opinion, a notion the Chief was discouraging. "The fact of the matter," Frankfurter wrote Learned Hand some years later, "is that Bob Jackson tried his hand at a justification for leaving the matter to Section 5 of the Fourteenth Amendment, 'The Congress shall have power to enforce . . . ,' etc., and he finally gave up."

The only real problem, then, was Reed. As late as February, Reed continued to work on the draft of a dissent, asserting that segregation in itself did not violate the "equal protection" clause of the Fourteenth Amendment.

Warren continued to work on him until the end of April. Reed's law clerk was at a meeting where "throughout, the Chief Justice was quite low-key and very sensitive to the problems that the decision would present to the South. He empathized with Justice Reed's concern. But he was quite firm on the Court's need for unanimity on a matter of this sensitivity."

After Warren had gently soaped up Reed, he rinsed him abruptly under a cold shower. "Stan, you're all by yourself in this now," he said bluntly. "You've got to decide whether it's really the best thing for the country."

Reed got the message. "There were many considerations that pointed to a dissent," he wrote Frankfurter a few days after the *Brown* decision was announced. "They did not add up to a balance against the Court's opinion. The factors looking toward a fair treatment for Negroes are more important than the weight of history."

If Jackson continued to entertain thoughts of explaining his vote in a separate opinion, the idea terminated abruptly when, on March 30, he was stricken by a serious heart attack.

Meanwhile, Warren faced some outside intervention, too. While the *Brown* decision was pending, President Eisenhower invited the Chief Justice to a White House dinner where—either cunningly or thoughtlessly—he seated him near John W. Davis, the lawyer who led the case in support of segregation. During dinner, Eisenhower remarked several times that he thought Davis was "a great man." After dinner, the President took the Chief by the arm and walked with him to a sitting room.

"These are not bad people," Eisenhower said of Southerners as they strolled. "All they are concerned about is to see that their sweet little girls are not required to sit in school alongside some big, black bucks."

Warren tried to view the President's comment generously, as a crude plea for moderation. He had, meanwhile, been the obvious choice to write the opinion for the Court. On April 20, Burton wrote in his diary that "after lunch, the Chief Justice and I took a walk around the Capitol and then went to his chambers where he uttered his preliminary thoughts as to author the segregation cases."

Later, Warren summoned the three clerks he had inherited from Vinson: Earl Pollock, William Oliver, and Richard Flynn. He told them the decision of the Court and that it was unanimous. He enjoined them to the strictest secrecy. He had told no one else, not even his wife. Warren directed Pollock to draft the *Brown* decision. Oliver was assigned a companion case, *Bolling*

v. *Sharpe*, which applied to school segregation in the District of Columbia. Flynn had the task of helping both clerks, especially in providing support through footnotes. Warren gave Pollock an outline that would serve as the basis for his *Brown* draft. It contained a line that, with minor editing and an altered phrase suggested by Frankfurter, would become the most famous sentence in the opinion:

> To separate them [children in grade and high schools] from others of similar age and qualifications solely because of their race generates a feeling of inferiority as to their status in the community that may affect their hearts and minds in a way unlikely ever to be undone.

If Warren's language, indicating his concern for the permanent damage to the "hearts and minds" of the youthful victims of discrimination, seemed bathetic, it demonstrated a politician's appeal to the hearts and minds of the American people. Without popular support for the decision, the Court's will might be flouted. Warren told Pollock he wanted the opinion short and to the point; use understandable English, he instructed; avoid legalisms. He wanted an opinion that could be understood by the man in the street.

Pollock prepared the *Brown* draft during the next twenty-four hours, working nonstop and without sleep; Oliver, meanwhile, wrote the much briefer *Bolling* opinion, while Flynn prepared supporting footnotes. In the District of Columbia case, the young clerks worked out the theory that allowed abolition of segregation in the federal city. There, the Fifth Amendment's "due process" clause applied; the "equal protection" language of the Fourteenth Amendment applied to the states, not to the District of Columbia. They wrote that "the concepts of equal protection and due process . . . are not mutually exclusive," though not "always interchangeable." Nonetheless, the deprivation of liberty without due process of law applied not only to bodily restraint but "to the full range of conduct which the individual is free to pursue, and it cannot be restricted except for a proper governmental objective." Segregation of schools failed to meet that test and was an arbitrary deprivation of the liberty of black children in the District of Columbia, violating the "due process" clause of the Fifth Amendment.

With a few minor changes, the drafts were the opinions read by the Chief Justice. On May 7, Warren wrote a memorandum of transmittal of the drafts to his colleagues, emphasizing that they were "prepared on the theory that the opinions should be short, readable by the lay public, non-rhetorical, unemotional, and, above all, non-accusatory." The next day, a Saturday, Warren personally delivered the drafts to the justices who were in the building that morning. Then he took a copy to Jackson's hospital room. The clerks carried copies to the others; Minton received his at his Washington, D.C., apartment, while Black accepted his copy on the tennis court at his home in nearby Alexandria, Virginia.

The following Saturday, May 15, the conference approved the segregation opinions, agreed they would be delivered after the weekend, on May 17, and sat down to one of Justice Burton's storied luncheons—this one, instead of the occasional feast of Maine lobster he provided, featuring as the main course a large salmon provided by Secretary of the Interior Douglas McKay. Burton recalled that the conference decided that no notice of the forthcoming opinions would be given to the justices' office staffs and that "most of us—including me—handed back the circulated print to the Chief Justice to avoid possible leaks."

On Monday morning, Warren returned to Jackson's hospital room to show him a copy of the final opinion and to secure his reaffirmed approval. Jackson, Warren remembered, "to my alarm insisted on attending the Court that day in order to demonstrate our solidarity."

Warren suggested to his clerks that they be in the courtroom when the session convened. Frankfurter told his clerks that *Brown* was coming down. On his way to the robing room, Clark had stopped to advise his clerks, "I think you boys ought to be in the courtroom today."

At noon, the red velour draperies behind the mahogany bench parted and, led by the Chief Justice, the members of the Court filed into the ornate marble-walled, Ionic-columned courtroom and proceeded to their plush green leather chairs. The courtroom was packed, as it had been for weeks in vain anticipation that *Brown* would be announced. Acute observers might have noticed the rare presence of family members of some of the justices; Warren's wife and eldest daughter were among them. Any doubt that this day was special was erased when Jackson made his dramatic entrance.

Nonetheless, Warren saw to it that the session began like any other. One hundred and eighteen attorneys (including Dean Acheson's son and Senator Roman Hruska of Nebraska) were admitted to the bar of the Court. Three unmemorable opinions then were read by Justices Clark and Douglas.

It was now ten minutes to one o'clock. Most of the news correspondents who covered the activities of the Supreme Court, told to expect a routine day, were chatting and sipping coffee languorously in the press room when Banning E. (Dick) Whittington, the Court's press officer, entered and announced, "Reading of the segregation decisions is about to begin in the courtroom." They raced up a long flight of stairs to the press section just as the Chief, at eight minutes until one o'clock, began reading in his unmistakable basso.

"I have for announcement," he said, "the judgment and opinion of the Court in Number One, *Oliver Brown et al.* v. *Board of Education of Topeka.*" Distinctly but colorlessly, he began to read the opinion. The question was "whether *Plessy* v. *Ferguson* should be held inapplicable to public education." It was not enough to determine whether "the Negro and white schools involved have been equalized, or are being equalized, with respect to buildings, curricula, qualifications and salaries of teachers, and other 'tangible' factors. . . . We must look instead to the effect of segregation itself on public education."

> Education is perhaps the most important function of state and local governments. . . . It is required in the performance of our most basic public responsibilities. . . . It is the very foundation of good citizenship. Today it is a principal instrument in awakening the child to cultural values, in preparing him for later professional training, and in helping him to adjust normally to his environment. . . . It is doubtful that any child may reasonably be expected to succeed in life if he is denied the opportunity of an

education. Such an opportunity, where the state has undertaken to provide it, is a right which must be made available to all on equal terms. . . .

Does segregation of children in public schools solely on the basis of race, even though the . . . "tangible" factors may be equal, deprive the children of the minority group of equal educational opportunities? We believe that it does.

At twenty minutes after one o'clock, the Associated Press flashed the word that the Court had decided that school segregation was unconstitutional. A few minutes later, the news was carried to the NAACP's Roy Wilkins and Thurgood Marshall in New York. The two reached for one another and, without a word, they kissed.

Two hundred and fifty miles to the south, Warren said the Court rejected the language in *Plessy* holding that segregation did not suppose racial inferiority; most decidedly, he said, quoting a court below, "separating the races is usually interpreted as denoting the inferiority of the Negro group."

Warren swept on to the opinion's denouement. "We conclude—" Warren skipped a beat, looked up, and departed from the text by enunciating ringingly, "unanimously—" and continuing, "that in the field of public education the doctrine of 'separate but equal' has no place. Separate educational facilities are inherently unequal."

Warren announced that arguments would be scheduled for the Court's next term on the questions of implementation that Frankfurter and Bickel had formulated earlier. It would turn out to be nearly a year before the Court could consider how best to implement its decision.

Initial reaction in the white South was, surprisingly, muted. Because Warren had treated the case as a class action, affecting not only the plaintiffs but "others similarly situated," the ruling would uproot long-established custom in Kansas, the District of Columbia, and twenty other states where segregation either was required by law or was permitted. In all, twelve million schoolchildren might be touched by the decision.

As hoped by the Court, border states like Kansas and Oklahoma responded calmly, predicting change would occur with minimal disruption. Governor Allan Shivers of Texas believed that compliance might take years—but Texas would comply. Governor Thomas Stanley of Virginia said he would convene a meeting of state and local officials "and work toward a plan which will be acceptable to our citizens and in keeping with the edict of the Court." Governor James F. Byrnes of South Carolina, a former justice, was "shocked"—but he confided to his former colleagues on the Court that he would cooperate. Governor Herman Talmadge of Georgia, however, sounded the kind of belligerent note that would grow into a chorus over the next year; Georgians, he drawled, "will fight for their right . . . to manage their own affairs" and "to insure continued and permanent segregation of the races."

President Eisenhower was disappointed. He began calling his appointment of Warren "the biggest damn-fool mistake I ever made." He feared that "if you try to go too far too fast . . . you are making a mistake." He argued to one of his aides in the White House that "I am convinced that the Supreme Court decision set back progress in the South at least fifteen years." To Vice President Richard Nixon, however, "civil rights is primarily a moral rather than a legal question." Eisenhower retorted that "we can't demand perfection in these moral questions. . . . The fellow who tries to tell me that you can do these things by force is just plain nuts."

Nonetheless, the old soldier moved as rapidly as he could in the sphere under his direct control. District of Columbia schools were integrated at once (although, as elsewhere in the nation, the nature and extent of that integration would remain a point of bitter contention for years). "Colored" and "White" signs denoting separate facilities on military posts disappeared. Blacks were hired for professional White House positions for the first time.

Over the ensuing months, some integration was reported in three hundred and fifty school districts in Arkansas, Delaware, Kentucky, Maryland, Oklahoma, Tennessee, Texas, and West Virginia. In other states, legislatures disinterred the antebellum rhetoric of John C. Calhoun and spoke of "interposition" as a way to reject state obedience to federal laws; it was a legal theory which, if not wholly discredited, was at least made moot by the Civil War. Before the Court even could consider the most propitious and least agonizing means of integrating schoolchildren, a seamstress in Montgomery, Alabama, Rosa Parks, tired after a long day's work, was riding a city bus when the driver directed her, according to the custom when the bus filled, to yield her seat to a white man. Mrs. Parks barely hesitated before refusing. At that moment, Eldridge Cleaver would write, "somewhere in the universe a gear in the machinery had shifted."

Propelled by the Court's school segregation decision, blacks and their white supporters throughout the country sensed the walls of racism beginning to crumble. In reaction to the gathering wave of freedom, bigotry started festering into hatred and, finally, violence. There would be skirmishes in Montgomery and Tuscaloosa—but it would be 1956 before the first full-scale battle erupted in Clinton, Tennessee, followed by the national shame of Little Rock in 1957. It would take the naked political lust and self-serving duplicity of Governor Orval Faubus of Arkansas to impel Eisenhower to take the sort of singular action in support of the Supreme Court that Warren had hoped would emanate from the White House three and a half years earlier.

Although the Court could have heard arguments the first week in October 1954 on the implementation of school integration, Warren had decided the previous summer to wait until late November, at least. Frankfurter had written the Chief in July, reminding him that because "segregation is exploited as a political issue . . . I suppose there will be no difficulty in hurdling the distorting opportunities of a fall election and hearing the case after the election is wholly behind us." Warren agreed "to place the cases on the calendar shortly after the fast-approaching 'sound and fury.'"

The planned delay was extended when, in October, a second heart attack proved fatal to Jackson. President Eisenhower promptly nominated John Marshall Harlan, grandson of the justice of the same name who had dissented in the *Plessy* v. *Ferguson* decision of 1896. With the off-year elections and the subsequent reorganization of Congress, it was March 1955 before Harlan's nomination was confirmed. Warren delayed the *Brown* reargument until April, allowing Harlan to join them, making for a full Court.

Briefs had been filed by six segregating states and by the United States. The government emphasized the need for flexibility and allowing the district courts to oversee the process of enforcing the decision; the Supreme Court, though, should insist on "an immediate and substantial start" toward integration.

The Court allowed an unprecedented fourteen hours for reargument over four days. John W. Davis had died a few weeks earlier. In his place, the lead-off attorney was S. Emory Rogers, a short, florid scion of an old landed southern family. He decided that the best hope for the South was to argue aggressively—rudely, if necessary—that southern whites found the prospect of integration repugnant.

To *Brown*'s assertion that "we cannot turn the clock back to 1868 when the [Fourteenth] Amendment was adopted, or even to 1896 when *Plessy* v. *Ferguson* was written," Rogers retorted that "I do not believe that . . . we can push the clock forward abruptly to 2015 or 2045." He advocated an "open decree"—one that returned the cases to the district courts without instructions specifying when and how the schools must be integrated.

"Is your request for an 'open decree,'" Warren asked from the Bench, "predicated upon the assumption that your school district will immediately undertake to conform to the opinion of this Court of last year . . . or is it on the basis—"

"Mr. Chief Justice," Rogers interrupted, "to say we will conform depends on the decree handed down."

Warren leaned forward, uncertain he was hearing correctly. Rogers' next words erased any doubt of his meaning.

"I am frank to tell you," he said somewhat airily, "right now in our district I do not think that . . . the white people will send their children to Negro schools. It would be unfair to tell the Court that we are going to do that. I do not think it is. But I do think that something can be worked out. We hope so."

Warren glared down icily. "It is not a question of attitude," he snapped, "it is a question of conforming to the decree. Is there any basis upon which we can assume that there will be an immediate attempt to comply with the decree of this Court, whatever it may be?"

"The question of compliance should be left to the lower court," Rogers said.

"But you are not willing to say here that there would be an honest attempt to conform to this decree, if we did leave it to the district court?"

"No, I am not," Rogers said bluntly. Then, raising his forefinger at Warren, he declared, "Let us get the word 'honest' out of there."

"No!" Warren roared, his face flushed. "Leave it in!"

"No!" Rogers shouted back. "Because I would have to tell you that right now we would not conform; we would not send our white children to the Negro schools."

Some of Rogers' co-counsel feared Warren might issue a contempt-of-court citation. As shaken as Warren was at the Southerner's sheer presumption and disrespect, he held his tongue. Rogers' defiance confirmed Warren's conclusion of the previous summer that "reasonable attempts to start the integration process is all the Court can expect." In a conversation at the time with one of Justice Reed's clerks, Warren said that "in view of the scope of the problem . . . an order to immediately admit all Negroes in white schools would be an absurdity because it is impossible to obey in many areas."

Warren and Rogers locked eyes for what seemed an eternity. Then the Chief Justice, biting his words, said, "Thank you," and the exchange ended abruptly.

The conference on the decree was conducted the following Saturday. Warren opened the meeting by saying the justices should discuss the issue as long as it was necessary; "I haven't reached a fixed opinion," he said, "and maybe we ought to talk this over the way we did in the main cases last year."

Following the style he had established more than a year before in the first conference on *Brown*, Warren then laid out the boundaries of a decision—this time by submitting a list of "some things we should and should not do."

To start, he issued his "don't" list:

- We should not appoint a master or indicate to the court below that it should do so—though, of course, that court has that power.

- We should not fix any date for completion of desegregation, nor suggest to the lower court that it should . . .

- We should not require the court below to call for a plan; it is perfectly feasible for a lower court to do so, but we should not require it.

- I would not make any procedural requirements; this is a court of equity . . .

Next, he listed "what appeals to me":

- Should we give guidance in an opinion or a formal decree? I think there should be an opinion with factors for the courts below to take into account rather than a formal decree.

- The opinion ought to give them some guidance. It would make it much easier and would be rather cruel to shift it back to them and let them flounder.

- These are class actions; thus enforcement may be had not merely by the named plaintiffs.

- The courts are entitled to take into consideration physical facts and financial problems—but I wouldn't suggest psychological or sociological attitudes.

- The courts must consider whether there has been any movement and progress.

- Give district courts as much latitude as we can, but also as much support as we can.

From the outset, Warren's style of clearly enunciating the options—most of which had been gleaned from previous Court discussions—had the effect of winning to his side nearly all his colleagues.

Reed said it was his "firm belief" that many southern leaders were "willing to give sympathetic consideration" to enforcement. Clark added he did not think there would be "too much trouble in Texas." Several justices emphasized the advantage of remaining unanimous in the enforcement decision as they had in the initial opinion.

Justice Black struck a discordant note, as he had in some of the previous discussions on the segregation issue. "If humanly possible," he said, "I will do everything possible to achieve a unanimous result." He harbored, though, deep reservations:

> I differ from your views [Black told Warren at the conference]. How to do and say as little as possible is my present desire. I was brought up in an atmosphere against federal officials, which is rooted in the race question. . . . The South would never be a willing party to Negroes and whites going to school together. There's no more chance to enforce this in the Deep South than Prohibition in New York City. Nothing is more important than that this Court should not issue what it cannot enforce.

Black said, "We should move gradually and make it as narrow as possible." To begin with, he opposed making the decree a class action; he urged limiting the writ to individual plaintiffs. At best, he said, there would be only "glacial movement" toward integration. "It is futile," he said gloomily, "to think that in these cases we can settle segregation in the South."

Warren again assigned the opinion to himself and the draft was written speedily. Justices suggested minor changes; Frankfurter's idea to issue an unsigned *per curiam* was rejected eight to one in favor of the Chief Justice issuing the opinion.

The only significant change was that first urged by Black and, subsequently, joined by Douglas. At the May 27 conference on the question, they insisted that relief be limited to the named plaintiffs in each case. That approach was certain to slow down the integration process, but the Southerner Black, supported by his friend Douglas, was certain that the success of integration, chancy at best, would otherwise be doomed.

The Chief delivered the decree on May 31, 1955, more than a year after issuing the *Brown* opinion. It directed the lower courts to balance the plaintiffs' interests in admission to schools "as soon as practicable" with "the public interest." Then, however, Warren made clear to Emory Rogers and the rest of the world that "it should go without saying that the validity of these constitutional principles cannot be allowed to yield simply because of disagreement with them."

The courts must "require that the defendants make a prompt and reasonable start toward full compliance." In determining if additional time is needed, "the courts may consider problems related to administration, arising from the physical condition of the school plant, the school transportation system, personnel, revision of school districts and attendance areas into compact units to achieve a system of determining admission to the public schools on a non-racial basis, and revision of local laws and regulations which may be necessary in solving the foregoing problems."

The decree then remanded the cases to the district courts to enter "such orders and decrees consistent with this opinion as are necessary and proper to admit to public schools on a racially nondiscriminatory basis with all deliberate speed the parties to these cases."

The bitterness, hatred, and violence that developed in the wake of the *Brown* decisions contributed to the final break between Warren and Eisenhower, and to the rift between the Chief and Frankfurter.

Despite the demonstrable need for resolute, unqualified support from the nation's popular President, Eisenhower, Warren complained, "never stated he thought the decision was right." Eisenhower, in 1956, said, "I think it makes no difference whether or not I endorse it." Two years later, Eisenhower conceded he may have told friends he wished the Court had moved more slowly.

And it had been Frankfurter who suggested using the words "with all deliberate speed," which he had borrowed from an old Holmes decision, to connote the Court's requirement for state action without imposing deadline constraints. In later years, when the indecisiveness of those words—and the consequent snail's pace at which integration proceeded—were roundly criticized for contributing to the welling up and solidification of opposition to integration, Warren said he blamed Frankfurter and his philosophy of judicial restraint for the problem. Of course, more blame lay with Black and Douglas, but Warren, when reflecting on his earlier Court actions he had come to regret, tended to censure "judicial restraint."

There was little restraint, however, in the way in which the Court proceeded to knock down segregation laws like a row of dominoes. In the District of Columbia segregation case, Warren had written that "in view of our decision that the Constitution prohibits the states from maintaining racially segregated schools, it would be unthinkable that the same Constitution would impose a lesser duty on the Federal Government."

Similarly, it would be unthinkable that if the Constitution prohibited racial segregation in schools, it would impose a lesser requirement on other public institutions.

Soon after *Brown*, the United States Court of Appeals for the Fourth Circuit held that, pursuant to the reasoning in *Brown*, Baltimore could not continue to segregate its public beaches. In November 1955, the Supreme Court unanimously affirmed this decision without issuing an opinion. At the same time, it unanimously reversed a decision upholding a segregated municipal golf course in Atlanta, citing as support only its decision in the Baltimore case.

The same month, a case was considered at the conference which persuaded Warren that, whatever else the Court might do in controversial cases, it must move decisively. The case was *Naim* v. *Naim*, in which a white woman in Virginia sought to have her marriage to a man of Asian descent annulled because it violated Virginia's miscegenation law. The couple had married in neighboring North Carolina concededly to evade the Virginia law forbidding their wedding, but the Virginia Supreme Court ordered the annulment and rejected the husband's claim that the statute violated the Fourteenth Amendment's equal protection guarantee. Three justices—Warren, Black, and Reed—voted to note probable jurisdiction of the Court. Four votes are needed to take a case and schedule it for argument; although Douglas indicated to Burton that he leaned toward taking the case, he held off voting when Clark requested another week to study the case.

When the justices reconvened to consider *Naim*, Frankfurter read a typed statement urging the Court not to take the case:

> What I call moral considerations far outweigh the technical considerations in noting jurisdiction. The moral considerations are,

of course, those raised by the bearing of adjudicating this question to the Court's responsibility in not thwarting or seriously handicapping the enforcement of its decision in the segregation cases. . . . To throw a decision of this Court into the vortex of the present disquietude would seriously—I believe very seriously—embarrass the carrying out of the Court's decree [in *Brown*].

After the conference, Frankfurter worked with Clark to draft a *per curiam* opinion remanding the case on technical grounds without considering the merits. The opinion stated that some questions relevant to the disposition of the case, such as whether the parties were citizens of Virginia at the time of their marriage in North Carolina, were not clearly addressed. The judgment was, therefore, vacated and returned to the state courts for clarification.

Everyone but Warren and Black agreed to the opinion. Black wrote a short dissent, which he withdrew at Warren's request. Warren himself was described by a law clerk as "furious. He thought that the failure to take the case was an evasion of the Court's responsibility." The clerk worked through one night on a draft dissent, but the next day Warren scrapped it and persuaded Black the same way. He thought it was inappropriate to file dissents from denials of certiorari or appeals.

The Court's majority, a Warren clerk said, feared the reaction in the South would have been that the justices "'first put blacks in the schoolroom, and then the next thing they had them sleeping with our daughters and marrying our daughters, and then they'll have the mongrelization of the races.' I don't think the Court in 1955 wanted to deal with that right away; it wanted to build up to it."

Warren strongly rejected that notion. He "thought that they really had to deal with the issue," the law clerk said. "He thought, 'It's too bad that it had come so soon, but we just can't have enforceable laws based on race and marriage.' He was very angry about that and thought they hadn't carried out their clear responsibility; they had to deal with these things, however impolitic it may be."

What happened was that the Virginia court, though instructed by the Supreme Court to return the case to the trial court to reopen and clarify the record, simply refused to comply with the mandate. It said Virginia law contained no provision for reopening the case, that the record was adequate, and that the earlier decision would stand.

Warren believed the Court got the sort of rebuff it deserved in that circumstance. When the Virginia court announced it was adhering to its previous decision and would not send the case to the trial court, Warren exclaimed in disgust, "That's what happens when you turn your ass to the grandstand."

If, during Warren's tenure, the Court might be accused again of exposing itself to slings and arrows, it wouldn't be due to inaction.

In 1956, the Court affirmed the judgment of a three-judge panel in Montgomery, Alabama, striking down the segregated bus system which, after the arrest of Mrs. Parks and her subsequent conviction and fine of ten dollars, plus four dollars in court costs, had become the object of a boycott by Negroes and the center of international attention. Warren told his law clerks the Court would affirm summarily, without hearing oral argument. The Court would cite three cases: *Brown* and the Baltimore and Atlanta cases. There was no hint of why the Court took the action, or the reasoning behind its decision.

"I thought at the time," one of the law clerks said, "that it was a pretty casual way for the Court to advance a major proposition of constitutional law—and I still do."

In the ensuing years, the Court ruled segregation invalid in public buildings, housing, transportation, and recreational and eating facilities. The Court, following Warren's direction, said as little as possible—but invariably struck down every segregation law that was challenged before it.

By 1963, an opinion could declare categorically, "It is no longer open to question that a State may not constitutionally require segregation of public facilities."

Warren used to recall that, when he arrived at the Court in 1953, the Supreme Court itself had a separate washroom for Negroes. When he retired nearly sixteen years later, virtually every vestige of racial discrimination had been rooted out of American law.

For that alone, Earl Warren would be vilified by one substantial segment of the population and venerated by another, assuring, whoever was right, his place in history. Soon, however, he would provide more ammunition to his enemies, and generate even greater adulation from his supporters. Not only had he become the center of the greatest domestic social revolution in America since immigration, but he soon would become the vortex of the near-hysterical xenophobia that was sweeping the country.

His critics put it simply, if crudely: Earl Warren was mongrelizing America from within, and he was selling it to the Communists from without.

NINE

One Communist Decision After Another

THE SUPREME COURT'S 1954 declaration that school segregation was unconstitutional transformed Earl Warren into a villain to many, but a hero to many more. Throughout that year and the next, especially after President Eisenhower suffered a severe heart attack in 1955, Warren was touted consistently in press speculation as the next Republican nominee for President.

The *Brown* opinion had been greeted throughout the world as majestic, its principal author championed as a Second Emancipator. To be sure, not every supporter of *Brown* was overwhelmed by Warren's personal performance. Judge Learned Hand, lauding the decision—and, in particular, the Court's unanimity—nonetheless suggested that the opinion indicated Warren possessed "a small capacity for verbal analysis." The opinion, he wrote Frankfurter, "will not satisfy the real eggheads."

Still, the decision's shock waves, when they were felt at all, would fall almost entirely on the states of the Deep South, which, Republican political kingmakers were keenly aware, had remained a solid Democratic stronghold since the Civil War, and were, therefore, no political loss.

Most of the remaining states, however, viewed legally enforced racial segregation as distant, foreign, and repugnant, something akin to apartheid in South Africa. It had no place in the American scheme of things—and Earl Warren symbolized a rekindled torch of liberty.

For obliterating racial discrimination from the law, the Court and its Chief were jeered by political and economic leaders in the South, but cheered almost everywhere else. At the same time, however, the Court began dealing in another judicial area —internal security—that would widen regional disaffection for the justices into a national phenomenon. Unlike the segregation cases, Court decisions in internal security—although, for the most part, focusing on narrow grounds and avoiding the sense of reforming zeal present in *Brown*—would stir primal fear not only among Southerners but among Northerners and Westerners as well.

Though little noticed at the beginning, its series of rulings favorable to Communists over the next few years would turn the Court from hero to harridan, and its Chief Justice from prospective President to public pariah.

Ironically, though widespread public vilification of Warren began with the Court's decisions in the Communist cases, the Chief's initial positions in these areas reflected traditionalism.

Another irony is that it was at the very conference at which Warren forged the Court's unanimous support for ending school segregation that the Chief also molded a majority decision requiring a witness to answer questions before the House Committee on Un-American Activities about his Communist Party membership, an opinion solidly in keeping with the temper of the times.

The witness had refused to answer the committee's questions, invoking "the First Amendment, supplemented by the Fifth." That was not enough, the lower courts held, to invoke the privilege against self-incrimination. The case, *Emspak* v. *United States*, was considered by the justices in their January 16, 1954, conference—the day after Warren had thrown his duck and pheasant luncheon to help his lobbying effort to win unanimous support for *Brown.*

"It gets down to the question of whether he actually claimed his privilege," Warren said of Emspak. "We should not indulge in technicalities, but he wants to eat his pie and have it. He did not want to testify, and yet not look guilty. We should not condone that action."

The others, except for Frankfurter, Black, and Douglas (who passed), indicated agreement with the Chief—although Jackson sounded a note that would be heard again in conference in the near future: "I wish committees would manage their work better and not abuse their power." Black echoed the sentiment; it was time, he said, "to draw a line on the powers of the Committee . . . and keep judicial and legislative powers separate."

Justice Reed, who was assigned the opinion by Warren, not only rejected Emspak's Fifth Amendment claim, he denied that the witness's refusal to answer questions about his Communist Party membership was protected by the First Amendment—an issue not raised at the conference and which the Court apparently wished to avoid.

Black, among others, bristled at Reed's assault on the First Amendment. "Except by outright repeal," he wrote his colleagues on April 23, 1954, "I cannot readily conceive of a way to give less effective meaning to the First Amendment than Justice Reed does in the opinion circulated in this case." He urged his colleagues "not to go along with this opinion until its devastating effect on free speech and press can be pointed out in dissent."

Black's objection led to an agreement at the May 15, 1954, conference to reargue the case; that was the same day the Court decided it would issue its *Brown* decision on the following Monday. When *Emspak* was reargued nearly a year later (joined by a similar case, *Quinn* v. *United States*), the Court was about to hand down its follow-up opinion in *Brown*—that integration should proceed "with all deliberate speed."

At the April 1955 conference on *Emspak* and *Quinn*, Warren announced, "I have changed my mind from last year." Following a characteristic of Frankfurter's juristic approach, Warren ad-

vised the conference to "set aside the First Amendment issue." It
was not necessary for a decision and should be avoided. Further,
the Court should assume the validity of the congressional resolution establishing the House Committee on Un-American Activities and acknowledge that its questions were pertinent. "We can
dispose of these cases on the slipshod method of the Committee
in questioning [and] a lack of direction by the Committee on
[the witness's] duty to answer the questions." Black agreed
that the "narrow grounds" would suffice, but Justices Reed,
Clark, and Minton, joined by Justice Harlan, who had succeeded
Jackson, disagreed. When Clark later changed his mind (as he
would do often in the years ahead), Warren had turned his own
five-to-four majority to uphold the committee into a six-to-three
Court to reverse.

Frankfurter later told Harlan, "I thought and think it was
right to charge these loose-mouthed, loose-mannered, and loose-
headed men on [Capitol] Hill with a little more responsibility in
the serious business of congressional investigations. That's all the
requirement [in *Quinn* and *Emspak*] gets down to."

Despite the Court's awareness of the volatile anti-Communist
mood permeating the nation, and its efforts to move cautiously in
the law where Communists were concerned, any action it might
take was bound to be perceived as an intrusion into politics. Decisions favoring the legal causes of Communists sowed the gathering storm over the Court; in the years ahead, it would reap the
whirlwind.

In 1938, organization of the House Committee on Un-
American Activities, with its vague charter to expose subversive
propaganda, was testimony that unreasoned fear of Communism's ability to subvert democracy had taken firm root in
America.

The next year, suspicion of Communists and their "sympathizers" was nourished; the Soviet Union, in a monstrous act of
duplicity, carved up Poland between itself and Nazi Germany
and then, on its own, invaded Finland. Nonetheless, a large number of Americans, suffering from the effects of the Great Depression, disillusioned by the pace of FDR's promised economic
cures, shocked by the growing power in Europe of Hitler, Mus-

solini, and Franco, supported the Stalinists and leaned toward Communism as a cure. By then, however, many Americans easily equated outspoken opposition to Fascism with Communism.

Despite the alliance with Russia during World War II, suspicion burst into virulence after the war when spies, whether previously faceless like Julius and Ethel Rosenberg or in sensitive positions of government like Alger Hiss, were accused and convicted.

At the same time, the Soviet Union was enslaving Eastern Europe and the Chinese Communists were pushing Chiang Kai-shek into the sea.

In January 1954, Senator Joseph R. McCarthy won the approval of seven of every ten Americans in a poll conducted by the Gallup organization. The Senate appropriated more than two hundred thousand dollars for his permanent investigations sub-committee—and supporters of the appropriation included John Kennedy, Lyndon Johnson, and Hubert Humphrey.

McCarthy's stock had never been higher. His supporters included not only Legionnaires and Daughters of the American Revolution but literati like Louis Bromfield and William F. Buckley, Jr. Their patriotic nerves had been jangled as societal and political change hurtled at them—from the establishment of the United Nations to the advocacy of fluoridation.

Songs were sung to him ("Nobody Loves Joe but the People") and political homage paid him (it was reported that eight senators owed their elections to McCarthy's support).

Apparently at the apex of his power, McCarthy had no place to go but down. And he started his inevitable slide when he bullied the Army for having drafted one of his aides, G. David Schine. When the Army resisted the senator's pressure, McCarthy and his counsel, Roy Cohn, resorted to the stratagem of all-out diversionary attack.

They accused high-ranking officers of protecting Communists in the service. An exchange of public allegations by McCarthy and denials from the Army climaxed when McCarthy's own committee decided to investigate the senator's actions.

The Army-McCarthy hearings were televised nationally—and,

for a time, McCarthy dominated them with "points of order" and tirades against the ubiquity of Communism.

But then the Army's special counsel, Boston attorney Joseph Welch, confronted McCarthy on the senator's publication of a classified document. Welch contended the senator's action was as reprehensible as the security leaks he railed against. Why did he do it? McCarthy refused to answer questions relating to the document or its publication.

> WELCH: Have you some private reservation, when you take the oath that you will tell the whole truth, that lets you be the judge of what you will testify to?
>
> McCARTHY: The answer is that there is no reservation about telling the whole truth.
>
> WELCH: Thank you, sir. Then tell us who delivered the document to you.
>
> McCARTHY: The answer is no. You will not get the information.

McCarthy, the man who had characterized witnesses invoking their constitutional rights as "Fifth Amendment Communists," now was himself refusing to answer questions under oath—and in front of some twenty million Americans.

Later, when McCarthy sensed that Welch was getting the best of him, the senator launched a personal attack on one of Welch's junior colleagues at the Boston firm of Hale & Dorr. McCarthy had discovered that Fred Fisher had once belonged to the National Lawyers Guild, an organization that had been characterized as subversive. But McCarthy had agreed not to bring up the matter if Welch promised not to explore Cohn's lack of a military record. Welch held to the agreement, but the cornered McCarthy, in lunging defensively, did not.

After Welch demanded that Cohn identify a single subversive or Communist in the Army, McCarthy interrupted. He identified Fisher as having once belonged to the Guild, which he described as "the legal bulwark of the Communist Party."

> I get the impression [McCarthy told Welch] that while you are quite an actor, you play for a laugh, I don't think you have any conception of the danger of the Communist Party. I don't think

you would ever knowingly aid the Communist cause. I think you are unknowingly aiding it when you try to burlesque this hearing . . .

Welch, stricken by the gratuitous smear of the young lawyer, proceeded to lecture McCarthy.

Little did I dream [Welch said, directly addressing the senator] that you could be so reckless and so cruel as to do an injury to that lad. . . . If it were in my power to forgive you for your reckless cruelty, I would do so. I like to think that I am a gentle man, but your forgiveness will have to come from someone other than me. . . . Have you no sense of decency, sir, at long last? Have you no sense of decency?

That was the beginning of the end of McCarthy, but he was not through yet. A petition bearing more than one million signatures, protesting McCarthy's censure, was delivered to the Capitol. A rally in New York questioning the loyalty of the Army's civilian leaders drew thirteen thousand cheering participants; sponsors included two governors, a former ambassador to the Soviet Union, and officials of the American Legion and the Daughters of the American Revolution.

Popularity polls indicated, nonetheless, that by August, the number who approved of McCarthy had plunged by twenty-two points. That was enough to persuade Republican Party leaders that their "hatchet man" for the 1954 congressional campaign ought to be the Vice President—and Richard Nixon's performance was not gauged to restore domestic tranquillity. Nixon reportedly accepted the job unenthusiastically, but he was a shrewd enough politician to agree, as he put it, that "every campaign has to have someone out front slugging." Once out front, he slugged away. Anyone who believed McCarthyism would decline as McCarthy's personal power ebbed received a rude shock.

Critics who said that Eisenhower's policies had led to a stagnant economy were accused by Nixon of "spreading pro-Communist propaganda." If too many Democrats were elected to Congress, "the security risks which have been fired by the Eisenhower Administration will all be hired back. . . . We recognize the Communist menace and this Administration is determined to crush that menace." He branded Democratic candidates as a "left-wing clique which has been so blind to the Communist conspiracy and has tolerated it in the United States."

As the Cold War was deepening distrust among nations and people, the Supreme Court was confronted with questions of law —law which had been born and codified in that very suspicion. In November 1955, the Court's conference considered *Pennsylvania* v. *Nelson,* a case in which Steve Nelson, the acknowledged head of the Communist Party in Pennsylvania, had been convicted and sentenced to twenty years in prison for violating the Pennsylvania Sedition Act prohibiting knowing advocacy of the overthrow of the United States government by force and violence. The Pennsylvania Supreme Court reversed Nelson's conviction because the Smith Act, passed by Congress in 1940, proscribed the same conduct and, therefore, superseded state law.

Warren said at the outset that he thought the United States clearly had superseded Pennsylvania and there would be "no loss to the United States if these acts are stricken." Frankfurter went further; though the Court did not have to decide it, he would probably disallow all local laws relating to treason. Reed did not see the "supersession" question as clearly as Warren did; Clark thought it was necessary for state and federal laws to "live together. . . . It's a question of policy. Shall we overturn the states, Congress, and the Department of Justice?"

In the end, only Reed, Minton, and Burton dissented. Clark changed his mind, while Harlan, Black, and Douglas concurred with Warren and Frankfurter. The decision focused on the question of supersession and left untouched similar laws elsewhere, except by implication; it clearly stated that if Congress had not legislated in the field, the states were free to do so—and there was nothing to prevent a federal law restoring to the states the powers the decision had taken away.

Still, the Court was criticized sharply by, among others, Representative Howard Smith of Virginia, the author of the Smith Act. Senator James O. Eastland of Mississippi, the new chairman of the Senate Judiciary Committee, declared the Court comprised "politicians instead of lawyers." Senator McCarthy said,

"We made a mistake in confirming as Chief Justice a man who had no judicial experience and very little legal experience." The Eisenhower administration announced it was supporting a Senate bill to nullify the decision.

Even when the Court upheld a federal statute requiring witnesses invoking the Fifth Amendment to testify in cases involving national security if, in return, they were granted immunity from prosecution, Frankfurter's opinion drew fire because of its staunch defense of the Fifth Amendment. The amendment, he wrote in *Ullmann* v. *United States,*

> . . . registers an important advance in the development of our liberty. . . . Time has not shown that protection from the evils against which this safeguard was directed is needless or unwarranted. This constitutional protection must not be interpreted in a hostile or niggardly spirit. Too many, even those who should be better advised, view this privilege as a shelter for wrongdoers. They too readily assume that those who invoke it are either guilty of crime or commit perjury in claiming the privilege. Such a view does scant honor to the patriots who sponsored the Bill of Rights as a condition to acceptance of the Constitution by the ratifying states. The Founders of the nation were not naïve or disregardful of the interests of justice.

Among the dissenters, Reed objected to Frankfurter's assertion in the opinion that "no constitutional guarantee enjoys preference." This was Frankfurter's way of enunciating his objection to Black's "preferred position" theory which contended that personal rights, such as the Fifth Amendment's privilege against self-incrimination, are elevated above economic rights or property rights. Frankfurter replied to Reed in a letter:

> When one talks about "preferred position," one means preference of one thing over another. Please tell me what kind of sense it makes that one provision of the Constitution is to be "preferred" over another? When is that true? When are two provisions of the Constitution in conflict so that one must be subordinated to the other? The correlative of "preference" is "subordination," and I know of no calculus to determine when one provision of the Constitution must yield to another, nor do I know any reason for doing so. Accommodating two provisions so

as to give effect to both is something else again. I do not think
there is a second-class citizenship among the different clauses
inhabiting the Constitution.

In *Slochower* v. *Board of Regents*, a Brooklyn College professor was discharged after he had invoked the Fifth Amendment
when a Senate committee asked him questions about his Communist Party membership. New York City law required the dismissal of any city employee who used the Fifth Amendment to
avoid answering a question relating to his official conduct. Warren told the conference in October 1955 that the New York law
"placed an unwarranted burden on these people. The premise
[of the law] is that the plea is one of guilt, and this is violative
of the Constitution." Harlan and Clark pointed out that the Fifth
Amendment had not been raised at the trial. Frankfurter helped
win Harlan and Clark to Warren's side by emphasizing that the
case could be decided on the grounds of due process; it was a violation of the "due process" clause, he argued, for New York to
assume guilt whenever the Fifth Amendment was invoked.

Frankfurter also persuaded the Court to avoid constitutional
issues in deciding whether the Communist Party could be forced
to register as a "Communist action" organization as required by
federal law. The statute not only required registration but imposed sanctions on those organizations ordered to register: loss
of tax exemptions, requirement to label mail or other distributed
matter as "disseminated by a Communist organization," prohibition against members who failed to reveal their affiliation from
holding passports and from employment in government, unions,
or the defense industry.

In conferences in November 1955 and March 1956 on *Communist Party* v. *Subversive Activities Control Board*, Warren argued
that the law violated the First Amendment as well as the Fifth
Amendment's guarantees of due process and privilege against
self-incrimination. "Was what was intended merely registration?
Registration alone—okay. Registration plus sanctions—that's out-
lawry, and that's bad."

Burton agreed that Congress "went overboard. . . . This is an
attempt to abolish the Communist Party."

Minton sharply disagreed. "Congress had found what everyone around this table should admit—what the Communist Party
is. I'd rather have a little of my liberty chipped away today than
have it all taken away tomorrow."

Harlan and Frankfurter thought the discussion was too far-
ranging; they thought only the registration requirement was presented to the Court and, by itself, it could be upheld. Typically,
Frankfurter was more disturbed by the splintered decision that
would result if the Court dealt with the constitutional issues.
From his count, it was five-to-four to uphold the constitutionality
of the registration provision. On March 31, 1956, he distributed a
memorandum ruing that the "diverse rhetoric" of a sharply divided Court in these cases certainly would generate "dissenting
views which, in their tenor, will not be preoccupied with spreading light and avoiding heat."

Frankfurter searched for grounds to remand the case without
reaching the constitutional questions. After two weeks, he succeeded. He seized on a motion, denied by the court below, alleg-
ing that if the Subversive Activities Control Board would admit
additional evidence, it would show that the testimony of three
key witnesses on which the Board had relied in determining the
Party was participating in and advocating subversive activities
was false. The case, Frankfurter said, should be sent back to permit the Board to receive the evidence in question. "I have come
to the conclusion," Frankfurter wrote his colleagues on April 2,
1956, "after considerable reflection and with great reluctance,
that the case must now be disposed of exclusively on [that]
ground without reaching the constitutional validity of this act."

Frankfurter made no bones about his delaying tactics. "I have
no doubt," he wrote, "that the Board will on the remaining evidence again reach the conclusion it has reached; nor do I doubt
that the Court of Appeals will promptly affirm such an order and
that the case will be back here."

The majority of justices approved of the Frankfurter approach.
His draft opinion, asserting that the Party should have the opportunity to produce the additional evidence, added:

> We assume, of course, that the members of the Board, like
> members of other tribunals charged with the reconsideration of

evidence, are men of conscience and intellectual discipline, capable of judging a particular controversy fairly on the basis of its own circumstances.

Douglas asked Frankfurter to delete that sentence, noting that "it casts aspersions (by implication) on the Board. It sounds as if we thought they were a slippery lot who need watching."

Frankfurter agreed, but maintained wryly, "No such thought ever crossed my mind."

Clark, however, objected to the charade. "Why should we go through this shadow boxing?" he demanded in a memorandum. "The disposition of this case, as proposed by Brother Frankfurter, is but another effort to shirk our plain responsibility to pass on constitutional questions. . . . As I remember, it was agreed that even if the case was reopened, the same judgment would result. Why stoop to such insincerity or demagogism?"

He, Reed, and Minton dissented from the Court's "pretext" to "avoid important constitutional issues." Frankfurter couldn't have put his intentions more concisely. The case returned to the Court and was, at last, decided—five years later; by then, 1961, the issue of subversion had been defused of most of its politically explosive force.

Frankfurter, though, was losing his early influence with Warren; where he had been able in the first years to restrain the Chief from giving full vent to his political instincts of fair play regardless of legal precedent or the threat to the Court's credibility, Frankfurter's pedantry and what seemed to be his occasional pettifoggery began eroding Warren's awe, admiration—and compliance.

In the fall of 1956, Warren led six of the justices to deal a blow to the Department of Justice in *Mesarosh* v. *United States,* in which five Communists had been convicted of violating the Smith Act. Two weeks before the case was scheduled for argument in the Supreme Court, the government moved to remand the case to the trial court to determine if a paid informer—a man named Mazzei, the government's principal witness—had testified truthfully. The Department of Justice had learned that Mazzei had testified falsely in other proceedings and it wanted to be certain that his testimony in *Mesarosh* would stand up.

The Court denied the motion and, instead, overturned the convictions and ordered a new trial. Warren delivered an opinion in which, one observer wrote, he "lectured the representatives of the Justice Department as if they were errant schoolboys." Warren wrote that "Mazzei, by his testimony, has poisoned the water in this reservoir, and the reservoir cannot be cleansed without first draining it of all impurity." The dissenters—Harlan, Frankfurter, and Burton—said the majority acted as though the government had conceded that Mazzei's testimony could not be relied upon. In an earlier letter to Frankfurter, Harlan said this basic misunderstanding had led the Court to an erroneous result:

> After all, the unsatisfactory discussion at our last conference stemmed from the initial mistaken premise that the government had conceded Mazzei's perjury at the trial. Even though this error was exposed, the discussion never got back on the track, and the stump speeches we heard really reflected, I think, that original error.

There was no misunderstanding in *Jencks* v. *United States* and, although the Court's decision later was largely undone by Congress, surprisingly little disagreement among the justices. Jencks was a union leader convicted of filing a false affidavit that he was not a Communist, a violation of the Taft-Hartley Act. The government's principal witnesses were Communist Party members, Harvey Matusow and J. W. Ford, who were paid by the FBI to make reports about Party activities. Jencks maintained that their written reports to the FBI would refute their testimony at the trial; they had testified that Jencks was a Party member at the time he swore he was not. Jencks asked that the reports be delivered to the trial court and then, if relevant to the defense, made available to him. The government refused to produce the reports.

The justices considered the case at five conferences, starting on October 19, 1956, and ending the following March 22. All agreed the reports should be made available, with a solid majority agreeing the reports should be given directly to Jencks rather than routed through the judge. "Only the defense is adequately equipped to determine the effective use" of the documents, the Court would rule.

Although two justices held they would give the documents to the judge rather than to Jencks, only Clark dissented. But it was a stinging dissent, averring the Court had granted criminals and Communists "a Roman holiday for rummaging through confidential information as well as vital national secrets."

It was reported that Eisenhower had "never been as mad in my life." Attorney General Brownell said the ruling created "an emergency in law enforcement." FBI Director J. Edgar Hoover said he would favor refusing to prosecute rather than open his files to accused subversives. Three months later, Congress passed a law specifying the types of documents that might be demanded by criminal defendants.

The opinion had been written by Justice William J. Brennan, who had come to the Court in that term to replace the retired Shay Minton. He regretted that "I may have been the instrument (and in my first year!) for demeaning the standing of the Court."

Frankfurter assured Brennan to the contrary. "The fact is," he wrote, "that I very largely blame myself for all the dust that the case has kicked up. . . . If I had my wisdom govern, I would have written a short concurrence with your opinion, sticking my pen into Tom [Clark]'s hot air and puncturing his balloon. . . . Then, Brownell & Company would not have made themselves the enslaved tools of Edgar Hoover."

However distasteful the Court's previous decisions on Communists may have been to the Administration and much of the citizenry, their impact was overtaken on June 17, 1957. That day, the Court handed down four decisions. It reversed the dismissal of a high-ranking diplomat from the State Department whose loyalty was challenged; it reversed the convictions of fourteen Communist leaders for violation of the Smith Act; and it reversed the convictions of witnesses held in contempt of the House Committee on Un-American Activities in one instance, and of a state legislature investigating subversion in another.

The State Department employee was Jonathan Service, an old China hand who, though found neither disloyal nor a security risk after extensive hearings by the State Department Loyalty Board, nonetheless was sacked by John Foster Dulles. A unanimous Court restored Service's job on the ground that Dulles had violated State Department regulations permitting him to fire an employee for security reasons only after the department's Loyalty Board had recommended dismissal.

Fourteen Communist leaders challenged their conviction for conspiring to overthrow the government by force and violence and organizing the Communist Party for that purpose. At the Court's conference on the case, *Yates* v. *United States*, Warren maintained "it has not been established that the Communist Party is 'force and violence.' The government has proved only membership in the Communist Party, not unlawful conduct. The only overt acts were attendance at public meetings and nothing was shown there to prove advocacy of force and violence."

Warren also questioned the clarity of the prohibition against "organizing." One of those convicted wrote editorials for a Party newspaper; "the editor of a paper by his editorials is not 'organizing,'" Warren maintained. Additionally, the Chief did not believe the charge of "advocacy" was sufficient to convict; he thought "it is a question of incitement." Finally, Warren objected that at a "crucial time" in the trial, "we find a congressional committee releasing an FBI report and a series of lurid articles."

Black said flatly that "the Smith Act provides for political trials—what the First Amendment was supposed to prevent."

Minton disagreed. "The Smith Act is not for political trials. It is to cope with a conspiracy hatched by a foreign government." Reed asserted "the Communist Party now is established as an advocate of force and violence. It is plain that they so urge."

Frankfurter agreed with Warren that the congressional committee "had fouled the air of this trial." Harlan, however, found the solution that carried a majority; he pointed out that if it was necessary for conviction to teach incitement, the instructions to the jury were inadequate. Harlan's subsequent opinion held that the Smith Act did not prohibit "advocacy and teaching of forcible overthrow as an abstract principle," but rather "any effort to instigate action to that end, so long as such advocacy or teaching is engaged in with evil intent." Thus, he wrote, the lower court did not properly instruct the jury as to the law.

Although *Service* and *Yates* alone would have raised cries of treason aimed at the Court, those decisions coupled with *Watkins* v. *United States* and *Sweezy* v. *New Hampshire* resulted in something akin to a national panic. Watkins was an organizer for the UAW who, when he appeared before the House Committee on Un-American Activities, testified candidly about his own earlier Communist activities and associations. He also answered questions about others he knew to be active in the Communist Party. But there he drew the line:

> I will not, however, answer questions with respect to others with whom I associated in the past. I do not believe that any law in this country requires me to testify about persons who may in the past have been Communist Party members or otherwise engaged in Communist Party activity but who to the best of my knowledge and belief have long since removed themselves from the Communist movement.
>
> I do not believe that such questions are relevant to the work of this committee nor do I believe that this committee has the right to undertake the public exposure of persons because of their past activities. I may be wrong, and the committee may have this power, but until and unless a court of law so holds and directs me to answer, I most firmly refuse to discuss the political activities of my past associates.

Watkins was held in contempt. Sweezy, a university professor, refused to answer questions of the New Hampshire attorney general, acting under a legislative mandate to investigate subversive activities, regarding the content of a lecture he had given at the state university and about the Progressive Party, its adherents and principles. He, too, was held in contempt.

At the Court's conference on March 8, 1957, Warren set the basis for the decision succinctly. "The committee must show why its questions are relevant and why they can get answers in this kind of case. And they do not have the right to expose for the purpose of exposure."

That struck at the heart of the House Committee on Un-American Activities. From the time of their inception, congressional committees created to probe "un-American activities" were given broad authority to find out whatever they could about people, political movements, or organizations believed to be subversive. The committees were to suggest means to overcome those influences that were undermining the country.

Early in their development, the committees' most powerful and most overtly utilized weapon was public exposure of those believed to be of questionable loyalty. When his resolution to create the House Committee on Un-American Activities was being debated, Representative Martin Dies said:

> I am not in a position to say whether we can legislate effectively in reference to this matter, but I do know that exposure in a democracy of subversive activities is the most effective weapon that we have in our possession.

Of the supporting justices (only Clark would dissent), all agreed to Warren's draft opinion except Frankfurter. Warren had maintained that Congress has "no power to expose where the effect is to abridge the First Amendment liberties of private citizens."

Frankfurter advised, "Don't begin with the First Amendment. Begin with due process and stay with it." He changed Warren's sentence to read that Congress has "no power to expose where the predominant result can only be an invasion of the private rights of individuals."

The former professor pointed out to Warren that Watkins' refusals to answer were not based on the First Amendment "and we do not have to adjudicate what the bearing of the First Amendment to congressional inquiries is."

Where the draft suggested an "application of the First Amendment to legislative inquiries," Frankfurter substituted "'protecting these rights from infringement by legislative inquiries.' We ought to assert limits on unjustifiable inquiry even though some of us may not find an infringement of the First Amendment."

Although Warren accepted nearly all Frankfurter's suggested changes, he remained dissatisfied with the breadth of the opinion. He wrote a concurrence, stressing the true basis of the decision was that congressional committees are obligated to demonstrate to witnesses the relevance of questions they are directed to answer.

The reversal in *Sweezy* also was cast in sweeping terms, with Warren contending the New Hampshire investigation "was an invasion of petitioner's liberties in the areas of academic freedom and political expression." At the conference, Warren had been appalled that the state attorney general "wanted to make this man state what his opinions were." In addition to that, the justices clearly wanted to strike at McCarthyism's insidious assault on academic freedom. Frankfurter asserted that "my chief concern here is the special position of educational institutions and teachers. . . . I can't think of a situation where a teacher should be hauled before a committee to ask, 'What did you lecture on?' " Harlan said the "state has a legitimate interest to find out what is being taught in state schools, but it can't put a block on teaching." Brennan said the case was "all bad. . . . The classroom is a sanctuary. In there is the first essential of the preservation of purity."

The New York *Times* entitled its editorial on the Court's June 17 actions "A Day for Freedom." It declared that "the Supreme Court has shown itself by far the most courageous of our three branches of government in standing up for basic principles." Senator Eastland, on the other hand, believed the Court "is attempting to consolidate all government power into its own hands." Retired Justice Minton wrote Frankfurter that the opinion would "make congressional investigations very difficult if not impossible."

At a Senate hearing, Eastland said, "The Supreme Court seems to be issuing one Communist decision after another."

"You're so right," Senator Joe McCarthy replied.

"What influence is there, except that some Communist influence is working within the Court?" Eastland asked rhetorically.

"Either incompetence," McCarthy said, generously for him, "or the influence you mention."

The Georgia legislature resolved overwhelmingly that Warren and his colleagues be impeached for "high crimes and misdemeanors." Senator Strom Thurmond of South Carolina echoed the call.

A week later, President Eisenhower wrote to Warren:

> I was told this morning that some enterprising reporter has a story that at a private party I severely criticized the Supreme Court, expressing anger. I have no doubt that in private conversation someone did hear me express amazement about one decision, but I have never even hinted at a feeling such as anger. To do so would imply not only that I knew the law but questioned motives. Neither of these things is true.

The next day at his press conference, Eisenhower conceded that "possibly in their latest series of decisions there are some that each of us has very great trouble understanding." Nonetheless, he called the Court "one of the great stabilizing influences of this country."

Years later, the Communist decisions continued to rankle Eisenhower. Whatever the general's disappointment with Warren as Chief Justice, his views on the Communist menace while he was President were demonstrably moderate compared to those of his Secretary of State, the most influential leaders in Congress, and a substantial segment of the American population.

While the two were flying to London in 1965 to attend Winston Churchill's funeral, Eisenhower conceded to Warren that he wished the Chief Justice had turned out to be a "moderate."

Warren asked him what decisions had contributed to his disillusionment.

"Oh, those Communist cases," Eisenhower replied.

"What Communist cases?" Warren demanded.

"All of them," Eisenhower replied tersely.

Warren tried to explain that "in the judging process we were obliged to judge Communists by the same rules that we applied to others."

Eisenhower didn't agree.

"What would you do with Communists in America?" Warren asked finally.

Eisenhower snapped unhesitatingly, "I would kill the sons of bitches."

TEN

Justice Tempered by Murphy

PRESIDENT EISENHOWER'S DISTASTE for the Supreme Court conformed with the seemingly inescapable conflicts between it and "strong" Chief Executives; history demonstrated how the Court, in the words of Robert H. Jackson, "has been in angry collision with the most dynamic and popular Presidents in our history. Jefferson retaliated with impeachment; Jackson denied its authority; Abraham Lincoln disobeyed a writ of the Chief Justice; . . . Wilson tried to liberalize its membership; and Franklin D. Roosevelt proposed to 'reorganize' it."

Even after returning to Monticello on concluding his presidency, Jefferson, in a letter to Madison, accused Chief Justice Marshall of "cunning and sophistry. . . . How dexterously he can reconcile law to his personal biases."

The vilification of justices over the years by Presidents, politicians, and the people has been equaled only by the invective some justices have reserved for one another.

Most of the internal abuse was kept from public view—but not always. On April 24, 1961, after Justice Black had issued an opinion for five justices reversing a murder conviction because of improper questioning by the prosecution, Frankfurter announced his dissent. Typically, Frankfurter extemporized, often adding acid-dipped barbs to his written comments. In this case, *Stewart* v. *United States*, Frankfurter attacked the majority opinion as an "indefensible example of judicial nit-picking [and] excessively finicky."

"That was not the dissenting opinion that was filed," Warren objected. "This is a lecture. This is a closing argument by the prosecutor to the jury. It is properly made, perhaps, in the conference room, but not in the courtroom."

"I'll leave it to the record," Frankfurter retorted.

Although Warren and Frankfurter had been crossing swords for years, relations between the two appeared to have now ruptured irreparably. In a burglary case decided in 1961, Frankfurter asserted that the majority opinion, from which he dissented, represented "absolutely novel doctrine. . . . I know what the Court has said, but I don't understand the meaning of it." Warren, again objecting to Frankfurter's elaborations on his written dissent, lectured his colleague tartly enough to provoke a critical editorial in the Washington *Post*.

The editorial referred to the "warmth of discussion" on the case at conference; Frankfurter noted in the margin next to the editorial that it was "a baseless assumption." He objected to "the Chief's wholly unconventional outburst."

The mounting attention to the polarization among the justices led to a 1961 article in *The Reporter* by Anthony Lewis; its principal source appeared to be Frankfurter. The journalist praised the work of the more conservative jurists like Frankfurter and Harlan, while taking issue with the work of justices like Warren and Black.

Black kept a copy of the article. In its margins, he commented acidly on its judgments. Where the reporter described a Harlan opinion as "a masterful piece of legal craftsmanship," Black wrote, "Is Mr. Lewis an expert on 'legal craftsmanship'? If so, admission into the mysteries of 'craftsmanship' depends neither on study time nor actual practice."

A reference to a Black opinion alleged the justice "had to distort the factual record . . . to reach his result." Black demanded in his marginalia: "Who thought this? Does he? If so, can he claim to be fair without offering proof . . . ?" When Lewis praised a separate Frankfurter concurrence in another case as "much more persuasive" than the majority opinion, Black wondered, "Persuasive to whom?"

Lewis' hope that Warren and Black could follow in the future "an unemotional . . . lawyerlike course" was greeted by Black's sneering rhetorical question: "Is this non-lawyer an expert on what is 'lawyer-like'?"

Publicly, Black painted the differences with bravado. "It's a grand fight," he declared at a dinner in his honor. "The Supreme Court does disagree. I hope it always will. It does have men who express their differences. I hope it always will have."

Privately, the differences in judicial tendencies strained and sometimes broke public decorum. The enemy camps began solidifying with the changing of the guard at the Supreme Court in 1955, 1956, and 1957.

When Jackson died in late 1954, it seemed clear from the outset that his replacement, John Marshall Harlan, would maintain Jackson's general adherence to the Holmes-Frankfurter school of judicial restraint. At the time, Frankfurter could carry a majority on most issues pitting activism against restraint. Reed, Burton, and Minton usually joined Frankfurter (who lavished praise on even unprodigious efforts if it secured their votes). Warren vacillated between the two camps; with Jackson's death, however, Warren began edging away from the often overbearing, irascible Frankfurter. More and more, Clark began making last-minute switches to Warren's position.

Harlan, however, generally provided Frankfurter with a solid fifth vote. Educated at Princeton University, a Rhodes Scholar, a successful Wall Street lawyer, and, for the year preceding his nomination to the high court, a judge on the United States Court of Appeals for the Second Circuit, Harlan adhered firmly to judicial restraint.

His grandfather had been a judicial maverick, an outspoken dissenter. Harlan the Younger, though, appeared to be a more moderate man than his grandfather, exhibiting temperance both in personality and in his judicial philosophy. He was, Frankfurter wrote a friend, "both on the Bench and in the conference as to the manner born."

Frankfurter, however, meanly refused to attribute his new colleague's talents to the first Harlan. "The present fashion to make old Harlan out a great judge is plumb silly," Frankfurter told a close friend in 1956. "I hope the grandson will be a much better justice than was his granddad—and I expect him to be."

Harlan certainly looked the part. Tall and erect, his features and feathery white hair aristocratic, his clothing conservative and tailored in London, Harlan exuded the dignity and aloofness associated with high judicial office. Yet he was warm and affable, able to develop close friendships—even with those with whom he clashed regularly on a philosophical or intellectual basis. A frequent sight at the Court's public cafeteria was Harlan and his sometime judicial foe, Hugo Black, standing together, waiting patiently in the food line, chatting and chuckling quietly, one a ramrod-straight patrician, the other a slightly rumpled southern good ole boy.

Once when Harlan was ill, the gregarious Texan Clark felt enough at ease with him to twit him gently in a get-well note:

> I hear, "milord," that you have been under the weather. . . . Your Lordship should be more careful of your whiskey and your habits.

Because they were intellectual equals and were compatible in judicial philosophy, Harlan and Frankfurter should have been as close as brothers. Indeed, Harlan tried to befriend Frankfurter; the professor's caviling nearly destroyed the effort. It was almost as if Frankfurter were genetically incapable of maintaining a serene relationship with another human being.

"One needs to see, to hear, to realize what an obstreperous person this man is," Dean Acheson once said of Frankfurter. One of the justice's close friends, Acheson nonetheless liked to describe what it was like "to have one's arm numbed by [Frankfurter's] vise-like grip just above one's elbow, to feel the intensity of his nervous energy."

Frankfurter longed for an ally in whom he could confide and with whom he could explore the complexities and paradoxes of the law. He could not, however, resist assaulting Harlan on a subject demonstrably dear (and, literally, near) to his colleague's heart—John Marshall Harlan the Elder. Under his judicial robes, across his neatly buttoned vest, John Harlan the Younger regularly wore the gold watch chain and fob that had belonged to his grandfather.

Still, Frankfurter needlessly and uselessly peppered Harlan with criticisms of the ancestor he revered:

> You will probably recall [Frankfurter wrote Harlan] that some time ago I expressed to you the belief that there is no evidence whatever that Harlan First thought that segregation was unconstitutional, and that it was my hunch that he would have sustained segregation.

Frankfurter wrote several letters on the theme that the elder Harlan, despite his dissent in *Plessy,* was no champion of racial justice, moving Harlan to reply irritably, "I think you push things too far."

Despite the warning growl, Frankfurter, like an aroused bulldog, would not let go; he even pursued Harlan into the sanctity of his summer home at Tanglewood, site of an annual music festival:

> Since cacophony is not alien to modern music, I dare to intrude upon you at Tanglewood with a disharmonious note. Duly mindful of all you say about *Plessy,* I am sorry to stand my ground. Whatever virtues may be attributed to Harlan First, no one, I submit, should credit (or charge) him with having been a close reasoner.

Frankfurter detested Douglas as early as 1940 for political activity. Douglas had written Frankfurter concerning "considerable talk in Washington about putting me on the ticket." Knowing that Frankfurter, too, was close to FDR, Douglas asked that "should the matter come your way, scotch it." Frankfurter's reaction was that Douglas had protested too much. In 1943, Frankfurter expressed "shock" to another FDR appointee, Justice Frank Murphy, a bluff, friendly Irishman, that Douglas was making the Court "a jumping-off place for politics." "Well, I don't like it," Murphy replied.

Frankfurter, searching for a metaphor he thought would impress Murphy, said "it's much more than a matter of not liking":

> When a priest enters a monastery, he ought to leave all sorts of worldly desires behind him. And this Court has no excuse for being unless it's a monastery.

Obviously, Frankfurter exempted from "worldly desires" the Brandeis practice of pursuing political interests indirectly by retaining persons off the Court, like Professor Frankfurter of Harvard, to promulgate them publicly.

Frankfurter's brewing disputes with Warren were brought to a boil shortly after the appointment in 1956 of William J. Brennan. Sherman Minton resigned and Eisenhower, trying to avoid his "mistake" in appointing Warren, continued the practice he started with Harlan of appointing sitting judges. Brennan had been a state judge in New Jersey for seven years. He had been a student of Frankfurter's at Harvard and Eisenhower, not to mention Brennan's former professor, probably thought the new justice would help retain the conservative majority.

But a compatibility developed between Brennan and Warren almost from their first meeting, a bond that would guide the Court's future over the next dozen years.

Warren escorted Brennan around the Court on Brennan's appointment in October 1956. When they reached the justices' third-floor lounge, Warren threw open the door. The room was dark except for a television set flickering in a corner. The Chief switched on the lights and saw most of his colleagues huddled around the small screen watching the World Series (the New York Yankees and Brooklyn Dodgers were at it again). When Warren started to make introductions, one of the justices called out, "Let's sit down so we can watch the game." After a moment's awkward silence, Brennan, affable and elfin, broke into a grin, shrugged, and, along with a delighted Warren, obliged.

Before the year was out, Brennan delivered his first opinion, *Putnam* v. *Commissioner*, a minor tax case involving a question of statutory interpretation. Nonetheless, four justices—Warren, Black, Douglas, and Harlan—disagreed initially.

"It is a healthy, even lusty firstborn," Frankfurter wrote when returning Brennan's draft. "I am glad to be its godfather."

Brennan's ability and willingness to mold his language to meet the objections of some of his colleagues—a talent that would become his hallmark on the Court and one on which the Chief Justice would rely frequently—succeeded in his maiden effort in winning to his side all but Harlan. "I hope," Warren wrote him, "that this opinion is the first of hundreds to be written by you for the strengthening of our institutions and for the welfare of our people."

For the time, the Frankfurter "wing"—those justices adhering to the professor's concept of avoiding constitutional questions where feasible, dodging controversy where practical, and ignoring personal preferences and prejudices where possible—held sway in the Court.

Indeed, on the "big" issues—particularly in the segregation cases—Frankfurter and his followers usually were found voting with Black and the activists. What separated Frankfurter from Black (and, with growing frequency, Warren) was his professorial penchant to search for technical grounds on which to decide cases while Black sought to assert broad constitutional principles.

Warren's declaration of independence from Frankfurter's propensity for judicial restraint was made early in 1957 in *Breithaupt* v. *Abram*.

Breithaupt was driving a pickup truck in New Mexico when he collided with a passenger car. Three people in the car were killed and Breithaupt was injured seriously. Authorities found a nearly empty pint of whiskey in the glove compartment of Breithaupt's pickup truck and medical attendants smelled liquor on the injured man's breath as he lay unconscious in the emergency room.

A state patrolman asked a physician to obtain a blood sample. The doctor withdrew about twenty cubic centimeters of Breithaupt's blood with a hypodermic needle and subsequent tests showed the blood contained 0.17 percent alcohol—well above the level at which people are considered to be under the influence of intoxicating beverages.

Convicted of involuntary manslaughter and sentenced to prison, Breithaupt later sought release by claiming that the blood test, made involuntarily, deprived him of his liberty without due process of law.

The decision of the Court to reject Breithaupt's claim was based on earlier key opinions fashioned by Frankfurter in criminal cases. In the 1949 *Wolf* v. *Colorado,* Frankfurter, for the Court, held that illegally seized evidence could not be barred from use in state criminal trials. In effect, that decision declared that the exclusion of such evidence in criminal trials was not required by the "due process" clause of the Fourteenth Amendment. Due process, Frankfurter had maintained in a 1947 opinion, incorporates "those canons of decency and fairness which express the notions of justice of English-speaking peoples." Excluding illegally obtained evidence from a criminal trial was not, Frankfurter determined, a basic notion of justice.

Three years later, in *Rochin* v. *California,* Frankfurter, speaking for the Court, made clear that not all illicit acquisitions of evidence were acceptable or admissible. In his initial memorandum on *Rochin,* the "stomach pump" case, Frankfurter wrote, "There are certain standards of civilized conduct below which the due process clause bars a state from falling." The question to decide in due process, Frankfurter maintained, was whether there was "a shock to the conscience in a particular case."

Taking blood from an unconscious man was not a "shock to the conscience," a majority ruled in *Breithaupt.* Clark, writing the opinion, maintained "there is nothing 'brutal' or 'offensive' in the taking of a sample of blood . . . under the protective eye of a physician."

Warren, who had joined the majority in *Irvine* v. *California* two years earlier in upholding the use of evidence obtained by breaking into someone's house and planting microphones there (a position opposed by Frankfurter), now turned completely to the Black-Douglas view. In a dissent, Warren objected to the limitation of constitutional rights to circumstances requiring physical force or resistance. "Only personal reaction to the stomach pump and the blood test can distinguish them," and imposing constitutional limitations on personal reactions "is to build on shifting sands."

Warren, later justifying his position to Alan Barth, a journalist and civil liberties advocate, offered a somewhat dubious assertion. "What's so bad about a stomach pump?" he asked rhetorically. "I've had my stomach pumped lots of times."

Now that Warren had become an activist devotee, Brennan was not far behind—and now there were four. But it was a solid four which, in any number of cases, through Warren's personal magnetism and Brennan's gift for incorporating a variety of viewpoints into the language of an opinion, could woo a fifth to their side and make a majority. Often, the fifth vote was Clark's. "When he went into a conference with an open mind," a Clark law clerk said of his justice, "he would often be influenced by the arguments of the Chief."

And it was a foursome that, as it grew more successful in controlling the Court, grew ever more damnable in Frankfurter's eyes. He once was overheard at a conference screeching—literally, for Frankfurter became high-pitched and loud during arguments—at Warren: "Be a judge, goddamnit, be a judge!" Frankfurter's own bitter animosity was reflected, albeit with a lighter touch, by Judge Learned Hand. In their correspondence, Hand often commiserated with Frankfurter about the Court. "It must be damnable," Hand wrote, "to be one of a bunch . . . of whom four . . . regard themselves as Teachers of the Four-Fold Way and the Eight-Fold Path . . . those Harbingers of a Better World." Hand referred to them as "the Jesus Quartet," "the Jesus Choir," "the Holy Ones."

"Oh," he rhapsodized in one letter, "to have the inner certainties of those Great Four of your Colleagues."

At the root of the deep gulf dividing judges like Frankfurter, Jackson, Harlan, and Hand on the one side from Warren, Black, Douglas, and Brennan on the other was conviction and dedication; if they erred, it was not because of apathy or estrangement from the nation's political and social concerns.

Often, their votes coincided; just as often, the reasons for those votes reflected their differences. In 1955, *Griffin* v. *Illinois* posed the question of whether a convict, too poor to afford a transcript of his trial and denied a free one, could receive an adequate appellate review. "We cannot have one rule for the rich and one for the poor" was the way Warren saw it at the conference on December 9, 1955. Frankfurter agreed in the vote; his separate opinion, though, made it clear he would not go beyond the circumstances of the case. A plurality of the Court, in an opinion by Black and joined by Warren, held that the ruling should operate retroactively. "Here we go again," Minton had sighed at conference, reflecting the opposition view. "There's no reason for us to tell them to furnish the transcript. This is not an inequality of law, but an inequality of riches."

Harlan had dissented on that point. He tried unsuccessfully to take Frankfurter with him. "Sorry I can't convince you in *Griffin*," he wrote. "If I followed my heart, I'd be with you, but what you have decided seems to me wholly unsound."

After the decision was announced, Harlan changed his mind:

> I think that I may say without impropriety [Harlan wrote Frankfurter] that I am glad that *Griffin* v. *Illinois* was decided as it was. . . . We needed a jolt. [But] we have not dealt with the problems of the old cases. I am glad, indeed, that you discussed the question in your opinion. We need a doctrine that will permit the right course to be shaped for the future uninfluenced by the fear of wholesale jail deliveries.

Ultimately, those differences in approach meant everything to Frankfurter; it was not the result of a particular case that counted so much as the judicial structure it would create for future cases; it was not for the Supreme Court to overstep its bounds—whether dealing with legislative, executive, or even its own judicial functions.

Responding to a remark that Warren meant as "a mere pleasantry while we were all in idle conversation," Frankfurter wrote:

> The Court can dispose of a case according to justice, on the assumption that the Court has jurisdiction. But it cannot dispense with the requirements of jurisdiction in order to do justice.

Frankfurter feared the activists were reviving the circumstances extant earlier in the century against which Justice Brandeis railed; the Court, he claimed, was exercising "the powers of a super-legislature." He accused Brennan of writing an opinion that, had he been a senator, "he wouldn't have to change a word in what he has written in a speech voting against the legislation."

For Warren, that kind of thinking resulted in "sweeping under the rug a great many problems basic to American life. We have failed to face up to them, and they have piled up on us, and now they are causing a great deal of dissension and controversy of all kinds." It was the Court's job, he said, "to remedy those things eventually."

Frankfurter believed this an utter misconception of the role of the Court. He wrote Brennan, "I do not conceive that it is my function to decide cases on my notions of justice and, if it were, I wouldn't be as confident as some others that I know exactly what justice requires in a particular case."

The attitude of Warren, Black, Douglas, and Brennan reminded Frankfurter of Justice Murphy, whom he called "Saint Frank." Murphy, Frankfurter believed, always voted with his heart in cases involving minorities and the poor, rendering, as one punster put it, "justice tempered by Murphy." Writing Reed, Frankfurter asserted that "the short of the matter is that today you would no more heed Murphy's tripe than you would be seen naked at Dupont Circle at high noon tomorrow."

Specifically, Frankfurter was nonplussed at Warren's inclination to reconsider the merits of cases involving injury to workers —especially railroad workers given the right, under the Federal Employers' Liability Act (FELA), to sue for injuries suffered on the job.

Frankfurter maintained that the Court was regularly reversing lower court decisions in these cases based only on "different assessments [of evidence]—a difference *not* to be resolved by the Supreme Court of the United States. . . . I do not think the correction of an erroneous decision, after two courts have dealt with the matter, is the proper business of this Court. . . . No doubt some of the lower court decisions which we bring here were decided erroneously against an employee. But this is not a Court for the correction of errors."

Warren, for his part, told a law clerk that "he felt that the [railroad] jobs used up the men and when they were no longer valuable, cast them aside. . . . He thought of the human cost of the railroads."

In a 1962 FELA case, an injured railroad worker had been denied damages by lower courts for the loss of a finger. The evidence pointed clearly to the worker's having been injured as a result of his own negligence. All nineteen law clerks recommended that the Court refuse to take the case. Nonetheless, at least four justices voted at a conference to grant certiorari. When Black returned to his chambers, he exclaimed jubilantly, "The justices beat the law clerks again."

Earlier, Minton wrote Frankfurter from retirement:

> There seems to be no end to the FELA cases. You all seem to have reached the position in the law of negligence where, a railroad employee has an urgent call of nature, the railroad company is negligent if [it] does not furnish him a safe gondola car to crap in.

Acheson saw some humor in the situation, too, if in somewhat less earthy terms than Minton. In London in 1958, Acheson wrote Frankfurter about a decision in the House of Lords that had ruled against a petitioner in a negligence case:

> It struck me that their Lordships of the Judicial Committee had not heard of [Warren's] rule in the Supreme Court of the United States to the effect that in negligence cases the defendant always loses. This is not to be confused with Clark's rule that in criminal cases the defendant always loses. It also occurred to me that if Mr. Justice Frankfurter had been sitting in the Judicial Committee he would have held that the appeal was improperly granted.

From Warren's perspective, Frankfurter was guilty of hypocrisy. The Chief maintained that Frankfurter, too, voted with his heart on some issues—especially those involving unlawful searches and seizures. In April 1957, Frankfurter wrote Warren complaining about Black's position that the Fourth Amendment's guarantee was not as important as those in the Bill of Rights dealing with personal rights as contrasted with property rights:

> The responsibility of this Court in relation to [the Fourth Amendment] is of as great importance as any aspect of civil

liberties. To the extent that I am charged with being "a nut" on the subject of the "knock at the door," I am ready to plead guilty.

Indeed, Frankfurter's dissent in *Irvine* v. *California* had been predicated on his finding that the surreptitious entry into a man's home constituted a "shock to the conscience" and, therefore, any evidence gathered from that entry must be excluded from the criminal trial.

Additionally, Frankfurter had cast an unusual vote, considering his record, in *Rowoldt* v. *Perfetto*, a 1957 case in which an old Jewish alien was ordered deported because he had been a Communist briefly some twenty years earlier. The conference was divided four to four. Frankfurter, despite a statute making any Communist membership a ground for deportation, sided with Warren, Black, Douglas, and Brennan to allow Rowoldt to remain in the United States. The old man's links to the Party, Frankfurter wrote for the majority, were not "the kind of meaningful association required . . . particularly in the case of an old man who has lived in this country for forty years."

What made the vote unusual was that Frankfurter had delivered several opinions upholding deportation of aliens with Communist Party associations. "You know," Warren told his clerks after the conference on the Rowoldt case, "I think Frankfurter is capable of a human instinct now and then. . . . [He] may well have thought, 'There, but for the grace of God, go I.' "

In his distress with Warren & Company, Frankfurter was not alone. Just as Jackson had provided him with intellectual solace in earlier years, Harlan offered him philosophical comfort after Jackson died. Although Harlan maintained friendly relations with most of his colleagues, he nonetheless was disturbed by the outward and unseemly displays of antagonism on the Court, as well as by what he considered thoughtless opinions.

In a conference in May 1959, for instance, Warren lashed out at Frankfurter for "deceiving" him about an opinion; Warren contended that a point Frankfurter had made in discussing the issue among the justices had not been included in the opinion. Frankfurter replied he could hardly consider it a deception; if

Warren thought it should be included, he could have suggested it on seeing the draft.

Harlan pushed a note over to Frankfurter:

> What the Chief said was utterly inexcusable—don't mistake me on that. But for your own health, you mustn't allow yourself to get sucked into that kind of stuff, if you don't mind my saying so.

In June 1957, the Department of Justice accused E. I. du Pont de Nemours & Company of violating Section 7 of the Clayton Antitrust Act. The statute prohibited a corporation from acquiring stock of another company where the effect might be to "substantially lessen competition" or to restrain commerce. At issue was du Pont's ownership of 23 percent of the stock of General Motors Corporation.

The previous year, Warren, Black, and Douglas had dissented from a majority holding that du Pont was not guilty of an antitrust violation in its manufacture of cellophane. Warren argued in conference that "since du Pont has the lion's share of that market, it must have monopoly power."

This time, Brennan would join the three dissenters; because three justices did not participate in the decision, that made a majority.

Du Pont argued that the applicable provision of the Clayton Antitrust Act prohibited companies from acquiring significant holdings in competing companies—that is, it was designed to prevent "horizontal" acquisitions. In this case, General Motors was a customer of du Pont's and the acquisition was "vertical."

The lower court sustained du Pont; Warren, in conference, argued it should not have done so. "When du Pont went into this," the Chief said, "it did so for the purpose of controlling a channel for the outlet of its products" to General Motors. Frankfurter pointed out that "it is not the law that 23 percent of stock is a clear violation." Brennan stressed that both companies had tried not to abuse the relationship; still, he did not think the purchase was solely for investment but, rather, to strengthen its position as supplier. Warren kept nudging Brennan to his own position; when it appeared he had netted Brennan, Warren assigned the opinion to him.

Brennan's opinion held the Clayton Antitrust Act forbade vertical acquisitions and, therefore, the du Pont purchase of 23 percent of General Motors stock was in violation.

Among those not participating was Harlan, who once had represented du Pont. On the Bench, while Brennan was reading his opinion, Harlan pushed a note to Frankfurter:

> Now that my lips are no longer sealed, if there was ever a more superficial understanding of a really impressive record than Bill's opinion in *du Pont*, I would like to see it. I hardly recognize the case as I listen to him speak. Between you and me, [this] for me has been the most disillusioning blot in the Court's processes.

When Reed retired in February 1957, Frankfurter wanted to make certain he won the support of his replacement, Charles E. Whittaker. Whittaker had been, like the President who appointed him, from a farm in Kansas. Unlike Eisenhower, Whittaker had quit high school at sixteen, had never gone to college, worked in a Kansas City law firm as a messenger and office boy, and eventually attended an unaccredited law school at night.

Serious, hardworking, "super-conscientious," as one justice would describe him, Whittaker was a successful lawyer whom Eisenhower named a district judge in 1954 and a judge on the United States Court of Appeals for the Eighth Circuit two years after that. As he had in his appointment of Harlan and Brennan, Eisenhower stuck gamely to his decision, after his disappointment with Warren, to appoint to the Supreme Court only those with prior judicial experience.

Frankfurter wrote a federal judge that "all this talk about the desirability of 'judicial experience' and promotion from the lower federal bench derives from uncritical conceptions about the history and work of the Court. It presupposes that because one cannot become a colonel unless he has been a major, one should not be put on this Court unless he has been on a lower court."

Despite Whittaker's obvious limitations, Frankfurter courted his vote with an almost embarrassing abandon. "Were I to retire tomorrow," he gushed in one note to Whittaker, "one of the most gratifying memories I would carry with me of my whole judicial life would be your behavior in *Yancy* [a Communist Party case].

It was judicial behavior at its finest." On another occasion, he told Whittaker, "No one on the Court more than you searches more consistently to reach results in cases solely on relevant judicial grounds." And yet again, "How gladdened I was by the clear-sightedness displayed so early in your days on the Court."

"It was clear to everybody on the Court—with the exception of Whittaker," one clerk recalled, "that he was being used by Frankfurter and that Frankfurter was ingratiating himself in order to secure Whittaker's vote."

Even Frankfurter's oiliness couldn't smooth Whittaker's bumpy road. "He used to come out of our conference literally crying," one justice said. "You know, Charlie had gone to night school, and he began as an office boy, and he'd been a farm boy, and he had inside him an inferiority complex which showed, and he'd say, 'Felix used words in there that I'd never heard of.'"

Douglas remembered that "in conference, Whittaker would take one position when the Chief or Black spoke, change his mind when Frankfurter spoke, and change back again when some other justice spoke."

In October 1957, the Court faced one of its first pornography cases. The question was whether the city of Chicago had the constitutional authority to censor a film it found to be prurient. Frankfurter decided to circulate one of his little satires:

No. 372—October Term, 1957

Times Film Corporation,
    Petitioner

v.

City of Chicago, Richard J. Daley,
    and Timothy J. O'Connor

The Court of Appeals in this case sustained the censorship, under an Illinois statute, of a motion picture entitled *The Game of Love.* The theme of the film, so far as it has one, is the same as that in Benjamin Franklin's famous letter to his son, to the effect that the most easing way for an adolescent to learn the facts of life is under the tutelage of an older woman. A judgment that the manner in which this theme was conveyed by this film

exceeded the bounds of free expression protected by the Fourteenth Amendment can only serve as confirmation of the saying
Honi soit qui mal y pense.

Less than a month later, Frankfurter received a note from
Whittaker:

Dear Felix:

    No. 372—Times Film Corporation,
    Petitioner v. City of Chicago et al.

    I join in your *per curiam* in this case.

Frankfurter, realizing Whittaker was serious, scribbled a note
explaining, "This was intended as a joke."

He had Whittaker's vote, all right, but Frankfurter could not
count on a majority the way he could in earlier days. And lack-
ing someone like Jackson, who disdained Black and Douglas at
least as much as he did, Frankfurter turned to Learned Hand to
thoroughly vent his spleen. In fact, Hand questioned Warren's
perspicacity from the start. Before long, he was calling Warren
"that Dumb Swede," "Pontifex Maximus," and "Judex Maximus."

"As to the 'Chief,'" Hand wrote in 1959, "somebody is writing
for him better than at the beginning, though the results
are ——."

When Hand wasn't deriding "Hillbilly Hugo," he was sniping
at "Good Old Bill." Referring to a review of a book by Douglas,
Hand said, "I was flattered . . . to find myself bracketed with
you as two termites, steadily devouring the underpinnings of all
free society, these being (as ought to be obvious to any but
biased heretics) finally to be measured by five out of nine
Peerless Champions of the Welfare of Democratic Society."

Frankfurter wanted Hand on the Court very badly, but it appears as if Frankfurter pressed the cause too strenuously when
there was an opening. Douglas wrote that FDR told him one
day, "Do you know how many people asked me today to name
Learned Hand? Twenty. And every one a messenger from Felix
Frankfurter. I won't do it." Francis Biddle, FDR's Attorney Gen-

eral, told Hand, "If Felix hadn't pushed, pushed, pushed, you'd have had a better chance." President Truman confided in Shay Minton that when he appointed Burton to the Bench in 1945, Hand had been his first choice—but the President decided that Hand was then too old.

Few men have devoted more consideration to what a judge should not be than Hand and Frankfurter. Hand wrote Frankfurter that the judges "whom I most dread are the men who conceive it to be the chief part of their duty to keep this society in the path of righteousness and high endeavor."

Frankfurter concurred.

> It is nothing new [he wrote in 1954] for lawyers to identify desire with constitutionality and to look to the Court to declare unconstitutional legislation that one does not like. Now the roles are reversed; the so-called liberals who threw their hats high in the air when Brandeis, in a dissenting opinion, said that the Court was not a third House of the legislature, now want the Court to strike down all legislation that touches civil liberties. The view [is] that the provisions of the Constitution dealing with individual liberties are absolutes in the sense that the Court is to enforce them "irregardless" of any concern for the legislative judgment.

Hand knew, of course, that for years he was a likely prospect for a Supreme Court seat. Conceding he "had the ambition to be on the Court," he added, "I should find it a trying position to be one of you nine at the moment."

In 1958, he wrote, "I will concede that for years I should have said that I wanted to be on your Court as much as I wanted anything that could come from the outside.

"But now I ask myself whether it can be a paradise.

"I know, I know. The fox said, 'Those grapes are sour, anyway.'

"But yet . . . but yet . . . maybe they really were."

ELEVEN

Burning the House to Roast the Pig

THE MIDDLE OF the twentieth century may have been neither the best nor the worst of times in the United States, but they seemed as perilous as any in the nation's first one hundred and seventy-five years.

When World War II ended, the wealth and power of America were unchallenged. Only four years later, Mao Zedong and his Communists had taken control of China and the Soviet Union had the Bomb.

By 1950, the nation learned there really were Soviet spies in their midst and GIs came face to face with Red Chinese troops in Korea.

Over the next two years, one of the nation's greatest war heroes was unceremoniously sacked by one of its least popular Presidents, organized crime was exposed on daytime television by Senator Kefauver, and Americans learned of a new doomsday weapon—the hydrogen bomb.

President Eisenhower ended the fighting in Korea in 1953. But it was a brief respite for a troubled people. Senator Joe McCarthy was striking fear into the hearts of those running the Pentagon, the State Department, colleges and universities, and the movie and television industries; racial unrest was heating to a boil; Ike suffered a heart attack; the Russians overran Hungary; the Edsel demonstrated the vulnerability of American business; Sputnik destroyed the myth of Russian scientific inferiority.

Through it all, America's middle-class standards—the quest for education and affluence, adherence to neo-Victorian sexual mores, an almost religious belief in the verities of family and flag —were challenged and ridiculed by a breed of self-styled writers and poets who called themselves "beat."

The unbending self-righteousness preceding the Civil War and the frenzied self-indulgence before the Great Depression may have persuaded most midcentury Americans to trust in the essential goodness of moderation: in business, in politics, in life style. Now, for the first time, a sizable portion of the country's youth denounced moderation as an evil—not by preaching revolution, but by deifying rootlessness and uncaring; not by advocating change in society, but simply by rejecting whatever appeared to represent middle-class conventions.

They urged secession from conformity in music, in religion, in dress, in sex—and it frightened those to whom conformity had become a refuge. Their "literature"—some of which, like Jack Kerouac's *On the Road,* struck artists like Truman Capote as "not writing . . . just typing"—was, for the most part, rambling and puerile (though an occasional poet like Allen Ginsberg would write of our foibles with originality and telling force).

Though the "beat generation" bequeathed little of value to the future, it represented the erosion of moderation in society and a growing manifestation of extremes—a polarization between fanatic apathy and compulsive action; the activists' ultimate victory was culminated in President Kennedy's inaugural pledge to "pay any price, bear any burden, meet any hardship, support any friend, oppose any foe to assure the survival and the success of liberty."

Society was rushing to rid itself of any perceived shackles to freedom—and conventional wisdom held that conventional wisdom was outdated. At the same time, optimism that America possessed the power, money, and brains to meet any challenge

was unbridled—and the Supreme Court reflected the growing belief that some of America's institutions could cure in a generation
age-old infirmities afflicting mankind.

The Court, like the people, eschewed moderation; unlike the
Skeptics, the justices thought it unnecessary to suspend judgment on most questions, at least, for long. There was one notable
exception, however, to the Court's growing penchant for superseding legislation—and that was in its dealings with a new problem brought on by the age: pornography.

In 1957, the Court confronted a Michigan law making it a
crime to sell or distribute books or magazines "tending to the
corruption of the morals of youth." A distributor named Butler
had been convicted of violating the law; he claimed his right to
free speech had been violated and that, further, the law should
not prohibit selling a book to the general public because of its
undesirable influence on young people.

Several justices urged deciding the constitutional questions,
but Frankfurter, as usual, urged crossing that bridge later. He
persuaded the entire Court to join him in deciding the case on
"narrow ground"—that making it an offense to make a book
available to the general public if it might have a deleterious
effect on youth was, in effect, limiting adults to reading only that
which was deemed fit for children. "Surely," Frankfurter wrote,
"this is to burn the house to roast the pig."

Justice Brennan "originally thought this should have full-dress
treatment. It is probably wise, however," he wrote Frankfurter
in February 1957, "to hold that treatment until we are forced to
it."

The Court faced the question squarely that spring when the
federal obscenity statute prohibiting mailing material that was
"obscene, lewd, lascivious, or filthy" was challenged as contrary
to the First Amendment.

Warren thought the claim "would go too far." In an April 26
conference, he said the federal government had a right to protect
itself. Brennan agreed, but thought the Court should define obscenity in terms of criminal law.

"The test," he said, "should be the 'dominant theme' test." A judge should apply the test "before it goes to the jury." Brennan's subsequent opinion enunciated the principle that "obscenity is not within the area of constitutionally protected speech or press." His test was "whether to the average person, applying contemporary community standards, the dominant theme of the material taken as a whole appeals to prurient interest."

Warren, in a concurring opinion, warned against using the test to limit "the arts and sciences and freedom of communications generally," but, as he said later, the decision in the case, *Roth* v. *United States*, was "the best we could do with what we had. . . . For all the sound and fury that the test generated, it has not been proved unsound."

The test was vague enough to allow flexibility—and to generate confusion. As one federal court put it, "the judiciary in our tormented modern civilization [is] also lost in a wilderness." Warren, despite his fear of encroachment on the First Amendment, abhorred pornography. He agreed with Frankfurter that both needed "a whiff of fresh air after the obscenity arguments" in Court. When his clerks were disputing Warren's views on the issue, the Chief told them, "You boys don't have any daughters yet."

Warren was not eager to view the materials in pornography cases. "Do we have to read all of them to determine if they have social importance?" he asked during a 1965 argument. "I'm sure this Court doesn't want to read all the prurient material in the country."

When, in 1966, Warren read the exhibits in the case of Ralph Ginzburg, publisher of *Eros* magazine, he was shocked. "Do you realize what's in there?" he asked a clerk. "This stuff is terrible." When dirty films were shown, Warren refused to view them. He would send a clerk or rely on the reports of his colleagues. "It's all garbage," Warren said. "How can you know," one justice asked him, "if you don't look at it?" "I *know* what that stuff is," he replied.

Most justices viewed most of the allegedly pornographic films most of the time; more "elevating" fare, though, didn't bring in the judicial customers. On April 6, 1967, Justice Douglas wrote his colleagues:

> Pursuant to our discussion at the last conference, I arranged with the Department of the Interior for the showing of the film *The Last Frontier*, which was shown last night in the conference room. You may be interested to know that one justice appeared, no law clerks, no one from the Clerk's office, no one from the Library, no one from the Marshal's office (except Mrs. Allen and Mr. Lippitt), four from the labor force, and four secretaries. There was a total of twelve from the entire building. Thus endeth my good neighbor policy for at least 1967, 1968, and 1969.

At the same time that "traditional" standards of morality were eroding, the nation's history of robust romance with the military began palling as well. The Korean War and its indecisive yet decidedly unheroic outcome had weakened the citizenry's once unquestioning devotion to its armed forces. And when that happened, the unchallenged hold of the military on its own members began to weaken as well.

The Court faced the question of military supremacy in 1956 and 1957.

The first case involved Robert Toth, an Air Force policeman in Korea. He had been honorably discharged and was working in a steel plant in Pittsburgh when he was arrested and charged with killing a Korean civilian. Toth had been on guard duty at the time the civilian was shot. The former airman was flown to Korea to be judged by a court-martial. The Uniform Code of Military Justice authorized courts-martial of civilians if they had committed serious crimes while in service.

Warren, at conference, saw no difficulty in affirming the court-martial power. "Congress made the reasonable choice of making the soldier subject to court-martial jurisdiction." He viewed the case as "just an extension of the old fraud statute of 1863" subjecting former servicemen to military jurisdiction for frauds against the United States, committed while in service. "It is less objectionable than the old fraud statute. It has a better test—serious offenses." All agreed with Warren except for Frankfurter, Black, and Douglas. (Jackson had died in the meantime, and Harlan had not yet been confirmed as his replacement.)

Justice Reed was assigned the opinion and (as he had in the *Emspak* and *Quinn* Communist cases) he snatched defeat from the jaws of victory. After Frankfurter looked at Reed's draft opinion, he circulated a dissent, joined by Douglas, which began:

> This case has nothing to do with the War Powers, nor do the legal questions it raises bring into relevance General Sherman's assessment of war. Considering his compassionate nature, even his experience might not have prepared him for the iron aspect of peace furthered by the Court's attitude toward the Bill of Rights.

Because of Harlan's pending confirmation, the dissenters persuaded the majority to wait until there was a full Court before deciding a significant case. The case was reargued subsequently and discussed at a conference on October 15, 1955. As he had in earlier Communist cases, Warren announced he had changed his position. "At the heart of the Constitution," he said, "is that courts-martial were for discipline and that is all. . . . The Constitution's 'necessary and proper' clause does not apply to it after service. . . . The case is of greatest importance for civil liberties. I don't believe [the provision] is consistent with jury trial of civilians." Warren's shift, Harlan's agreement, and Clark's change of mind made a six-to-three Court for Toth.

Black wrote the opinion for the Court; in his draft, he quoted Thomas Jefferson viewing "trial by jury as the only anchor ever yet imagined by man by which a government can be held to the principles of its Constitution." Frankfurter persuaded Black to remove the quote because it "strikes me as a bit of humorless hyperbole. I cannot regard the jury, any more than any other political device, as the final word of wisdom or as indispensable to the free human spirit. . . . I cannot for the life of me believe that the Constitution is less regnant in Baltimore, where, as a matter of long tradition, trial by jury is waived in all but two or three percent of the criminal cases (including capital), than it is here in Washington, or in Alabama, or in Massachusetts."

When, in separate incidents, Mrs. Dorothy Krueger Smith and Mrs. Clarice B. Covert were accused of murdering their soldier

husbands on overseas American military bases, they were tried
and convicted by military courts-martial under a provision subjecting to military justice "all persons serving with . . . or accompanying the armed forces without the continental limits of
the United States." The women independently claimed it was
unconstitutional to try civilians in military courts.

The justices, among themselves, referred to the incidents as
"The Case of the Murdering Wives." When the cases first were
discussed in conference on May 4, 1956, Warren argued strongly
against the provisions of the Uniform Code of Military Justice
which gave the military judicial authority over the dependents of
servicemen.

"It's hard to believe that a housewife and youngsters in England and Tokyo are members of the armed services for military
justice," Warren asserted. "The fact that they use the PX means
nothing. . . . That's not in keeping with our traditions."

Black agreed that "it stretches the Constitution" to subject
non-soldiers to military jurisdiction; Reed, Douglas, and Frankfurter voiced similar doubts. Minton maintained that since 1891,
in the *In re Ross* case, the Court had ruled that constitutional
guarantees may not apply outside the territorial United States.
Burton agreed.

Reed reconsidered, however, and Clark and Harlan joined his
view favoring military jurisdiction. Reed, as the senior justice in
the majority, assigned the opinion to Clark. Clark stressed cases
like *Ross*, which upheld congressional power to create "legislative" and consular courts to try certain crimes abroad. "The
power to create a territorial or consular court," he wrote, "must
necessarily include the power to provide for trial before a military tribunal." Where United States courts are not available,
"Congress may well have determined that trial before an American court-martial . . . was preferable to leaving American servicemen and their dependents . . . subject to widely varying
standards of justice unfamiliar to our people."

On reading Clark's draft, Frankfurter wrote Harlan that "a
respectable—that is, a lawyer-like opinion" supporting the convictions could be written. He added reprovingly, however:

I have just read Tom's opinion and I'm appalled. This [is a] far-
rago of irresponsible, uncritical . . . far-reaching, needlessly dangerous incongruities. I cannot believe that this opinion will be allowed to go down with your concurrence—until it does!

But Harlan did concur, and Clark's opinion spoke for a majority of five justices. Neither Frankfurter nor the dissenters—Warren, Black, and Douglas—filed opinions because the decision had
been handed down as the Court prepared to leave on its summer
recess. The petitioners asked for a rehearing—a routine practice
invariably denied. This time, though, the dissenters started plot-
ting in early September to get the case back. Both Black and
Frankfurter prepared dissents designed to encourage a rehearing.

Frankfurter, ever the political strategist, urged the others who
disputed the Clark opinion to keep mum on their plans: "There
is, I think, a very good reason why it should not be known outside ourselves that such a dissent has been prepared. Therefore,
I am seeing to it that this gets to you in person, for it is just as
well that not even the law clerks know about this at the moment."

Douglas wrote Frankfurter in September 1956, "I hear the majority [in *Reid* v. *Covert*] is having conferences on the petition
for rehearing. So maybe trouble for them is brewing."

Black later circulated a memorandum stating the issue and
trying to win a fifth vote for rehearing:

> The issue in these cases is whether Congress can constitutionally
> authorize the military trial of civilians during times of peace for
> alleged crimes. . . . Study and reflection since the Court's deci-
> sions have strengthened our view that this Court's holdings in
> these cases have given the military authorities new powers not
> hitherto thought consistent with our scheme of government.

By October 9, Frankfurter and Warren persuaded Harlan to
join in the vote for a rehearing to allow counsel, in the manner of
Brown, to respond to some questions from the Court relating to
the historical evidence on military jurisdiction in such cases,
whether there is a distinction between civilian employees of the
military and civilian dependents, why it was practical to maintain military jurisdiction, and where the line should be drawn to
differentiate between major crimes and petty offenses.

Before the Court scheduled its rehearing for February 1957, both Minton and Reed had retired, reducing the five-justice majority to a minority of three. At the March 1 conference, Warren said, "The simple question is whether Congress has the right to declare these dependents a part of the armed forces of the United States and are subject to court-martial. This goes beyond anything; it's contrary to the history of the United States and England. Congress does not possess the power to declare them in the armed forces."

Black was assigned the opinion; it condemned broadly the court-martial jurisdiction over civilians. Clark decided to make a stab at getting the vote of the new justice, Brennan. Only eight justices would participate, for the case had been reargued before Whittaker joined the Court. If Clark and Burton, who had been in the majority before, could hold on to Harlan's vote and win Brennan's, the evenly divided Court would sustain its previous decision upholding the convictions and the military's authority to have tried the civilian wives.

Clark argued in a letter to Brennan that if the Court struck down the provision, the government would have to secure new agreements with foreign countries; under the Status of Forces agreements with the NATO countries and Japan, the United States retained the authority to try its own military personnel and their dependents for crimes committed in host countries, provided the hosts waived jurisdiction, which they usually did.

> The only remaining alternative [Clark wrote] would be to let prosecutions proceed in the local courts of the foreign sovereign. This might be okey [*sic*] in England. But in France one is presumed guilty rather than innocent, and in Spain local courts are certainly no protection whatever. Likewise, in the Middle and Far East we would have great difficulty. We should hesitate to repudiate our opinion of last June—and more so the power of the Congress that has been exercised *unquestioned* for over forty years. It will have a disastrous effect on our foreign relations with sixty-three countries, cause the NATO agreement to be scrapped . . . and undermine the morale of our armed forces in these foreign installations.

Clark's arguments troubled Brennan enough to delay his decision. In the end, he joined Black's opinion. Harlan and Frankfurter decided to write concurring opinions, limiting the opinion
to the question of whether courts-martial could try capital cases
involving civilians. So the Court was six to two to reverse the
wives' convictions.

From his recent retirement, Minton, one of those who had
voted in the first place to sustain the convictions, wrote Frankfurter:

> All you succeeded in doing was to turn out a couple of cold-
> blooded murderers without the Court arriving upon any principle
> of law. [You] seem strangely to have found some difference be-
> tween capital and other crimes not to be found in the Consti-
> tution.

A more troubling question faced the Court in June 1957. An
American soldier named Girard had shot and killed a Japanese
woman while trying to frighten her away from an Army range in
Japan. Under an executive agreement with Japan, Girard had
been turned over to the Japanese authorities for trial. A federal
court issued an injunction barring Girard's delivery to the Japanese.

"Am I wrong," Frankfurter asked Warren, "in deeming high
the probability that not many days will pass before the case of
Specialist Girard will be here?" Because it was "such a sensa-
tional case," Frankfurter urged Warren to "assure the continued presence of the majority of the Court members" in Washington so they would not have to be "brought back from far and
near."

The Department of Justice appealed directly to the Supreme
Court; it argued that the government of the United States was
bound by its agreement to turn Girard over to the Japanese.

On June 20, Solicitor General J. Lee Rankin, who would be arguing the government's case if the Court agreed to grant certiorari, visited Warren. The Chief Justice informed the others of
what took place:

> The Solicitor General was in to see me . . . to express the belief
> of the government that it is a matter of paramount importance in

foreign relations, not only as between this country and Japan, but also as between it and all of the other nations with which it has similar agreements. . . . It is believed by the President personally that if this country cannot legally waive jurisdiction in such matters, other nations would not waive (as they have done in the vast majority of cases) because to do so would demean them before the world.

Rankin's lobbying, though ethically questionable, appeared to have been successful. Because the Court's "Red Monday" decisions on June 17, 1957, had caused such voluble criticism, Warren persuaded the justices to maintain a low profile on the Girard case. He assigned Brennan to write a unanimous *per curiam* maintaining that the United States had validly ceded to Japan its sovereign authority to punish crimes committed by American servicemen against Japanese civilians. Mercifully for the Court, already pilloried for its Communist decisions and, depending on the source, for moving either too fast or too slow in the realm of racial discrimination, the *Girard* case aroused little protest.

The rapid changes in social mores, accelerated by the mushrooming popularity of television, and the threatening rumbles of major discord in the South seem to have obscured the anticipated chauvinistic response to allowing an American GI to be tried in a Japanese court.

As national tensions grew tauter, they were reflected in growing dissension among some justices, notably Frankfurter and Douglas.

In October 1957, the justices considered *Lambert* v. *California,* a case of whether the city of Los Angeles could require the registration with the police of every person who had been convicted "of an offense punishable as a felony." At first, the justices seemed unanimous in wanting to reverse because the statute was too vague; the words, Douglas wrote in a draft opinion, "are the equivalent of Arabic script or a formula written in mathematical symbols." Clark objected; he thought the reversal should be based on the ground that due process was violated when the registration requirement was applied to a person who had no actual knowledge of the duty to register.

Four justices dissented from that interpretation. Frankfurter wrote that "a whole volume of the United States Reports would be required to document in detail the legislation in this country that would fall or be impaired" by the majority decision.

After he issued the dissent on December 16, Frankfurter received a note from Douglas requesting "a citation of the statutes that would fall." Frankfurter replied, "You ask me for ordinances just like the Los Angeles ordinance. I have no doubt that there are such. But that isn't the game I am playing."

Later the same day, Douglas replied to the reply:

> The reason that I asked you for some statute which would run afoul of *Lambert* other than the ordinance involved was your statement on the bench that it would [take] much, much too long to list the statutes which would fall as a result of [the decision]. I thought you might be willing to disclose their identity— at least, the identity of a single one.

Frankfurter responded still later the same day:

> I stand on what I wrote in my earlier letter. I would go to the stake for the accuracy of my statement.

Likely to the chagrin of the messengers, Douglas dispatched yet another response that afternoon:

> Nobody in this office wants you to go through the ordeal by fire— especially at Christmas time. I, too, would go to the stake for the accuracy of my quotation of what you said from the bench [about] the statutes which would fall. . . . To be more specific, you stated from the bench the list would fill a volume. So when we ask for just one, we are not asking for very much out of that long tabulation.

The late hour put off Frankfurter's next sally until the following morning:

> Of course you are accurate in indicating what I said from the bench in *Lambert*. I stand on what I said there. The whole point of my dissent is that many statutes should fall if the reasoning in *Lambert* governed other instances, but my forecast is that they won't. I am sorry that what I wrote is opaque.

Douglas had the last word on the subject later on December 17:

> I guess my writing must be the opaque one. For all I wanted was a citation of one statute that would fall if the reasoning in *Lambert* were followed.

The carping between the two and, indeed, between Frankfurter and all the activists continued beyond the *Lambert* case. During oral arguments one day in 1960, Frankfurter posed a series of sharp questions to one of the lawyers. Each time the lawyer started to answer, Douglas broke in with a helpful reply.

"I thought *you* were arguing this case," Frankfurter snapped at the lawyer.

"I am," the counsel replied, "but I can use all the help I can get."

TWELVE

Serving Up the Law on a Silver Platter

THE COLD WAR abroad, coupled with racial animosities and expanding super-patriotism at home, was exacerbating domestic tensions in the United States in the late 1950s and early 1960s. The Supreme Court, personified by its Chief Justice, had become the principal target for vilification by those who were frustrated by the failure of World War II to bring peace and security and by the demonstrable diminution of America's world leadership in military power and scientific achievement.

Like many politicians, Warren publicly laughed off criticism but fumed at it in private. "He was rock-hard," Justice Byron White said of Warren. "It was hard to rile him." Another justice recalled, however, that Warren "was a person who had deep-seated and permanent resentments and dislikes—and he held to them stubbornly."

Inevitably, even the most self-disciplined public figures occasionally allow their private peeves to spill into the open; in Warren's case, it was more like a flash flood.

At a Washington cocktail party in July 1959, Washington correspondent Clark Mollenhoff "was innocently, or naïvely, in the process of making what I believed was a routine introduction of Chief Justice Warren to Earl Mazo."

Mazo, like Mollenhoff a Washington-based journalist, was the author of a just-published, generally flattering biography of Vice President Nixon.

Before the introduction was completed, Mollenhoff recalled, Warren grew furious. "You are a damned liar," Warren said, stunning both journalists. Mazo's book, he charged, was "a dishonest account to promote the presidential candidacy of Nixon. I don't care what you write about Nixon as long as you don't try to build him up over my body."

Actually, Warren did not appear extensively in Mazo's book. The author reported, without much comment, Nixon's efforts for Eisenhower and alleged "double-crossing" of Warren in 1952, and how, two years earlier, Nixon had "wormed" from Governor Warren an indirect endorsement of Nixon's candidacy for the Senate. But Warren told one of his law clerks that the book was "nothing but a whitewash of Nixon" and that, when he met Mazo, "I got very irritated."

Indeed, when the Chief Justice, concluding his outburst at the cocktail party, raised his clenched fists and leaned toward Mazo, several startled onlookers thought he might strike the reporter. Actually, Warren pressed his wrists together as if he were handcuffed. "You people are persecuting me," he bawled, "because you know I can't strike back."

Warren's volatile reaction to Mazo's book seemed to indicate the extent to which nerves had become increasingly frayed in the United States since the summer and fall of 1957. It was a difficult time for the country and for the Court.

In August 1957, the Soviet Union successfully tested a multi-stage intercontinental ballistic missile. On October 4, the Russians launched Sputnik. Before the month was out, they announced they had perfected a new hydrogen warhead for the ICBM. Americans were scared and humiliated. They believed their government had failed them, their scientists had sold them out, and, most particularly, their educators were second-rate. Suddenly, Johnny couldn't read or do arithmetic—or, if he could, he wasn't as good at it as Ilya.

The Supreme Court, meanwhile, seemed to be taking the side of the Communists, while in Little Rock, the military appeared to be making war against Americans instead of Russians in a battle that was soiling the nation's honor in full view of the civilized world.

That battle had its origins on August 20, 1957, when Governor Orval Faubus of Arkansas called on Deputy Attorney General William Rogers in Washington to ask how the federal government intended to forestall violence in Little Rock when newly integrated schools opened two weeks later. Rogers registered surprise. No one had suggested before that there was a possibility of violence in Little Rock. The mayor had indicated all was well; the integration of schools was to take place over a seven-year period and, in the first year, the blacks who would attend previously all-white schools had been handpicked carefully. Any trouble, Faubus was told, would be handled by local authorities; if there was a conspiracy to thwart integration, the governor or others could seek federal injunctions.

When asked why he expected violence, Faubus said his information was "too vague and indefinite to be of any use to a law-enforcement agency."

It wasn't too vague, however, for him to ask of, and receive from, a state court an injunction to stop Little Rock's integration plan because, in the governor's unsupported view, it would lead to bloodshed. A federal court promptly overruled the action, and the Little Rock Board of Education proceeded with its plan to initiate integration by admitting nine black boys and girls to Central High School along with two thousand white students. Although there were no signs of unrest, Little Rock's mayor and police chief developed their own plan on how to deal with any demonstrations.

Faubus did not intend to allow the local authorities to deal with what, until then, was a nonexistent problem. On September 1, Winthrop Rockefeller, Arkansas' best-known citizen (who would become governor himself some years later), rushed to see Faubus. Was it true, he asked, that the governor intended to activate the National Guard to block the Negro students from entering Central High School? It was, Faubus disclosed. Rockefeller pleaded with Faubus to change his mind. Faubus refused. He was running for a third term, he said, and he would be defeated if he permitted integration to proceed unimpeded.

The next evening, just before the schools were to reopen, National Guardsmen surrounded the school and their commanding officer established his command post in the principal's office. The governor told a television audience his action was based on a "deluge" of information that Little Rock was on the brink of riot. The mayor, Woodrow W. Mann, protested vigorously. "There was no indication whatever," he said. "We had no reason to believe there would be violence."

On September 3, the nine black students were turned away from the school. One of the students was called a "burr-head," but there was no violence. The governor had claimed that citizens, mostly black youths, were buying up all the knives in the city; the FBI found knife sales were less than usual for the time of year. Without fanfare, integration began without incident in the Arkansas communities of Fort Smith, Ozark, and Van Buren. The FBI issued a five-hundred-page report to the federal district court maintaining there was no evidence to support the claim of impending violence.

The governor was ordered to appear in court to explain why he was interfering with the school board's integration plan. After being served with the federal summons, he wired President Eisenhower, asking for "understanding and cooperation." Eisenhower wired back that "the only assurance I can give you is that the federal Constitution will be upheld by me by every legal means at my command."

Still, the President agreed to meet Faubus at the summer White House in Newport, Rhode Island, on September 14, the twelfth day on which the high school was occupied by Guardsmen and a week before he was scheduled to defend his actions in court. Eisenhower's chief of staff, Sherman Adams, thought after the meeting that Faubus "would not be unreasonable or difficult to deal with."

Nothing, however, had changed when Faubus' lawyers appeared before the United States district court in Little Rock. The governor had been promising ever since making his telecast that he would present his evidence of impending violence in open court. Now, given the chance, Faubus backed away. His lawyers announced the position "that the Governor of the State of Arkansas cannot and will not concede that the United States in this court or anywhere else can question his discretion and judgment."

It was a tired argument—one which the Supreme Court had rejected one hundred and thirty-nine years earlier when, in the 1819 decision in *McCulloch* v. *Maryland,* Chief Justice John Marshall, for a unanimous Court, enunciated what he called "a principle which so entirely pervades the Constitution, is so intermixed with the materials which compose it, so interwoven with its web, so blended with its texture, as to be incapable of being separated from it, without rending it into shreds."

> This great principle [Marshall wrote] is that the Constitution and the laws made in pursuance thereof are supreme; that they control the Constitution and laws of the respective States, and cannot be controlled by them.

The judge, Ronald Davies, after hearing from the mayor, police chief, and school superintendent that there was racial peace in Little Rock, ruled that school integration had been "thwarted by the Governor" and "there would have been no violence in carrying out the plan of integration." Faubus, heeding the court's command, withdrew the National Guard from Central High School later that day, September 20.

By then, however, Little Rock had become a media center. News of the pending confrontation circled the globe. Hundreds of people—many of them curious, but many others clearly malicious—surrounded the school. The seventy Little Rock policemen were unable (and some, perhaps, were unwilling) to contain the crowd when some toughs attacked five blacks approaching Central High. The blacks were reporters, though, and while they were being mauled, the nine black students entered the school without incident. Outside, though, tumult continued to build; other reporters, white and black, were harassed or worse, and the mob threatened to break into the school if the black youngsters were not ejected. By noon, the mayor ordered the black students sent home—and the crowd dispersed.

Faubus claimed the event "vindicates my good judgment"; others maintained the violence was a self-fulfilling prophecy.

Mayor Mann of Little Rock requested federal help. The President, who had made little secret of his distaste for *Brown* v. *Board of Education,* was, nonetheless, resolved to enforce federal law and to stand firm against the mob.

> The very basis of our individual rights and freedoms [Eisenhower said on national television] rests upon the certainty that the President and the executive branch of government will support and ensure the carrying out of the decisions of the federal courts even, when necessary, with all the means at the President's command. Unless the President did so, anarchy would result.

On September 25, the Arkansas National Guard was placed in federal service by the Secretary of Defense, and the Army Chief of Staff, General Maxwell Taylor, ordered elements of the 101st Airborne Division, under the command of Major General Edwin Walker, into Little Rock. (Walker would become controversial in another context later—first, as a John Birch Society supporter while still on active duty and, when retired, as a leader of a demonstration against the admission of James Meredith to Ole Miss. At Little Rock, General Walker, whatever his personal devils, faithfully executed the orders of his commanders; his troops dispersed the mob, restored order, and assured that the nine black students could attend school safely.)

Governor Faubus, who had left Little Rock during the crisis— he had attended the Georgia-Texas football game in Atlanta over the weekend, then went to the resort of Sea Island, Georgia, to attend the Southern Governors' Conference—returned in time to claim that federal troops had bludgeoned innocent bystanders, threatened schoolgirls with bayonets, and leered at naked girls in Central High's locker room. J. Edgar Hoover said Faubus was "disseminating falsehoods." The governor never produced evidence to support his allegations. By November, the Army withdrew nearly all troops from Little Rock and the black students began attending school without an escort.

It had been the first time since Reconstruction that federal troops had been dispatched to quell southern intransigence. Whatever the truth or falsehood of Governor Faubus' claims, Southerners rallied to him and to the ghost of a dirty, bloody civil war which they chose, with blurred, myth-befogged memory, to recall as noble and glorious.

In their warped fervor, they displaced as heroes men of courage and grace—Jefferson Davis, Robert E. Lee, Stonewall Jackson—in favor of shallow bigots like Faubus, John Kasper, Bull Connor. The fabled battlefields—Antietam, Richmond, Gettysburg—gave way to the steamy streets of Clinton, Birmingham, Selma.

Still, a unanimous Supreme Court—supported by the determination of the White House to enforce the Court's decisions—held out hope to white and black Americans of good will that their nation would defend the Constitution and its promise of freedom and equality.

The Court's unanimity in racial questions bent perilously in the wake of Little Rock. In January 1958, with some troops still guarding Central High School, the Court considered *NAACP* v. *Alabama*, in which Alabama's attorney general ordered the organization to turn over to him the names and addresses of all its members in the state. The justices agreed the order violated First Amendment rights of NAACP members. After the conference, though, Justice Clark decided to dissent "on the ground that the state's interests have not been adequately put to us." Warren and the others tried to persuade Clark to withdraw his dissent. This issue, Frankfurter wrote Clark, "doesn't seem to me a good enough starting point for a break in the unanimity of the Court in what is, after all, part of the whole segregation controversy. The sky is none too bright anyhow. The mere fact that you are dissenting would be blown up out of all proportion to what you yourself would subscribe to." Just before the decision was announced in June, Clark made it unanimous.

By then, all troops had left Little Rock. But the school board, which had displayed such fortitude in the white heat of crisis, backed away from its integration plan in the face of Faubus' growing popularity. (In a few months, Faubus would be elected to a third two-year term as governor—and he would be elected four more times after that until he retired and drifted into obscurity.) A federal district court granted the school board a two-and-a-half-year postponement for implementation of integration, agreeing it was wise to wait until "tempers had cooled."

In August, the Court of Appeals for the Eighth Circuit reversed that ruling, but the parties appealed. The Supreme Court justices gathered hurriedly on August 28 (they were not scheduled to reconvene until October) to try to resolve the issue before the opening of school on September 2—a year to the day when Faubus had sent the National Guard to Central High to keep out the nine black students.

The Court could not resolve the issue that day, setting additional arguments for September 11. Nonetheless, there was a heated exchange between Warren and Richard C. Butler, the school board's lawyer.

Butler, in arguing for the two-and-a-half-year delay, maintained that the people of the state were confused as to who had authority in the matter and, therefore, were disinclined to support the Court's ruling.

"If the governor of any state says that a United States Supreme Court decision is not the law of the land," Butler averred, "the people of that state have a doubt in their mind—and a right to have a doubt."

Warren was incensed. "I have never heard such an argument in a court of justice before—and I have tried many a case through many a year. I never have heard a lawyer say that the statement of a governor as to what was legal or illegal should control the action of any court."

Almost immediately, the Arkansas legislature was summoned into special session to pass a number of segregation laws—among them the authority for the governor to close public schools that were about to be integrated, and power to transfer public school funds to private, segregated schools. The United States Attorney General notified the school board in Little Rock that the Department of Justice would cooperate to prevent violence. On Butler's advice, school openings in Little Rock were postponed until September 15; the attorney, assuming the likelihood of the Supreme Court ordering integration to proceed without delay, thought it unwise to open the schools on a segregated basis; conversely, he wanted the support of the Court ruling—and the firm backing of the Justice Department—before allowing integrated schools to be seized by Faubus.

The Washington *Post* editorially characterized the school board as courageous—and Frankfurter agreed. The school board, he wrote Warren, "showed a good deal of enterprise and courage to stand up against Faubus and Company." He suggested that when the arguments were heard on September 11, Warren take note of the action to delay the school opening.

> My own view [Frankfurter wrote] has long been that the ultimate hope for a peaceful solution of the basic problem largely depends on winning the support of lawyers of the South for the overriding issue of obedience to the Court's decision. Therefore, I think we should encourage every manifestation of fine conduct by a lawyer like Butler.

Warren rejected Frankfurter's idea. He told Brennan and some others that he would not go out of his way to praise a lawyer who, as Warren saw it, argued that southern obstruction justified delaying integration.

Frankfurter was angry.

> I am bound to say [he wrote Harlan] that Butler's advice to his school board was much wiser than the views the Chief Justice expressed to you fellows at luncheon. Of course Faubus has been guilty of trickery, but the trickery was as much against the school board as against us. And, in any event, the fight is not between the Supreme Court and Faubus—though, apparently, this is the way it lay in the Chief Justice's mind. I am afraid his attitude toward the kind of problems that confront us are more like that of a fighting politician than that of a judicial statesman.

From the Bench on September 11, Warren made plain his disdain for Arkansas' "defiance" of *Brown* v. *Board of Education.* He also asked Butler whether, if the two-and-a-half-year delay was granted and "the climate of opinion is as it is now, would you be in here asking for another two and a half years?"

The conference met immediately after the arguments and was over in half an hour. Frankfurter and Harlan wrote a brief *per curiam* sustaining unanimously the Court of Appeals decision denying the delay of the integration plan. The announcement of the decision, made promptly because school was to open imminently, added that supporting views would be issued later.

Again, Clark considered dissenting—this time because he questioned the haste with which the Court had acted. He wrote out a planned dissent, which, however, he never circulated:

> My action is not to be construed in any respect whatsoever as a change of position from that taken in *Brown,* etc. I adhere steadfastly to my vote there believing that every American citizen goes first class. Under our Constitution, there is no steerage. However, as I understood *Brown,* integration was not to be accomplished through push-button action but rather by "deliberate speed." The case should be considered in its regular course, not by forced action. Of all tribunals, this is one that should stick strictly to the rules. To do otherwise is to create the very situation that the Constitution prohibits, the existence of a preferred class.

Brennan wrote the opinion in the case—*Cooper* v. *Aaron*— which held that all officials are bound to obey the law as ultimately propounded by the Supreme Court. Harlan suggested including a paragraph pointing out that since the *Brown* decision, three new justices had come to the Court (Harlan, Brennan, and Whittaker), but "they are at one with the justices still on the Court who participated in the original decision as to the inescapability of that decision."

Brennan didn't like it. "I feel that any such reference to the three new members would be a grave mistake," he said at a September 19 conference. "It lends support to the notion that the Constitution has only the meaning that can command a majority of the Court as that majority may change with shifting membership. Whatever truth there may be in that idea, I think it would be fatal in this fight to provide ammunition from the mouth of this Court in support of it."

Brennan lost; the Harlan suggestion was adopted. Frankfurter, taking up a suggestion by Harlan, proposed that the opinion be signed by the entire Court. Only Douglas objected, pointing out that opinions always had been issued in the name of a single justice. He was outvoted, eight to one. (In 1974, Brennan suggested to Chief Justice Burger that the entire Court sign the opinion in the Nixon tapes case, but Burger dismissed the idea.)

Warren read the opinion on September 29, its vibrant language made more dramatic by the announcement that all nine had written the opinion. "The federal judiciary is supreme in the exposition of the law of the Constitution," he read. Obedience of the states to the principles of *Brown* is "indispensable for the protection of the freedoms guaranteed by our fundamental charter for all of us. Our constitutional ideal of equal justice under law is thus made a living truth."

The justices filed out of the courtroom. Only they knew that, for the first time in more than four years, the Court would speak in more than a single voice in a segregation case. The source of that break with a powerful, if young, tradition would be known to the public a few days later when a concurring opinion was announced. It was the man who, unknown to that public, had been the justice who, except perhaps for Warren, had been most responsible for unanimity on segregation—Felix Frankfurter. And it appeared that Frankfurter, after having argued against those of his colleagues who had threatened to steal away, however gingerly, from unanimity on segregation, turned on his own arguments for no more substantial reason than his inflated ego.

Frankfurter, Justice Burton recalled after the final conference on the case on September 29, "wants to say something more. We are unable to dissuade him, but did succeed in getting him not to announce it from the Bench today."

Frankfurter circulated his opinion on October 3. Warren thought the opinion added nothing of substance to the Court's opinion, which Frankfurter had joined. He asked Black to try again to dissuade Frankfurter from filing separately. As one justice recalls it, the former professor pompously explained that "respect for law in the South depended on southern lawyers, and that the leading ones were his former students. It was necessary for him to write personally to persuade them."

Black and Brennan then said that if Frankfurter persisted, they would issue a statement:

> Justices Black and Brennan believe that the joint opinion of all the justices handed down on September 29 adequately expresses the views of the Court, and they stand by that opinion as delivered. They desire that it be fully understood that the concurring opinion filed this day by Justice Frankfurter must not be accepted as any dilution of the views expressed in the Court's joint opinion.

Warren didn't think issuing the statement was a good idea, but Black and Brennan were adamant. Then Harlan defused the explosive situation by passing around a whimsical opinion "concurring in part, expressing a *dubitante* in part, and dissenting in part." He said he concurred in the Court's September 29 opinion, "in which I have already concurred." He doubted Frankfurter's wisdom in filing separately, "but since I am unable to find any material difference between that opinion and the Court's opinion . . . I am content to leave his course of action to his own good judgment." He dissented from Black and Brennan issuing their rejoinder, "believing that it is always a mistake to make a mountain out of a molehill. *Requiescat in pace*." Frankfurter filed as planned, but Black and Brennan were persuaded by Harlan to let the matter drop.

Even before the Little Rock case was argued, Burton, growing increasingly ill with Parkinson's disease, had planned to retire after his seventieth birthday in June, when he would be eligible for a pension. Warren persuaded him to stay on until the new Court term officially opened in October. After Burton submitted his resignation, Eisenhower made clear that he wanted another justice with previous judicial experience. This appointment would mean that a majority of the Court would be Eisenhower appointees—all, except Warren, with previous service on the Bench. Even though Brennan also had disappointed the President, selection of someone with a judicial background seemed the most prudent course.

From the beginning of the discussions in the White House, Judge Potter Stewart, an Ohio Republican who sat on the Court of Appeals for the Sixth Circuit (having been appointed by Eisenhower four years earlier), seemed the odds-on favorite. Stewart, at forty-three, was, but for Douglas, the youngest Supreme Court appointee in over a century.

Stewart, after taking a postgraduate year at Cambridge, England, graduated with honors from Yale Law School in a class that included Congressman Gerald Ford of Michigan. Eisenhower named him to the appellate court after Stewart had served two terms on Cincinnati's City Council.

A gregarious man who never lost his zest for politics, Stewart almost immediately became the press's favorite justice. He always found time to meet with journalists and help them to understand the issues that faced the Court in reaching their decisions.

From the start, Stewart was notable for pungent observations and a judicial philosophy that defied categorization.

Stewart's description of hard-core pornography in a 1964 case was that he would not attempt to define it, "but I know it when I see it." In a 1961 antitrust case involving a shoe company, the question was raised whether dress shoes competed with casual shoes. The Solicitor General, pressing the case, contended they did; indeed, the company president had arrived at the trial court wearing dress shoes one day and casual shoes the next. "Maybe," Stewart observed, "it was direct examination one day and cross-examination the next."

With the Court evenly divided on most cases between two camps—Warren, Black, Douglas, and Brennan being the activists and Frankfurter, Harlan, Clark, and Whittaker generally favoring restraint—Stewart became the "swing man," sometimes voting with one camp, sometimes with the other. He conceded he did not possess an easily defined philosophy. "I am a lawyer," he would say to those who asked if he was a judicial liberal or conservative. "I have some difficulty understanding what those terms mean even in the field of political life, and I find it impossible to know what they mean when they are carried over to judicial work."

Throughout his tenure on the Court, Stewart maintained a healthy perspective on his role, never permitting self-importance to consume him. For one thing, he remained convinced that the President who appointed him to the Court never really knew who he was. President Eisenhower, Stewart said, used to think he was Justice Whittaker. As for Warren, Stewart recalled, the Chief Justice "was never sure if I was from Cleveland or Cincinnati," and when a group of lawyers from Ohio were being admitted to the bar of the Court, Warren said he was pleased to welcome attorneys "from Justice Stewart Potter's state." (Stewart was not the only justice whose name slipped Warren's mind; in 1965, Warren referred from the Bench to Arthur J. Goldberg as "Justice Goldwater.")

With two judicial factions, each numbering strong-minded men among them, playing tug-of-war for Stewart's vote and support, the new, young justice found himself in what Frankfurter described as "an intellectual traffic jam. He terrifically feels the burden of his work," Frankfurter wrote his friend Learned Hand. "I also think, however, that he is concerned how he appears to the world outside and, more particularly, he doesn't want to appear to be lining up with John [Harlan] and me." Frankfurter added that "John is confident this is true."

Whatever Stewart's concern with his public image, he voted independently enough to avoid identification with either group. One case in which he sided with Frankfurter to produce a bare majority was *Bartkus* v. *Illinois,* in which the defendant was acquitted of robbery by a federal court jury only to be convicted subsequently in a state court and sentenced to life imprisonment. He claimed the conviction violated the constitutional protection against double jeopardy. Lower courts rejected the claim.

Warren urged reversal on grounds that the Fourteenth Amendment "bars a retrial after a federal acquittal."

Frankfurter argued that "both criminal justice and federalism are involved here. The same act is a transgression against two sovereigns." Each might prosecute independently, he said.

Supporting Warren were Black, Douglas, and Brennan. Backing Frankfurter were Harlan, Clark, and Whittaker. Stewart, who had the swing vote, wanted more time to consider the issue.

Warren and Brennan pressed the point that the federal authorities participated in the Illinois trial—that, in essence, the "state" trial really was a second federal prosecution, and that clearly was unconstitutional. Brennan, in a letter to Frankfurter, reminded him "how vigorously I balk at the extent to which the federal government made use of Illinois officials to effect Bartkus' conviction."

Frankfurter found this "surprising." The state, he said, was simply "exercising its independent constitutional powers, although it had evidentiary help and, if you please, encouragement from federal officials—a help and encouragement, to repeat, the desirability of which has been preached from the housetops for most of my professional life."

Brennan disliked how Frankfurter "not too delicately implies that my circulated dissent misrepresents the record."

> Even though the state, by its "free will" decided to prosecute [Brennan wrote in a memorandum for the conference], if that prosecution is instigated by the federal government and the state case prepared and guided by federal authorities, this is enough to void the state conviction. Such a situation, for all practical purposes, is one in which federal resources, federal power, and federal energies are utilized to put an accused twice in jeopardy for the same criminal conduct.

Stewart sided with Frankfurter's group, and Bartkus' conviction was upheld by a single vote.

The issue of criminal rights was beginning to command more and more of the Court's attention—and to engender considerable dissension. But, sometimes, the justices could unite even on that hot topic. In *Spano* v. *New York*, a man was convicted of murder after a confession had been wrung from him after eight hours of intensive police interrogation. Spano had surrendered to the authorities; his attorney had left him in their custody after cautioning him not to answer any questions.

At a conference on the case on May 1, 1959, Warren led the argument for reversing the conviction. "When one surrenders to the D.A.," he said, "with instructions not to talk—and they know he has such instructions from a lawyer—they can't query him for hours until they get a confession. In the totality of this picture, due process was denied." All the justices agreed with the Chief, who assigned the opinion to himself. He wrote so eloquently in denouncing the police action that Clark was moved to write, "You've got even hardhearted me to crying."

There was anything but unanimity when, in the spring of 1960, *Elkins* v. *United States* reached the Court. Elkins had been convicted in a federal court of wiretapping. The evidence against him included recordings seized in his home by state police officers who had entered without a search warrant. The lower courts refused to suppress the evidence, relying on the "silver platter" doctrine established in 1914; it allowed federal judicial use of evidence seized in violation of the Constitution—if it had been seized by state authorities.

Warren opened the conference with the assertion that he would abolish the "silver platter" doctrine. He made clear that it would not be necessary to overrule *Wolf* v. *Colorado,* a 1949 case which ruled that state criminal proceedings could utilize "tainted" evidence, even though federal courts could not. Rather, he said the Court could establish a new rule simply by exercising its supervisory power over lower federal courts to ensure proper standards of procedure and rules of evidence. Further, Warren said that he would apply the federal standard regardless of whether the state had an exclusionary rule—a rule under which tainted evidence was excluded from introduction at the trial.

Black, Douglas, and Brennan joined the Chief. Frankfurter, Harlan, Clark, and Whittaker wanted to uphold Elkins' conviction. Stewart was the swing man again—but this time, he swung to Warren. "This [wiretapping] is a federal crime," he said. The federal standard should prevail.

Stewart wrote the opinion, including a passage that, as Brennan saw it, seemed "a square dictum that Congress could change the exclusionary rule as to federal seizures under the Fourth Amendment." Stewart rewrote the draft, eliminating "all discussion of what the Constitution might or might not require in this general area."

The minority questioned the appropriateness of "reversing out of hand a course of adjudications in this Court that began with a unanimous decision more than forty-six years ago." When the majority refused to alter its decision to nullify the "silver platter" doctrine, Judge Henry J. Friendly wrote Frankfurter, "I can now better understand some of the reservations you expressed about your latest colleague. A more conceptualistic approach I have never seen."

Frankfurter circulated a satirical "dialogue" (prepared by one of his clerks) in which the Doctor observes, "I am much more puzzled by the opinion than I was disappointed by the result." The Student asks, "Why then do you boggle over the *Elkins* case?" The Doctor replies, "Just as in most instances a case is an offspring, so it may also become an ancestor. It projects itself into the future."

Elkins would do just that in the field of criminal law—and in a year's time. And so would other cases that were beginning to touch on areas of man's supreme privacy—his church and his bedroom.

In *McGowan* v. *Maryland*, the Chief Justice decided that Sunday Blue Laws were constitutional because they were supported by "a proper economic and social objective." Choosing a particular day for closing most business establishments was all right; "the fact that the day conforms to the usages and habits of most people doesn't make this an invasion of religious beliefs or a preference for particular ones." Warren wanted to go further and rule that legislation in this area was acceptable as long as it did not operate "predominantly" to support religion. Black persuaded him that the point should be simply whether or not a law operated to aid religion—period. Douglas alone dissented. He argued that all Sunday Blue Laws were at variance with the First Amendment. "I think we're entitled to our religious scruples," he said at conference, "but I don't see how we can make everyone else attune to them. I can't be required to goose-step because eighty or ninety percent goose-step."

The justices became more exercised when a husband and wife and their physician challenged the constitutionality of a Connecticut statute prohibiting the use of contraceptive devices and forbidding doctors from issuing advice on their use. The law had been on the books since 1879—but there had never been any prosecution to enforce it.

Warren indicated he didn't like the law, but he saw the suit as "an abstract principle. We don't want to decide a contrived litigation." Frankfurter, Clark, Whittaker, and Brennan sided with him.

Stewart objected. "I don't think this law is a dead letter when, as a practical matter, there's no [birth control] clinic in Connecticut."

Harlan shed his usual reserve. "I can't say this is a feigned business," he said, objecting vigorously to dismissing the cases. "This is a full adjudication. . . . I think the statute is egregiously unconstitutional on its face. The argument submerged the real constitutional question. . . . The right to be left alone is embodied in due process. Despite the broad powers to legislate in the area of health, there are limits. This is more offensive to the right to be let alone than anything possibly could be."

Frankfurter wrote the opinion for the five-member majority, dismissing the complaints on the ground that the Connecticut law had never been enforced, and there was, therefore, no real case for adjudication—only a hypothetical situation.

"Good riddance," Clark exulted in joining the opinion. "Sign me up."

Before the next year was out, another large segment of America might have wished good riddance to a Supreme Court that increasingly "intruded" in other areas once left solely to the states—criminal justice and voter apportionment. And Tom Clark, until then widely considered a social and political conservative, especially because of his harsh dissents in cases upholding the rights of Communists, and Potter Stewart, still a judicial enigma but generally voting on the side of Frankfurter, would play a crucial role in providing accused criminals with enormous protection and extending political power to those whom the legislative bosses had effectively disenfranchised.

THIRTEEN

Mapping a New America

WHEN CLEVELAND POLICE forced their way into Dollree Mapp's home on May 23, 1957, they touched off a series of events that both characterized and influenced the turbulence that rocked the United States in the 1960s.

The authorities had conducted a search for a suspected criminal. Instead, they found some obscene books. Dollree Mapp was arrested and convicted of violating an Ohio statute prohibiting the possession of obscene materials.

New concepts of the nature of obscenity, of morality, of sexuality had begun sweeping America and much of the world in the 1960s. The 1932 Hemingway line in *Death in the Afternoon*—"I know only that what is moral is what you feel good after and what is immoral is what you feel bad after"—had been adopted as revealed truth by millions. Promiscuity flourished and, with it, community efforts multiplied to limit or bar nearly anything that struck elders as pornographic.

At first, it appeared as if the *Mapp* case would hinge on whether or not the courts believed that the Ohio law had gone too far—that, in practice, it infringed on Dollree Mapp's First Amendment rights to free speech.

In the end, however, *Mapp* v. *Ohio* would alter drastically the methods by which society might limit illegal activities in its midst. Abe Fortas called it "the most radical decision in recent times." And, as a precursor of far-reaching decisions which were perceived as tipping the balance of justice against law-abiding citizens and in favor of criminals, *Mapp* v. *Ohio* would have a strong impact on the nation's politics before the decade was out.

Mrs. Mapp had refused to admit the police to her home unless they had a warrant. They returned in three hours—still without a warrant. This time, they forced their way through a door, handcuffed Mrs. Mapp for being "belligerent," and searched the house for evidence of gambling and for someone "wanted for questioning." They found the allegedly obscene books and arrested Dollree Mapp. At the trial, she offered evidence that the books, along with some clothing, had belonged to a former boarder who had left no forwarding address. Nonetheless, she was convicted and sentenced to prison.

Until *Mapp* reached the Supreme Court, it was the established law that the United States Constitution did not prohibit prosecutors from using, in state-level criminal proceedings, evidence obtained from unreasonable search and seizure. From 1914, when the Supreme Court ruled in *Weeks* v. *United States*, evidence thus obtained in violation of the Fourth Amendment could not be used in federal proceedings. But, in his 1949 *Wolf* v. *Colorado* opinion, Frankfurter had written that the Fourteenth Amendment did not extend that prohibition to the states.

Frankfurter, in that opinion, raised the question of whether "the basic right to protection against arbitrary intrusion by the police demands the exclusion of logically relevant evidence obtained by an unreasonable search and seizure because, in a federal prosecution for a federal crime, it would be excluded. As a matter of inherent reason, one would suppose this to be an issue as to which men with complete devotion to the protection of the right of privacy might give different answers."

Frankfurter went on to assert that "in fact most of the English-speaking world does not regard as vital to such protection the exclusion of evidence thus obtained."

At the time the *Weeks* decision was handed down, twenty-six of the twenty-seven states which had passed on the admissibility of unlawfully obtained evidence had opposed the *Weeks* doctrine. In the thirty-five years between that decision and Frankfurter's opinion in *Wolf*, forty-seven states reconsidered *Weeks* or passed on it for the first time; in all, thirty opposed the doctrine and seventeen agreed with it.

Frankfurter maintained there were other means of protecting the right of privacy in communities—including internal police discipline "under the eyes of an alert public opinion":

> We cannot brush aside the experience of states which deem the incidence of such conduct by the police too slight to call for a deterrent remedy not by way of disciplinary measures but by overriding the relevant rules of evidence.

In succeeding years, the Court consistently excepted cases in which physical force that "shocked the conscience" was used to obtain evidence. But it stood fast with *Wolf* even in cases involving illegal entry into and "bugging" of a private home to obtain evidence (*Irvine* v. *California*) or taking a blood sample from an unconscious suspect and then using it against him (*Breithaupt* v. *Abram*).

When *Mapp* was discussed at a Court conference on March 31, 1961, Warren said the Ohio law barring knowing possession of obscene material "cuts across First Amendment rights. It's too broad a statute to accomplish its purpose, and on that basis, I'd reverse." Stewart agreed. "If this stuff isn't covered by the First and Fourteenth, it's hard to see what is," he said.

Douglas also agreed, but added that he was prepared to go further and overrule *Wolf*. Warren and Brennan suggested they would join that effort—but the idea died (or so it seemed) for lack of support. At that point, Douglas, Warren, and Brennan agreed to reverse the *Mapp* case on First Amendment grounds. Warren assigned the opinion to Justice Clark.

After the conference disbanded, Clark boarded the elevator with Brennan and Black.

Turning to his colleagues, Clark said, "Wouldn't this be a good case to apply the exclusionary rule—and do what *Wolf* didn't do?"

The others asked if he was serious. Clark said he was; he had shifted to Douglas' position. That made four for overturning *Wolf* and extending the exclusionary rule to the state courts as well as to federal cases.

Black suggested he might go along, although not eagerly. Black (who had concurred with the *Wolf* opinion) never believed that Fourth Amendment rights were as sacrosanct as rights protected by the First Amendment; he told Clark he might have difficulty joining him on Fourth Amendment grounds alone.

When Clark circulated his draft in late April, several of the justices were plainly surprised. "As I am sure you anticipated," Stewart wrote Clark, "your proposed opinion in this case came as quite a surprise. The idea of overruling *Wolf* was not even discussed at the conference where we all agreed, as I recollect it, that the judgment should be reversed on First Amendment grounds." Stewart ultimately voted to reverse the conviction—but he wrote that he did so because the Ohio statute was not consistent with the rights of free thought and expression.

Brennan, however, was ecstatic. "Of course you know I think this is just magnificent and wonderful," he wrote Clark after reading the *Mapp* draft. "I have not joined anything since I came with greater pleasure." Black decided that no assertions in Clark's draft "raise insuperable barriers for me."

Clark's draft quoted Cardozo: " 'The criminal is to go free because the constable has blundered.' The criminal will go free, if he must, but he will be freed by the law. Even Titus has rights."

Much of the draft's more eloquent passages were deleted ultimately, but they indicate the majority's mind-set:

> In violations of what other rights do we abide unfettered judicial employment of the fruits of official lawlessness? In none, save those of the core of the Fourth Amendment. The ignoble but doubtless efficient route to conviction left open to the state tends by its very efficiency to destroy the entire system of constitutional restraints on which the liberties of the people rest.

Black decided to concur in a separate opinion, as Douglas did. Douglas' concurrence noted that after *Wolf* was handed down, "there was a storm of constitutional controversy." On reading this, Frankfurter noted wryly, "I wonder in what weather bureau this 'storm' was recorded?"

Frankfurter's concept of judicial restraint was damaged by the *Mapp* opinion; Clark's unexpected move to overrule *Wolf* threatened the already tenuous majority of judicial "conservatives." Harlan represented Frankfurter's views when he wrote Clark, "Your proposed overruling of *Wolf* is, I submit, both unnecessary and undesirable. This course threatens a jail delivery of uncertain but, obviously, serious proportions."

Clark stood by his guns in replying to Harlan:

> If the right to privacy is really so basic as to be constitutional in rank, and if it is really to be enforceable against the states, then we cannot carve out of the bowels of that right the vital part—the stuff that gives it substance—the exclusion of evidence. It has long been recognized and honored as an integral part of the equivalent right against federal action.

"I hope," Clark concluded, "that you will restudy the opinion, John, and find logic and reason in it." Harlan did not. Frankfurter and Whittaker joined his strong dissent.

Mapp marked the beginning of what would become a political and public phobia—a belief that "crime in the streets" was out of control and that the courts were at least partly responsible for an erosion in public morality.

Widespread uneasiness with the Court had begun with the sweeping segregation decisions; although these decisions were applauded by a majority of Americans, a substantial minority disputed them for reasons ranging from racism to whether the Court was overstepping its authority. Public restiveness grew with the Communist decisions and with the Court's handling of pornography cases. Now the issue was whether the Court was somehow encouraging crime. And, before long, other disturbing questions would be raised: Was the Court trying to supersede the states? Was it denying God? Was there no end to its sense of limitless power?

What the people could not see, of course, was that the justices themselves, albeit on a more sophisticated level, were confronting the same issues and asking the same questions of one another, often with rancor and spite. The line between state and federal power was the subject of continuing, fundamental debate in the Court almost from its inception—and the arguments among justices often were spirited and ungentlemanly. Through the years, nearly all justices retained a sensitivity to public concerns, from the Dred Scott decision to *Brown* v. *Board of Education,* often deciding or ignoring cases because of their awareness of the possibility of popular rejection.

But the overriding devotion of nearly all the justices, no matter how they approached the law or differed philosophically, was to the guarantees of individual rights. And though there were differences among them as to what constituted essential rights, what state or individual actions violated those rights, and whether some rights were more basic than others, on one point there was virtual unanimity among the one hundred justices appointed during the nation's first two hundred years: the Supreme Court was entrusted by the Founding Fathers with securing those rights for even the least among us.

In early 1962, the Court continued what it had begun with *Mapp*—ensuring the rights of defendants in criminal trials. This time, the question was whether a defendant could get a fair trial unless represented by qualified counsel.

Thirty years earlier, in 1932, the Court considered the case of *Powell* v. *Alabama,* widely remembered as the case of the Scottsboro Boys. The year before, Victoria Price and Ruby Bates, two young white mill workers, were riding the rails, along with white and black drifters and field workers, from Chattanooga to Huntsville. A fight broke out, during which most of the white boys were thrown from the freight train.

A sheriff's posse stopped the train in Jackson County, Alabama, and arrested nine Negroes. The two white girls claimed they had been raped. Physicians found no proof of the claim, but by the time the trial started a week later, a mob of ten thousand people had gathered, Alabama militia armed with machine guns ringed the courthouse, and a nearby band played "There'll Be a Hot Time in the Old Town Tonight." Until the morning of the trial, no lawyer had been assigned to the case. All the defendants were illiterate, all were under twenty-one, all swore they were innocent.

The Supreme Court threw out the inevitable convictions by a seven-to-two vote. "In a capital case," Justice George Sutherland wrote for the majority, "where the defendant is unable to employ counsel, and is incapable adequately of making his own defense because of ignorance, feeblemindedness, illiteracy, or the like, it is the duty of the court, whether requested or not, to assign counsel for him as a necessary requisite of due process of law." Sutherland added that it would not be sufficient to appoint a lawyer "at such a time or under such circumstances as to preclude the giving of effective aid in the preparation and trial of the case."

The cases were sent back for retrial and, again, the defendants were convicted—even though Ruby Bates swore that her original story was a lie. Later, she led a demonstration to the White House to appeal for the freedom of the nine blacks. In 1935, the Court threw out the convictions again—this time because qualified Negroes had been barred from jury duty. Ultimately, some of the Scottsboro Boys were released when rape charges were dropped, others were paroled, and one—Haywood Patterson, after being convicted four times and serving sixteen years—escaped and never was captured.

For the next decade, it was widely assumed that *Powell* v. *Alabama* had made the right to the assistance of counsel in a criminal trial one of the mandatory requirements of due process of law and that it had been "incorporated" into the Fourteenth Amendment. ("Incorporation" is the extension to the states of a right guaranteed in the United States Constitution; in its *Mapp* decision, for example, the Court "incorporated" the Fourth Amendment's guarantees into the Fourteenth insofar as the use of illegally obtained evidence is concerned.)

In 1942, however, the Court ruled in *Betts* v. *Brady* that the right to counsel was not, in fact, required in state criminal cases. In upholding the conviction of an indigent defendant who had been denied court-appointed counsel, the Court noted that the state's constitution did not require such appointment and that examination of the record demonstrated that his trial had been fair. "The due process clause of the Fourteenth Amendment does not incorporate, as such, the specific guarantees found in the Sixth Amendment [right to counsel]," the Court declared. "That which may, in one setting, constitute a denial of fundamental fairness, shocking to the universal sense of justice, may, in other circumstances, and in the light of other considerations, fall short of such denial."

That was the way it stood for another twenty years. Then *Carnley* v. *Cochran* reached the Court. Carnley had been convicted by a Florida court of incest and indecent assault upon a child. He maintained the conviction was invalid because, despite his inability to pay for a lawyer, he had not been provided counsel. Although Carnley was illiterate and unfamiliar with legal procedure, the state court ruled that the defendant technically had waived his right to counsel. Carnley, defending himself, made no objections during the trial and, as Justice Brennan noted later, "there was no cross-examination worthy of the name."

At the Court's conference of February 25, 1962, Warren noted the conviction could be reversed on the facts of the case, or the justices could consider overruling *Betts* v. *Brady*. Black, who had dissented in *Betts*, wanted to "meet *Betts* and overrule it."

Frankfurter demurred, first because "this comes within *Betts* v. *Brady*" but, more important, he did not want to reconsider *Betts* on the basis of *Carnley*. "I can't imagine a worse case, a more unsavory case," Frankfurter said, referring to the incest conviction, "to overrule a long-standing decision."

Douglas and Brennan strongly supported Black; Whittaker said he would go along, but only prospectively. Clark and Stewart said they would reverse within *Betts* as Frankfurter had suggested. Harlan said he would overrule *Betts*, "but with my tongue in my cheek." He argued that the contention that "'you can't have a fair trial without a lawyer' is a fiction if one remembers the quality of representation provided."

Meanwhile, Brennan pressed Frankfurter to consider overruling *Betts*.

I think I'm prepared [Frankfurter replied to Brennan], in view of the change of climate and of legislation, to spell out my view of due process and overrule *Betts* v. *Brady*.

With the stage set for a historic decision by the Court, Justice Whittaker resigned in March 1962 and Frankfurter was incapacitated by a stroke the following month. That still left a four-to-three majority favoring overturning *Betts*—but Warren and Brennan agreed it would be unwise to issue a ground-breaking decision with a bare majority of a seven-member Court. They decided instead to reverse *Carnley* within the *Betts* rule.

Black went along, but wrote separately because, he told Brennan, he feared leaving the impression "that challenges to *Betts* v. *Brady* are no longer advisable, and that the right to a lawyer under state law depends entirely upon a 'shock-the-conscience' due process concept." His concurrence was necessary, Black said, because:

> From my viewpoint, we get a wholly incomplete repudiation of *Betts* v. *Brady* if it is at the cost of leaving as the only standard that of the accordion-like meaning of due process on which FF [Frankfurter] and his brethren rested in *Betts, Rochin,* and other like cases. . . . I am at present completely persuaded that unless I write, the accordion followers will cite *Carnley* as a plain holding that accepts that concept. That philosophy, I think, more and more leaves this country no bill of rights except as doled out by this Court.

The Court waited only a year before formally acting on what it had decided earlier—to require that defendants in criminal trials be represented by counsel. The case was the celebrated *Gideon* v. *Wainwright*.

In 1961, Clarence Earl Gideon was accused of breaking into a poolroom in Panama City, Florida. He asked the trial court to appoint a lawyer to defend him, but the judge refused. The Florida Supreme Court upheld the conviction, ruling that state law required the appointment of counsel for indigent defendants only in capital cases. Gideon became a "jailhouse lawyer," spending hours poring over law books in the prison library. In 1961, about the time the Court was considering *Carnley*, Gideon sent an IFP petition, written on the stationery of the Division of Corrections of the State of Florida, to the Supreme Court of the United States. There, it joined the mass of other *in forma pauperis* petitions awaiting the scrutiny and judgment of one or another recent law school graduate fortunate enough to have become a clerk to the Chief Justice of the United States.

Gideon's petition was marked for history—but not by accident, or through the perspicacity of one of the clerks, or even because of the brilliant argument of Abe Fortas, the gifted Washington attorney appointed by the Supreme Court to argue Gideon's case. Gideon's case was selected much earlier by the Chief Justice—before he even knew of its existence.

Shortly after *Carnley* was announced, Warren, aware that a majority of the Court had favored overturning *Betts*, determined that the Court should address that question again as soon as possible. He wanted a case in which the facts were less "unsavory" than those in *Carnley*.

He alerted his law clerks to be on the lookout for an appropriate case. By the fall of 1962, no one had yet spotted the petition from Gideon. But as Warren's new clerks arrived, one of the Chief's outgoing clerks instructed them, "Keep your eyes peeled for a 'right-to-counsel' case. The Chief feels strongly that the Constitution requires a lawyer."

Soon, the petition was located, certiorari was granted, Fortas was appointed to argue the case on January 15, 1963. Three days later, the conference agreed unanimously—including the previously unconvinced Harlan and Clark—that the time had come for *Betts* v. *Brady*. It was made fully retroactive, but Warren prudently suggested it was "better not to say 'the right to counsel applies in every criminal case' if we don't have to here. Maybe it's best just to decide this case." Thoughtfully, he assigned the opinion to Black, who had dissented twenty-one years earlier in *Betts*. "When *Betts* v. *Brady* was decided," Black said gratefully, "I never thought I'd live to see it overruled."

If public anger at the Warren Court began building with the segregation and the Communist cases, and was heightened by the criminal cases, it reached a boiling point with a case in which most of the justices, including Warren, uncharacteristically overlooked the political and public implications—*Engel* v. *Vitale*.

In 1951, the Board of Regents of the state of New York wrote a simple classroom prayer:

> Almighty God, we acknowledge our dependence upon Thee, and we beg Thy blessings upon us, our parents, our teachers, and our country.

The Board made plain it was not advocating any instruction in formal religion, which, members said, had no place in the public schools. Indeed, the members only recommended its use to local school boards. But the Board thought that by "teaching our children, as set forth in the Declaration of Independence, that Almighty God is their Creator," the young people would derive the "best security" possible in the unsettled times following World War II.

Some school boards, like the one in New Hyde Park, agreed—albeit belatedly. The board decided in 1958 to have each school day open with the recitation of the prayer. Steven Engel and four other parents objected; they asked the New York courts to order that use of the prayer be discontinued. The parents contended that the classroom ceremony was offensive to many families who were Jewish, Unitarian, members of the Society for Ethical Culture, and atheists. They insisted the use of the prayer violated the New York and United States constitutions.

William J. Vitale, Jr., and other school board members argued the prayer provided moral training for good citizenship. Any child who wished to leave or not participate would be excused, they said.

The New York courts held that by adopting the prayer, the schools were neither favoring one religion over another nor teaching religion—as long as no child was compelled to pray.

On December 4, 1961, the Court agreed to hear the case. Only Whittaker and Stewart opposed granting certiorari. "I can't agree to hear this case," Whittaker said, displaying surprising emotion. "I feel strongly—very deeply—about this." Stewart agreed fully with the court below. Warren said he could not "get excited" about the case; the official prayer, he said, seemed as harmless and venial as starting the school day with the pledge of allegiance to the flag.

The tenor and number of *amici curiae,* however, should have sounded a warning gong in the heads of the justices.

Engel's brief argued that studying American history, including the devoutness of the people, was a proper exercise in public schools—but worshipping God was not. When state officials like members of the Board of Regents composed and instituted a prayer, Engel maintained, they took on the work of clergymen— and that was forbidden by the Constitution. He quoted James Madison dismissing the notion "that the civil magistrate is a competent judge of religious truths or that he may employ religion as an engine of civil policy. The first is an arrogant pretension . . . the second, an unhallowed perversion of the means of salvation."

Jewish representatives maintained that prayer was by its nature sectarian; the form of the prayer and the use of certain words might alter the essence of religion. No governmental authority, they argued, could enter this realm.

The Board of Regents rejected these claims. The Regents argued that to whatever extent possible, and without violating the separation of church and state, schools must provide moral and spiritual leadership to students. These were weapons against rising delinquency and crime, they said.

Vitale and the New Hyde Park school board maintained that public schools should not be forced to eliminate "any recognition—even on a voluntary basis—of the existence of a Divine Being."

Parents opposed to Engel's view maintained in their brief that a handful of people were trying to "force all others to conform to their views" by insisting on "the total and compulsory elimination of God's name from our schools."

On April 6, 1962, the Court's conference voted overwhelmingly to support Black's contention that the official prayer was patently violative of the First Amendment's clause forbidding the establishment of religion. Only Stewart disagreed at the conference, citing the pervasiveness in government of opening meetings with prayer, including the invocation which opened Supreme Court sessions.

Later, however, Black was questioned on his view from an unexpected quarter. On June 11, only two weeks before the decision was announced, Douglas confessed he was troubled by the case. "If we would strike down a New York requirement that public school teachers open each day with prayer," Douglas wrote Black, "I think we could not consistently open each of our sessions with prayer. That's the kernel of my problem."

Douglas' difficulty was answered by what the Chief had said during oral argument when a similar point was raised. The school board's lawyer compared the New York prayer to the Court's invocation—"God save the United States and this honorable Court." Warren commented from the Bench, "I wonder whether it would make a difference if we were to require every litigant and lawyer who comes in here to say the same prayer your school district requires."

When Black delivered the opinion on June 25, 1962, only Stewart dissented, arguing the decision denied children the opportunity to share "the spiritual heritage of our nation."

The protest which erupted in the wake of the decision continued unabated for at least two decades; no session of Congress passes without an effort to overturn the Court's decision through adoption of a constitutional amendment. The volume of mail attacking the decision was the greatest in the Court's history. Warren remembered many letters condemning the decision. Clark, in an almost unprecedented step, publicly defended the decision in a San Francisco speech.

Two years later, when the Court prohibited Bible reading and recitation of the Lord's Prayer in public schools, reaction was more muted—but it ran deep. By then, millions of Americans, most of them unfamiliar with the law, were nonetheless well aware that the Supreme Court—for better or worse—was an intrinsic part of their lives.

And their lives would never be touched more intimately than they were by a decision that aroused still more controversy— *Baker* v. *Carr*. Through it, more Americans gained greater political leverage than through any other action since the founding of the Republic, save the adoption in 1920 of the Nineteenth Amendment giving women the vote.

That decision and its progeny (*Gray* v. *Sanders, Reynolds* v. *Sims*) shifted political power at a stroke from fewer than 30 percent of the population—people living in small towns and on farms, mostly white, suspicious of big business and big government—to the majority who lived in cities and their suburbs, whose interests focused on public education, on attracting industry, and on dealing with the problems associated with blacks and Hispanics and others among the urban poor.

On June 25, 1969, two days after he retired as Chief Justice, Earl Warren declared in an interview, "I think the reapportionment, not only of state legislatures but of representative government in this country, is perhaps the most important issue we have had before the Supreme Court." *Baker* v. *Carr* was, Warren recalled in his memoirs, "the most important case of my tenure on the Court."

Through it, the geographical, political, and racial makeup of legislatures and of Congress changed drastically in ensuing years, bringing down political dynasties and disrupting small political cliques. With that, on the other hand, went political continuity; by 1982, more than a third of those in the United States House of Representatives had served less than four years.

In a number of areas of the country, legislative apportionment had become ludicrous. In 1950, for instance, one member of the Vermont legislature had 49 constituents while one of his colleagues represented more than 33,000 people. In Connecticut, fewer than 10 percent of the population could elect a majority of the state legislature. In 1955, the Colorado legislature appropriated $2.4 million for 18,000 pupils in a semi-rural county while giving $2.3 million to aid 90,000 students in Denver.

Malapportionment—or the design of voting districts to perpetuate the political party or officeholders in power—is nearly as old as the Republic, and has become identified with Governor Elbridge Gerry of Massachusetts. In 1811, Gerry reluctantly signed a bill readjusting the representative districts in his state so as to favor the Democrats over the Federalists, even though the Federalists cast nearly two-thirds of the votes in Massachusetts.

According to an 1890 book, *Political Americanisms*, the artist Gilbert Stuart (who had painted George Washington) fancied that one of the resulting districts of about a dozen counties, given a few well-placed strokes of his pen, would look just like a salamander. Boston *Sentinel* editor Benjamin Russell glanced at it and said, "Salamander? Call it a Gerrymander!"

The epithet became a political war cry and Stuart's caricature appears in nearly every dictionary and reference book in America. Although the governor pronounced his name with a hard "g," the gerrymander came to be pronounced as if it began with a "j". (Though his name is linked irrevocably with political villainy, Gerry was a signer of the Declaration of Independence and was one of James Madison's Vice Presidents.)

The "silent gerrymander" became at least as important as the conscious effort to draw political lines to favor the party in power. That phenomenon resulted merely from failing over the years to redraw districts to keep pace with the movement of people from the rural areas to the cities. The failure was challenged in 1946 in *Colegrove* v. *Green*. The Illinois constitution of 1870 provided that the state be divided into fifty-one senatorial districts, each of which would select a senator and three representatives. After each census, the legislature would redraw the lines to reflect population changes.

By the turn of the century, it appeared that very soon more than half the population of Illinois would be concentrated in the Chicago metropolitan area. Downstate legislators, constituting a comfortable majority of the legislature, simply refused to yield their political power by agreeing to any redistricting after the apportionment of 1901. The Illinois courts refused to interfere, stating it had no power to compel the legislature to act on a "political question."

At the same time, the Illinois legislature failed to redraw congressional districts as required after each census when Congress reapportions seats in the House of Representatives among the states. As a result, by 1946 one congressional district in Chicago had a population of over 900,000 while a southern Illinois district had just over 100,000 residents. The Court was asked to enjoin Illinois officials from conducting an election in November 1946

under the 1901 apportionment; that would have compelled the
state to elect all its congressmen at large, thus giving greatest
weight in the election to city dwellers.

Frankfurter spoke for a plurality (with Black, Douglas, and
Murphy dissenting) when he said "the petitioners ask of this
Court what is beyond its competence to grant."

> It is hostile to the democratic system to involve the judiciary in
> the politics of the people. And it is not less pernicious if such ju-
> dicial intervention in an essentially political contest be dressed
> up in the abstract phrases of the law. The petitioners urge with
> great zeal that the conditions of which they complain are grave
> evils and offend public morality. The Constitution of the United
> States gives ample power to provide against these evils. . . .
> The short of it is that the Constitution has conferred upon
> Congress exclusive authority to secure fair representation by the
> states in the popular House and left to that House determination
> whether states have fulfilled their responsibility. If Congress
> failed . . . the remedy ultimately lies with the people. . . . To
> sustain this action would cut very deep into the very being of
> Congress.

Frankfurter followed with his memorable warning, "Courts
ought not to enter this political thicket." He continued by enunciating the essence of his political philosophy:

> The remedy for unfairness in districting is to secure state legisla-
> tures that will apportion properly, or to invoke the ample powers
> of Congress. The Constitution has many commands that are not
> enforceable by the courts because they clearly fall outside the
> conditions and purposes that circumscribe judicial action. . . .
> The Constitution has left the performance of many duties in our
> governmental scheme to depend on the fidelity of the executive
> and legislative action and, ultimately, on the vigilance of the
> people in exercising their political rights.

Despite *Colegrove*, complaints about malapportionment continued. Georgia's "county unit system" was challenged in *South
v. Peters* in 1950. Under that system, all one hundred and fifty-
nine counties were assigned a minimum of two electoral votes,
however small their population. But no county received more
than six electoral votes, no matter how large. The result was to

effectively disfranchise urban populations in congressional and statewide elections. The Court, following *Colegrove,* ruled that "a state's geographical distribution of electoral strength among its political subdivisions" was a political question.

A decade later, Charles W. Baker of Memphis, Tennessee, and nine other qualified voters asked a federal court to order Tennessee Secretary of State Joe C. Carr and other officials to alter the state's election procedure.

The Tennessee constitution required electoral districts to be changed every ten years so that each legislator would represent approximately the same number of voters. Like its counterpart in Illinois, the Tennessee General Assembly had not passed a reapportionment law since 1901.

As in earlier cases, the mathematics of *Baker* v. *Carr* was fundamental to the case. In 1901, Memphis' 43,000 voters had seven representatives; the surrounding eight counties, with 43,000 voters, had eleven. By 1950, Memphis had 312,000 voters and still was entitled to seven representatives. The surrounding twenty-four counties also had 312,000 voters—but were allotted twenty-six representatives.

Tennessee was little different from Illinois or Georgia or, as Frankfurter had shown in an appendix to his 1946 *Colegrove* opinion, California. As Warren recounted in his memoirs, California "was one of the most malapportioned [states] in the nation." It remained that way partly because Governor Warren, in 1948, defeated a proposed reapportionment plan. "It was frankly a matter of political expediency," Warren conceded. "I was just wrong as Governor."

A federal court threw out Baker's claim, but on November 21, 1960, Chief Justice Warren, supported by Justices Black, Douglas, and Brennan, voted to hear Baker's appeal. The other five voted not to take the case.

The argument was made the following spring, and at the April 20, 1961, conference, Warren stated flatly, "I think the case ought to be reversed."

The Court had two questions: first, did federal courts have jurisdiction in apportionment cases, and second, did the merits justify specific remedies? Warren made it plain he wanted to go beyond the jurisdiction question. "I don't see why we should say merely that there is jurisdiction," he told the conference. "I'd say the case stated a cause of action. . . . I'd let the Court determine the remedy."

Black, Douglas, and Brennan fell in behind the Chief. But Frankfurter made an impassioned argument against tampering with *Colegrove*. One of the justices there said that "Frankfurter unleashed a brilliant tour de force, speaking at considerable length, pulling down reports and reading from them, and powerfully arguing the correctness of *Colegrove*."

Clark and Harlan agreed fully with Frankfurter. Whittaker, however, believed the Court did, in fact, have jurisdiction. But he did not think the *Colegrove* principle should be abandoned by less than an overwhelming majority. He cast his vote with Frankfurter.

That made Stewart's the pivotal vote. But he said at the conference he was unable to make a decision. He urged that the case be reargued during the new term starting in the fall of 1961. The justices agreed.

On April 24, four days after the conference, Frankfurter began lobbying for Stewart's vote. "I cannot but deeply believe," he wrote Stewart, ". . . to open up these undetermined and indeterminate questions is bound to bring the Court in conflict with political forces and exacerbate political feeling widely throughout the nation." If the Court decided the judiciary could take jurisdiction in apportionment cases, "the clash and tension [among] Court and country and politicians," Frankfurter warned, "will assert themselves within a far wider area than the segregation cases have aroused."

Frankfurter dismissed the "jaunty analogue that we were offered between progress in [public] acceptance of our segregation decision and this reapportionment problem. There is all the difference in the world between asking the courts to differentiate between black and white, and asking courts to make the appraisal of factors which [are] relevant to this problem."

Baker v. *Carr* was reargued on October 9, 1961. Frankfurter circulated a sixty-page memorandum which had been drafted by one of his former clerks, Anthony G. Amsterdam. Only one justice, Brennan, responded to it. Brennan sent Frankfurter an eleven-page chart depicting the wide disparities between the population in Tennessee's counties and their legislative representation.

"I should think at the very least," Brennan wrote Frankfurter, "the data show a picture which Tennessee should be required to justify if it is to avoid the conclusion that the 1901 [Tennessee apportionment] act, applied to today's facts, is simple caprice."

Brennan's chart had an impact on his colleagues, even those who did not yet agree with his position in the case. Clark, for one, later said the chart showed that "Tennessee's apportionment is a crazy-quilt without rational basis."

Harlan, Frankfurter's strongest ally in the case, took up the cudgels. On October 11, he wrote to Stewart and Whittaker because "unless I am much mistaken, past events in this case plainly indicate that your votes will be determinative of its outcome.

"From the standpoint of the future of the Court," Harlan asserted, "the case involves implications whose importance is unmatched by those of any other case coming here in my time (and by those in few others in the history of the Court, not excluding the desegregation case). I believe that what we are being asked to do in this case threatens the preservation of the independence of the Court.

"The only sure way of avoiding this is to keep the gate to the [political] thicket tightly closed. The responsibility is entirely in our laps, and to me, it would be a sad thing were we, by our own act, to plunge this institution into what would bid fair, as time goes on, to erode its stature."

Stewart, though, had been leaning away from the Frankfurter view since the April 20 conference. He was troubled by the notion that, even in the face of patent violations of the "equal protection" clause, the courts were without jurisdiction. Carried to an extreme, he told Frankfurter, an apportionment could be devised to restrict voting to men over six feet tall.

Frankfurter answered that he understood "the legitimate fear of an abusive extension of a doctrine." He said that courts always can deal with extremes "as and when they arise [in] circumstances different 'in kind.' Disallowing all Christian Scientists or Jews to vote, or to reduce votes in any county that has Christian Scientists or Jews, would present circumstances different 'in kind.'"

At a conference of the justices on October 13, 1961, the same lines of demarcation were drawn. Warren declared *Baker* v. *Carr* presented "a violation of equal protection. I don't think we have to decide the merits. . . . All we have to decide is that there is jurisdiction. We don't have to say that the state must give complete equality."

Warren rejected the central argument that elections involved political questions beyond judicial competence. He reasoned that Congress "put us in it" when it made the courts referees in inquiries involving the denial of the vote on racial grounds. "All we need here is to say that this shows an arbitrary and capricious practice," Warren said. He said he would rule that the courts have jurisdiction, and leave it to the district court to determine the specific remedy.

Black maintained that *Colegrove*, from which he had dissented, "is a weak reed on which to hang the notion of a settled rule of law." He said he agreed with the 1849 case of *Luther* v. *Borden*, in which the Court refused to decide the "political question" of which of two contending factions was Rhode Island's lawful government. "Two factions claimed to be the state," Black said. "It wasn't a dispute over a law passed *by* a state—but which *was* the state. But it's different when you attack a law that's not an attack on the state's form of government. Here it's simply a question of whether the law passed bears so unequally, capriciously, as to deny equal protection."

Douglas relied on the 1960 decision in *Gomillion* v. *Lightfoot*, which invalidated the districting of Tuskegee, Alabama. That case, Douglas argued, established that courts have jurisdiction in apportionment cases.

Ironically, Frankfurter had written the *Gomillion* opinion for a unanimous Court. Frankfurter had written that Alabama's challenged law had altered the shape of Tuskegee from a square to "an uncouth twenty-eight-sided figure" removing from Tuskegee nearly all its black voters, but none of its white voters.

The law, he wrote, resulted in "fencing Negro citizens out of town so as to deprive them of their pre-existing municipal vote." The district court had dismissed the claim because of *Colegrove.* But Warren maintained the case did not have to be decided on the basis of *Colegrove*—and Frankfurter, who wrote *Colegrove,* strongly agreed.

"The state seeks cover under the *Colegrove* line of cases," Frankfurter argued. "The statute passed here [may appear] an act narrowly dealing with redistricting but, actually and demonstrably from objective manifestations, it is a function of separating black from white." The case was decided on the basis of the Fifteenth Amendment, which prohibits racial discrimination in voting.

Nonetheless, Douglas argued that *Gomillion* clearly demonstrated that the Court had jurisdiction in apportionment cases. To Frankfurter, *Gomillion* was one of those cases which presented "circumstances different 'in kind.'"

Brennan said he concluded that *Baker* v. *Carr* should be reversed because of the inferences drawn from his chart—that whatever might be true in other cases, here the apportionment defied rational explanation.

Warren, Black, Douglas, and Brennan made four for reversal.

Frankfurter spoke only briefly. To decide that courts have jurisdiction in apportionment cases, he said, "is fraught with such consequences that, to me, are so dangerous to our system that I'd stay out."

Harlan, however, argued intensely to demonstrate the undesirable consequences of reversing the lower court. He added he did not believe that equal protection required mathematical equality of representation. He said there were geographical considerations as well.

And Clark voiced his firm support of Frankfurter. He added, somewhat gratuitously, that what was at stake, at least in the South, was whether the whites would control the power structure. Whittaker voted again to stay with the Frankfurter wing, despite his personal belief that the courts might, indeed, have jurisdiction.

Frankfurter, Harlan, Clark, and Whittaker made four for affirmance.

Stewart, as junior justice, spoke last. He, too, was concerned that the Court's involvement in apportionment questions might attract sharp criticism and some erosion of its stature. On the other hand, he said, he agreed the malapportionment was so extreme it could have no rational basis. Given that extreme circumstance, Stewart said, "the district court did have jurisdiction."

That made it five to four for reversal.

Stewart emphasized he would decide only that the courts had jurisdiction. "I can't say whether we can or can't frame appropriate relief. On the merits, I couldn't say that equal protection requires representation approximately commensurate with voting strength. So the state doesn't have to justify every departure from a one-man, one-vote basis." In addition, Stewart emphasized his view that there is "the greatest burden of proof on a plaintiff to show an arbitrary and capricious system."

(The term "one man, one vote" used by Stewart at the conference ultimately came to symbolize the underlying principle in the Court's reapportionment decisions. The term, modified by Douglas to "one person, one vote," was not actually used in a Court opinion, however, until the 1963 *Gray* v. *Sanders* decision striking down Georgia's use of a county unit electoral system in electing governors and senators. The case against Georgia was argued by the United States Attorney General, Robert Kennedy. Present for the occasion were his wife, mother, two sisters, his brother Teddy, four of his children, and his sister-in-law—the First Lady. Kennedys outnumbered the justices, eleven to nine. The phrase "one-man, one-vote" first was used in England early in the nineteenth century in a campaign against "plural voting" which permitted two ballots to those men who could show a business or university "qualification.")

Warren delayed assigning the *Baker* v. *Carr* opinion. Although Black and Douglas had dissented in *Colegrove*, both believed strongly the Court should decide the merits of the case, not merely that the courts had jurisdiction. Such an opinion, however, would have lost Stewart's vote—and the majority. Black thought that unless Stewart wrote the opinion, the junior justice

might waver in his vote. Conversely, Douglas said he would refuse to join a Stewart opinion because of Stewart's insistence that
the plaintiff bore the burden of proof in apportionment cases.
After two weeks of conferences and consideration, Warren assigned the opinion to Brennan.

Frankfurter's four principal antagonists—Warren, Black,
Douglas, and Brennan—wanted to decide that the Tennessee apportionment law violated the "equal protection" clause and that
the Fourteenth Amendment "requires what Hugo called 'approximately fair' distribution or weight in votes."

Stewart, however, would vote to reverse only if the decision
was limited to holding that the district court had the authority to
entertain Baker's complaint. Because Stewart's vote was necessary for a bare majority, "The Four," as Frankfurter derisively
called them, agreed that Brennan must limit his opinion to the
jurisdictional issue.

Brennan completed his draft in January 1962 and sent a copy
to Stewart. After Stewart telephoned his approval, Brennan
couldn't contain his pleasure. "There was a broad Irish grin on
his face," Douglas recalled, "when he told me that the fifth vote
was secure." Additionally, Stewart agreed to drop his insistence
that the question of burden of proof be discussed in the opinion.
"Potter now agrees with me," Brennan wrote the rest of the majority, "that we should not pass on any issues except [those] actually requiring decision at this time."

Stewart also agreed, to Black's surprise, to join despite Brennan's lengthy discussion of why the "political question" doctrine
did not bear on jurisdiction in apportionment suits. Brennan
believed the exposition necessary "if we are effectively and
finally to dispel the fog of another day produced by Felix's opinion in *Colegrove* v. *Green*."

Brennan circulated his opinion on January 31. Frankfurter
flipped through his copy and marched directly to Clark's chambers. "They've done as I expected," Frankfurter snapped. "I'm
circulating my dissent without delay." He did so the next day.
Two days later, Clark wrote Frankfurter, "Your dissent is unan-
swerable, except by ukase."

Frankfurter snatched up the telephone. To secure Clark's vote irrevocably, he suggested the Texan "prepare something on the failure to exhaust other remedies," meaning that Tennessee voters could seek relief from Congress or through voter action.

Clark went to work. He told the other justices that the decision must be delayed to allow him to write something in dissent in addition to Frankfurter's opinion. Because he, Warren, and Brennan were leaving for a ten-day judicial conference in Puerto Rico, Clark said the decision would be completed by late February, at the latest. "We leave for sunnier climes," Clark wrote, "so I shall have to set the task aside until I return. In light of the waiting period Tennessee has already experienced, I hope my delay will not too long deprive it of a constitutional form of government—that is, control by the 'city slickers.'"

While the three were gone, Harlan decided to try once more to dissuade Stewart from joining those favoring reversal. "I am trying my hand at a piece," Harlan wrote Stewart, "directed to the proposition that the kind of 'rights' asserted by the petitioners in this case are *not* assured by the Federal Constitution—a thesis with which I once understood you to agree. . . . Wait (if your mind is still open) [for] what I am writing before casting what will be the decisive and, if I may say so, fateful vote in this case."

Stewart told Harlan he always kept an open mind; nonetheless, he notified Brennan of his concurrence on February 1. That gave Brennan his majority. Upon his return from Puerto Rico, however, Brennan found himself plunged into intensive lobbying to hold the majority together.

First, Douglas circulated a concurrence which discussed standards of apportionment. That upset Stewart, who did not want his vote to be read as support for mathematically equal representation. He told Brennan he would have to write his own separate concurrence.

Brennan tried to dissuade Stewart. For one thing, two concurrences in a five-to-four decision might seriously confound the lower courts. For another thing, he was afraid Stewart, whose vote was shaky at the start, might finally decide to remove himself from Brennan's opinion altogether, leaving only a plurality in the case.

After hearing Brennan out, Stewart would agree only to circulate the concurrence privately to the majority first; that, at least, would give Brennan time before Frankfurter and Harlan might try to pounce on the wavering Stewart to nudge him into some second thoughts on the issue.

When Douglas learned of Stewart's reaction to his draft concurrence, he telephoned Brennan and offered to temper the opinion if that would keep Stewart from writing separately. Brennan consulted Warren, who agreed it would be a good idea for Douglas to make some significant changes. Stewart was impressed by the significance of Douglas' changes; but he told Brennan he had decided to go ahead with his own opinion anyway.

Then Stewart responded to Harlan's draft dissent. To emphasize his position, Stewart said he would modify his concurring opinion to say that in other cases, where the facts of the case were not so irrational, he would agree with Harlan. Brennan rushed to see Stewart. Both he and the Chief thought such language would seriously jeopardize the impact of the decision. Stewart agreed to drop the idea.

In mid-February, Stewart circulated his draft concurrence to all the justices, and Frankfurter distributed his dissent, which was joined by Clark, Whittaker, and Harlan, who also had sent around his separate dissent. The stage was set—but everyone had to wait three weeks while Clark worked on his expected dissent.

Douglas urged his colleagues to move as quickly as possible. "This is an election year," he wrote the others. "If the lower court is to have an opportunity to act, the case should be disposed of soon."

The others were of two minds; they didn't appreciate Clark's delay, but they didn't think he ought to be pressed while he considered the case.

But Clark had not been procrastinating. He was thoughtfully assessing the material that was to have been the substance of his dissent. On March 7, he wrote Frankfurter:

> Preparatory to writing my dissent in this case—along the line you suggested of pointing out the avenues that were open for the

voters of Tennessee to bring about reapportionment despite its Assembly—I have carefully checked into the record. I am sorry to say that I cannot find any practical course that the people could take in bringing this about except through the federal courts.

Having come to this conclusion, I decided I would reconsider the whole case, and I am sorry to say that I shall have to ask you to permit me to withdraw from your dissent. I regret this, but in view of the fact that the voters of Tennessee have no other recourse, I have concluded to issue a concurring opinion.

While he was considering the case, Clark had jotted down what was to him the essential reason for changing his mind:

Here a majority of representatives ignores the needs and desires of the majority, and for their own selfish purpose hamper and oppress them—debar them from equal privileges and equal rights. That means the failure of our constitutional system.

Clark notified Harlan. "I am sorry that I cannot go along," he wrote, "but it does not change the result, anyway."

In fact, Clark's change of heart—had it come sooner—might have changed the outcome to a considerable degree, and with it, the face of the nation.

When he notified Brennan of his switch, Clark wrote that he was issuing an opinion "concurring in part and dissenting in part. My difference with the majority narrows down to this: I would decide the case on its merits. Instead of remanding it for the district court to determine the merits and fashion the relief, I would do that here. There is no need to delay the merits of the case any further."

Clark's position meant there was a majority of five justices who would rule on the merits. But Brennan and Warren decided they had to consider the undertaking they had given to Stewart. Brennan discussed the issue with Stewart. "Potter felt that if [Clark's changes] were made, it would be necessary for him to dissent from that much of the revised opinion. I therefore decided it was best not to press for the changes."

Brennan persuaded Clark to limit his statement to a concurrence and to remove the portions dissenting from the majority.

Clark insisted on keeping the line that he would have invalidated the Tennessee law on the merits.

Had Clark determined earlier that he would have reversed on the merits and fashioned relief at the Supreme Court level, the majority almost certainly would have required the states to adopt a "federal system" of apportionment. That system—in which one house was apportioned according to population while the second, the Senate, elected its members geographically—was favored strongly by Warren. That was the system in California, in numerous states, and, of course, for Congress.

If it is true that mathematical equality of representation in both houses of a legislature constitutes justice, *Baker* v. *Carr* is an example of justice delayed not being justice denied. In 1964, the Court decided in *Reynolds* v. *Sims* that the "federal system" did not provide fair representation in the state legislatures. They required that both houses of the legislatures be apportioned according to population. Had it not been for Clark's initial opposition to *Baker* v. *Carr*, it is likely that *Reynolds* v. *Sims* never would have reached the Court, and that the "federal system" would have become the constitutional standard.

Frankfurter's dissent in *Baker* v. *Carr* was a *cri de coeur* generated by his realization that his judicial philosophy of restraint had been overwhelmed. He believed that "evil genies [would] be released by the decision" and he warned in his dissent of "the mathematical quagmire . . . into which this Court today catapults the lower courts of the country."

Even before the decision was announced, an emotionally exhausted Whittaker collapsed and entered Walter Reed Army Medical Center. Two weeks later, Frankfurter, defeated intellectually on the Court, was ravaged physically as well when he suffered a stroke.

But the majority was elated. The concept of judicial activism had triumphed. A solid majority of the Court believed that justice demanded that the letter of the law be enlarged or restrained so as to effectively accomplish an equitable end.

On March 26, 1962, as the opinions in *Baker* v. *Carr* were being read from the Bench, Warren scribbled a note to Brennan. "It is a great day for the Irish," it read.

Then, before he passed it along, he scratched out part of it and wrote:

"It is a great day for the country."

FOURTEEN

The New Majority

FRANKFURTER AND HIS enforced rule of judicial restraint had reigned over the Court from his appointment in 1939 for fifteen years—challenged regularly, but never seriously threatened, by Black and Douglas.

His grip started loosening when Warren, a strong-willed, self-confident man thoroughly accustomed to command, ascended to the Bench.

Brennan's appointment in 1956 guaranteed Frankfurter's eventual decline.

Starting then, the solid four activists—Warren, Black, Douglas, and Brennan—enjoyed increasing success in wooing to their side one or more of Frankfurter's erstwhile supporters (usually Clark or Stewart) to achieve a majority.

Frankfurter, the quintessential judicial politician, was forced to work harder than ever if he was to keep his troops in line. Almost always, he could depend on Harlan, whose dedication to the philosophy of restraint was as strong as his own.

The others remained unpredictable. Clark, a political conservative, was nonetheless strongly and regularly influenced by Warren; his frequent changes of position were considered open-mindedness by his friends and weak-mindedness by his opponents.

Stewart eschewed the very notion of judicial philosophy; his political background suggested a conservative temperament, but he vigorously refused to be categorized as a judicial liberal or conservative.

And although Whittaker was a staunch admirer of Frankfurter who found it more comfortable to follow than to attempt independence, the former professor alternately flattered and bullied him to make sure of his vote.

Perhaps because of the greater strain on a general rallying his faltering troops to do battle, Frankfurter's health declined as his position of power weakened.

Concomitantly, his demands on wavering colleagues to stand firm with him grew more strident than ever.

In *Mapp* v. *Ohio*, for instance, Frankfurter bitterly accused Clark of having "flopped" to the side of the "incorporation enthusiasts." They were the jurists who accepted Black's controversial theory, enunciated in a 1947 dissent in *Adamson* v. *California*, that the framers of the Fourteenth Amendment intended to apply all the requirements of the Bill of Rights to the states.

Frankfurter consistently opposed the view that the "due process" clause of the Fourteenth Amendment thus "incorporated" all the specific guarantees of the Bill of Rights. Rather, he maintained that the amendment required the states to extend to their citizens only those guarantees in the Bill of Rights so fundamental that they were, in Justice Benjamin Cardozo's words, "of the very essence of a scheme of ordered liberty."

Frankfurter revered the Fourth Amendment—with its guarantee of "privacy against arbitrary intrusion by the police"—as "basic to a free society. . . . The knock at the door," he wrote in *Wolf* v. *Colorado* in 1949, "whether by day or by night, as a prelude to a search, without authority of law but solely on the authority of the police, did not need the commentary of recent history to be condemned as inconsistent with the conception of human rights enshrined in the history and the basic constitutional documents of English-speaking peoples."

Nonetheless, he argued, it did not follow logically that evidence obtained through illegal search and seizure could or should be prohibited from state criminal prosecutions as it had been in federal cases since 1914.

Frankfurter's reasoning had ruled for a dozen years until it was overturned in *Mapp*. In *Baker* v. *Carr*, however, Frankfurter bent every effort to keep from losing an even more fundamental principle which he had established in 1946 in *Colegrove* v. *Green*—that the Supreme Court had no business meddling in political questions like reapportionment.

Almost from the start of that battle—when Stewart indicated he would side with "The Four"—Frankfurter knew he was beaten. Although both he and Harlan never stopped hoping they might convert Stewart, Frankfurter spent more time trying to hold his four-vote minority. His strategy in keeping the decision to a bare majority was that it would be more difficult for a future Court to expand on the decision—and easier to overturn it.

His overzealousness backfired when he lost Clark. And the pressure he put on Whittaker, whose vote in *Baker* v. *Carr* never had been solid, aggravated the strain Whittaker already was undergoing in trying, unsuccessfully, to cope with writing a highly complex antitrust decision Warren had assigned him.

In mid-March, Whittaker, at the urging of his physicians, resigned from the Court, effective April 1, 1962.

Almost immediately, the White House started considering replacements. Attorney General Robert Kennedy first proposed elevating Judge William H. Hastie from the federal appellate bench. Hastie, a black, had been Frankfurter's student at Harvard.

The Attorney General called on the Chief Justice to get his opinion of Hastie. Warren, Kennedy recalled, "was violently opposed to having Hastie on the Court. . . . He said, 'He's not a liberal, and he'd be opposed to all the measures that we're interested in—and he would just be completely unsatisfactory.'" The Kennedys, who already were concerned that naming a black would be "too obvious" politically, dropped Hastie from their list.

Next, they considered Paul Freund of Harvard University. Again, they ran into Warren's opposition. Warren thought that Freund, the foremost disciple of Frankfurter's judicial philosophy, would be an even more effective ally of the Frankfurter wing than Whittaker had been.

Finally, the President focused on his old friend Deputy Attorney General Byron White, who, as "Whizzer" White, had been an All-American halfback at the University of Colorado in 1937.

The two had met two years later in London. White was attending Oxford on a Rhodes Scholarship and Jack Kennedy was the twenty-two-year-old son of the United States Ambassador to the Court of St. James.

The onset of World War II separated the young men when White was recalled to the United States. They met again, however, in the South Pacific. "One of the jobs I had to do," White recalled, "was write the report on the accident when his boat was sunk."

After the war, White completed his legal studies at the Yale Law School and was appointed as a clerk to Chief Justice Fred Vinson. He and Kennedy, who was serving his freshman term in the House of Representatives, soon renewed their friendship.

They stayed in touch over the years as White returned to Colorado to practice law and Kennedy advanced his political career. In 1960, White became national chairman of Citizens for Kennedy. His reward in the razor-thin victory over Vice President Nixon was the post of Deputy Attorney General of the United States.

He had been in the job less than five months when he earned the lasting admiration of the Kennedys.

On Mother's Day, 1961, an interracial group of young men and women calling themselves Freedom Riders were routed from Greyhound and Trailways buses in Alabama and beaten by Ku Klux Klansmen and other hoodlums.

Governor John Patterson, a square-jawed racist who had been elected in 1958 over his more moderate opponent, George Wallace, by appealing openly for the support of the Klan, said, "I cannot guarantee protection for this bunch of rabble-rousers."

Because the Freedom Riders had vowed to pursue their protest of segregation in interstate transportation by continuing their trip to Montgomery, Robert Kennedy dispatched his friend

Tennessean John Seigenthaler to try to change Patterson's hard-line position.

It seemed as if Seigenthaler had succeeded. Before the scheduled arrival of the Freedom Riders at Montgomery's Union Bus Terminal, he reported to the Attorney General that Patterson maintained he had "the means, ability, and the will to keep the peace without outside help."

Floyd Mann, who commanded Alabama's Highway Patrol, also pledged to the Attorney General that his troopers would keep the peace.

Mann was as good as his word. As the bus traveled from Birmingham to Montgomery, the Highway Patrol kept suspected agitators at a safe distance. As the bus neared Montgomery, both Mann and the FBI alerted Montgomery Police Commissioner Lester B. Sullivan.

Sullivan, however, had no plans to dispatch his policemen to the bus terminal, where more than a thousand hostile whites had gathered. "We have no intention of standing police guard for a bunch of troublemakers coming into our city," he told reporters.

Across from the bus terminal, John Doar, a Justice Department attorney, had stationed himself at a telephone where he could report the developments directly to Washington. As Robert Kennedy and Byron White listened at the Justice Department, Doar reported the arrival of the bus:

> The bus is in. The people are just standing there, watching. . . . Now the passengers are coming off. They're standing on a corner of the platform. Oh! There are fists, punching! A bunch of men led by a guy with a bleeding face are beating them! There are no cops. It's terrible! It's terrible! There's not a cop in sight. People are yelling, "Get 'em, get 'em." It's awful.

Mann's state troopers finally arrived, but were too outnumbered to effectively disperse the crowd. Even Seigenthaler was victimized. As he went to aid two young women who were being beaten, he was dragged to the ground and knocked senseless. He lay bleeding on a sidewalk for half an hour before an ambulance arrived to transport him to a hospital. Police Commissioner Sullivan explained later, "Every white ambulance in town reported their vehicles had broken down."

The Attorney General was furious. He felt Patterson had betrayed him. He asked Byron White to take the next plane to Montgomery and restore order.

White established his headquarters at Maxwell Air Force Base outside the Alabama capital. As quickly as possible, he assembled four hundred riot-trained federal agents from surrounding states—United States marshals and their deputies, revenue agents, border patrolmen, and guards from federal prisons. He notified the governor they would protect the Freedom Riders in the absence of adequate response by local and state authorities.

Patterson reacted angrily. He called a meeting of state law-enforcement authorities and opened it to the press. Its purpose, he announced, would be to instruct his people to arrest any federal official who violated Alabama law. White attended the meeting, precipitating a tense confrontation between him and the governor.

The governor demanded that White give him information about the Freedom Riders. White refused.

PATTERSON: You know where some of these Freedom Riders are, don't you?

WHITE: Yes. In the hospital.

PATTERSON: Do you know where the others are?

WHITE: No, I don't.

PATTERSON: If you knew where some of these people are, would you inform us?

WHITE: I will never know where these people are.

In fact, as much of the nation was aware, the Freedom Riders were at Ralph Abernathy's First Baptist Church, where Martin Luther King would address a rally in their support. As he had warned, Sullivan had failed to deploy policemen to guarantee the free and peaceful assembly.

With an onlooking crowd of whites turning surly, White dispatched about a hundred of his federal force to the scene; they arrived in private cars, postal trucks, and a prison truck. They wore business suits, but were armed with pistols, clubs, and tear-gas canisters.

When the mob surged toward the church, hurling stones and bottles, the governor declared martial law. Meanwhile, with the church jammed with nearly two thousand people, the federal force feared there might be an effort to burn it down. Forming a skirmish line, the federal agents fired tear-gas volleys to disperse the attackers.

The line held until state troopers and National Guardsmen arrived; after that, the crowd was dissipated and the threat of violence was ended.

Patterson maintained in a heated telephone call to Robert Kennedy that the Attorney General had fomented the violence by sending the Freedom Riders into Alabama and then by invading the state.

"Who's invading you, John?" Kennedy demanded. "You know better than that. . . . You can say that on television. You can tell that to the people of Alabama—but don't tell me that. Don't tell me that, John."

Violence had stalked the Freedom Riders, but no one had been killed. At the initiative of the Attorney General, the Interstate Commerce Commission issued regulations requiring an end to segregation at all railroad depots, bus terminals, and airports. By the time Byron White was named to the Supreme Court, overt racism in interstate travel had disappeared—and he had played a crucial and courageous role in its eradication.

If, however, Warren had hoped that White would provide him the solid fifth vote he needed to establish an activist majority, he was disappointed.

Like Stewart's, White's judicial philosophy—if he had one—defied categorization. If anything, White appeared inclined to conservatism—at least when contrasted with the activism characterizing "The Four." In the years ahead, White would vote against Warren's position as often as with it. Of his relationship to the Chief Justice, he recalled, "I wasn't exactly in his circle."

Warren, however, did not have long to wait for his circle of authority to close.

Eleven days following the announcement of the decision in *Baker* v. *Carr,* Frankfurter, working in his chambers after the conference on the school prayer issue, collapsed at his desk. He had suffered a stroke—and, over the next five months, he would be stricken with two heart attacks. His health destroyed, Frankfurter would resign from the Bench in August 1962.

As Frankfurter was carried from the Supreme Court to a waiting ambulance that April day, an era passed with him—a quarter century marked by constructive restraint which he personified as the heir to Holmes, Brandeis, Stone, and Cardozo.

If any such lofty thoughts crossed his mind, though, Frankfurter gave no hint. As he was borne on a stretcher toward the ambulance, he complained loudly that someone had left his shoes behind in the office.

"Twenty years ago, or even ten, it would have been inconceivable" for the Supreme Court to hand down *Baker* v. *Carr,* a leading lawyer was quoted in the New York *Times.* Since Warren's arrival nine years earlier, however, such a decision "had been inevitable," he said.

Critics of the Court's growing activism roundly denounced the decision. "Another major assault on our constitutional system," Senator Richard B. Russell of Georgia complained. "If the people really value their freedom, they will demand that the Congress curtail and limit the [Court's] jurisdiction." Arthur Krock of the New York *Times* condemned the seeming "Big Brother function of the Court."

Frankfurter's friend Dean Acheson, asked for his views by President Kennedy, recalled saying that "the Court had taken on in the desegregation decisions about all the legislative and executive governmental work that it could handle for the time being, and it seemed to me unwise to pick out another task, the end of which no one could see."

The President disagreed. "The legislatures would never reform themselves," Acheson remembered Kennedy saying. "He did not see how we were going to make any progress unless the Court intervened."

Publicly, the President defended the Court's decision in *Baker* v. *Carr* ("The right to fair representation [is] basic to the successful operation of a democracy"), as he would support its *Engel* v. *Vitale* decision some two months later ("It is very important . . . that we support Supreme Court decisions—[and] a very easy remedy . . . is to pray [to] ourselves").

Warren, who resented President Eisenhower's often faint-hearted support of segregation decisions, rejoiced in the new President as a consistent and clear-voiced champion.

His joy came unsalted, though, when Kennedy chose his Secretary of Labor, Arthur J. Goldberg, to succeed Frankfurter. For the next year—the year in which he completed a decade as Chief Justice—Warren's position would carry the Court in every major decision. Perhaps as important, Frankfurter had been a source of constant irritation to Warren.

The two had clashed loudly at conferences and acidly on the Bench. The animosity sometimes even clouded Warren's judicial objectivity. At a conference on November 11, 1960, Frankfurter wanted the Court's reaction to a lengthy memorandum he had circulated previously on *Monroe* v. *Pape*, a case concerning civil rights violations by Chicago policemen. The case, he said in a note accompanying the memorandum, was of "far-reaching importance" and his memorandum was "the result of weeks of investigation, discussion, and formulation."

"I haven't read Felix's memo," Warren responded. "But I have looked at his conclusion—and disagree with it."

"Are you surprised," Harlan asked Frankfurter in a note, "that some of your brethren are able to reach 'firm' conclusions on your memo on two days' study and reflection? And that [Warren] should be ready to decide *without* reading the memo?"

Goldberg, rather than clashing with Warren, became a powerful supporter in the effort to push back the frontiers of constitutional law. "There is nobody I felt closer to than Warren," Goldberg recalled of his associations on the Court. The two, he said, voted together more frequently than any other two justices.

From the moment Warren notified them that Frankfurter would not be returning to the Court, the brothers Kennedy knew that Goldberg would be their choice to replace him. Robert Kennedy said he and the President agreed on "the necessity of replacing Frankfurter with a Jew [and] if a Jew was placed on the

Court, it should be Arthur Goldberg. . . . The President said he had talked to Arthur and that Goldberg was anxious to get the appointment."

The appointment culminated an American success story. Goldberg was the youngest of eleven children of an immigrant Russian fruit peddler on Chicago's South Side. Young Goldberg was graduated first in his class from the Northwestern University Law School, became counsel to the AFL-CIO, an early Kennedy supporter, and the new President's Secretary of Labor.

Even before he backed Kennedy's candidacy, Goldberg cultivated the Chief Justice. He invited Warren to join his family at a Passover seder. Warren brought his own yarmulke. Goldberg learned that during Warren's political years, Nina Warren customarily packed a skullcap for the governor—among other paraphernalia for the unexpected that a superb politician would have available.

To Goldberg, Warren was the epitome of the ultimate good in American jurisprudence. "After he got away from Felix's influence and became his own man," Goldberg said, "Warren . . . decided to use his own conception of law, morality, and realism, and did not worry about what critics said. He just decided —and followed the pattern of voicing and voting his genuine convictions.

"Felix was a technician, but always was fearful that the Court would injure itself. This was his principal concern—always. Well, it's not the function of a Supreme Court justice to worry about the Court injuring itself. It's the sworn duty of a Supreme Court justice to do justice under law and apply the Constitution."

Performing that duty, however, meant different things to different justices. Less than six months after Goldberg took his seat on the Court, Frankfurter wrote his former clerk Alexander Bickel, "The men who are overruling prior decisions of a Court which contained Holmes, Hughes, Brandeis, and Cardozo are such wholly inexperienced men as White and Goldberg—without familiarity with the jurisdiction or the jurisprudence of the Court either as practitioners or scholars, or judges."

Five months later, Harlan wrote Frankfurter that a speech by Goldberg to the American Bar Association "left me cold. Respect for the Court is not something that can be achieved by fiat, but must come from its own performance. Who knows that as well as you do?"

And after Goldberg had been on the Bench for two years, Shay Minton wrote Frankfurter, "How they must miss you! Goldberg is a walking Constitutional Convention! Wow, what an activist he is!"

The replacement of Frankfurter by Goldberg was crucial to several cases before the Court.

In 1960, in the case of *Mendoza-Martinez* v. *Kennedy*, the Court first considered the constitutionality of a law revoking the citizenship of anyone who left the United States to evade military service during a war or national emergency. A tentative majority of the Court was prepared to uphold the statute—but the case was sent back to the lower courts on a technicality.

It reached the Court again in late 1961. Stewart prepared an opinion for a bare majority upholding the constitutionality of the law. He was joined by Frankfurter, Clark, Harlan, and Whittaker. By the time the decision was ready to be handed down in the spring of 1962, Whittaker had become ill, leaving the Court tied at four. The justices decided to put the case over for reargument.

The case came to conference again barely two months after Goldberg's swearing-in. Warren stated the position of himself, Black, Douglas, and Brennan. "You can't take citizenship away without an unequivocal act of expatriation. You can't punish this way." Clark, Harlan, Stewart, and White (who had replaced Whittaker) disagreed. Frankfurter had voted earlier to uphold the law—but Goldberg joined the Chief and was assigned the opinion.

In November 1961, the Court considered *NAACP* v. *Button*, a case arising out of a Virginia law construed to bar organizations from retaining lawyers in actions to which they were not parties.

Warren said the "purpose is to circumvent *Brown*, obviously," and wanted to strike down the law. Black maintained the statute's legislative history revealed a discriminatory purpose—to preclude effective litigation for civil rights. Brennan maintained the statute could be invalidated on First Amendment principles of free association and that an opinion need not rely on discriminatory intent.

Frankfurter led the argument to affirm the state courts. "I can't imagine a worse disservice than to continue being the guardians of Negroes. There's no evidence here that this statute is aimed at Negroes as such." Consequently, he maintained the law was a valid exercise of the state's regulatory power over the legal profession.

The conference voted five to four to support the Virginia law. Before the decision could be announced, though, Whittaker had fallen ill and Frankfurter had been hospitalized. The case was reargued and considered within two weeks of Goldberg's arrival at the Court. Both he and White supported the Chief and Brennan. What would have been a bare majority upholding Virginia's law turned into a six-to-three decision to declare it unconstitutional on First Amendment grounds.

At the same conference on October 12, 1962, the justices considered another case which had been set aside because of the illnesses of Whittaker and Frankfurter. It was *Gibson* v. *Florida Legislative Investigation Committee.*

A special committee of the Florida legislature was created to investigate Communist infiltration into organizations such as the NAACP. The president of Miami's NAACP branch refused to obey an order to produce membership and contribution records; additionally, he declined to disclose whether any of fifty-two persons named by the committee were members of the Miami NAACP branch. The branch president was sentenced to a six-month jail term and fined $1,200. The Florida Supreme Court upheld the judgment.

The Court first considered the case in December 1961. Warren argued the decision should be reversed based on the 1958 decision in *NAACP* v. *Alabama,* in which it was held the First Amendment forbade the state from scrutinizing the organization's membership records. Warren was backed by Black, Douglas, and Brennan.

The Frankfurter wing voted the other way, though. Clark, articulating the position, said, "There was an interest here of the state. There was a resolution of the NAACP saying that Commu-

nists were trying to infiltrate them—and also testimony by
witnesses about colored people attending Communist meetings."

When the conference reconsidered the issue, White voted as
Whittaker had a year before. But Goldberg voted with Warren.
The new majority held that the legislative committee had failed
to show any substantial relationship between the NAACP and
the Communist Party. What would have been a five-to-four decision to punish the NAACP official turned into a five-to-four vote
to exonerate him.

Two criminal cases were also decided differently on October
12, 1962, than they would have been had final decisions been
reached before Frankfurter and Whittaker were incapacitated.

In one case, *Wong Sun* v. *United States,* federal narcotics
agents broke up a heroin ring which they believed centered on a
laundry operated by a Chinese-American, James (Blackie) Toy,
on San Francisco's Leavenworth Street. Toy and his alleged con-
federate, "Sea Dog" Wong Sun, were linked to heroin finds; both
men made incriminating statements. They were convicted.

"The Four" were clear in the view that the arrests were illegal. When the agents identified themselves to Blackie Toy, he
slammed the door and raced into his bedroom with the officers
giving chase.

"Now, wait a minute!" Warren interjected when the legality of
the arrests was defended. "This guy was a Chinaman in San
Francisco who was awakened at six o'clock in the morning by a
couple of guys in plain clothes. They say they're narcotics
agents. He's scared. He slams the door shut. He runs back to his
bedroom, standing next to his wife, who was asleep in one bed.
His kid was asleep in another bed. These guys start to ask him
questions. And now you're gonna tell me that the statements he
makes in those circumstances can be admitted in evidence
against him? You can't do that!"

At the April 6, 1962, conference (Frankfurter's last), the former professor argued that the arrests were, in fact, legal because
they were based on "probable cause." He was supported by
Clark, Harlan, and Stewart. It was White's first conference, so he
passed. The four-to-four division (which, if allowed to stand,

would affirm the lower court), plus Frankfurter's subsequent absence, persuaded the Court to hear the case again.

This time, "The Four," who maintained there had been no probable cause, were joined by Goldberg in deciding the arrests were illegal. Toy's bedroom statements were inadmissible, they ruled, and the convictions must be vacated.

White angrily argued that that view "constitutes a major step toward excluding any post-arrest statements made in the presence of the police and goes far beyond any previous tests which this Court has applied to determine the voluntary nature of statements made while in custody."

Clark dismissed the majority's notion that the authorities would not have known who Blackie Toy was had it not been for a tip from a suspect trying to save his own skin. The majority, he chided, displayed a "total lack of acquaintanceship with the habits and practices of Chinatown."

Brennan produced a map of San Francisco. He pointed out that Toy's Leavenworth Street laundry was located in an area known as Russian Hill—nowhere near Chinatown. Clark revised his statement, saying the arresting officers were "familiar with San Francisco and the habits and practices of its Chinese-American inhabitants."

Finally, in *Townsend* v. *Sain,* the Court decided that if a convict in a criminal case did not receive a full evidentiary hearing in state court, he was entitled to one in a federal *habeas corpus* proceeding. Townsend, a drug addict, had confessed while still under the influence of drugs. Initially, however, the Court had voted five to four to deny the *Townsend* petition on the ground that the state courts had heard him out and decided against him.

Again, the replacement of Frankfurter and Whittaker turned the tables. White's vote accorded with his predecessor's, but Goldberg switched from the Frankfurter view. Warren's position, representing the new majority, was that the federal courts should do more than rely on state-court records, and should be willing to question the facts themselves.

"Judges, both federal and state, and state prosecutors . . . are bound to wail," Brennan predicted.

He was right. Alabama's Chief Justice charged the Warren

Court was remaking the Constitution and using the Fourteenth Amendment for the "systematic destruction of state sovereignty." Senator James Eastland, chairman of the Senate Judiciary Committee, introduced a bill to strip the Supreme Court of its review power over state criminal laws. The Council of State Governments proposed a constitutional amendment to create a Court of the Union comprising state Chief Justices to review Supreme Court decisions.

Warren waited a year to respond. In September 1963, he told the California Bar Association, "Where the Supreme Court of a state is vigilant concerning constitutional rights, the Supreme Court of the United States is equally vigilant in supporting its decisions."

To Warren, 1963 had been a shining success. But clouds lay ahead. The "sit-in" cases, in which blacks challenged the right of retailers and restaurateurs to practice segregation, drove a wedge between two of the staunchest allies of long standing in Supreme Court history—Black and Douglas. And before the year was out, President Kennedy would be dead. His murder cast a pall over the nation that would permeate the remainder of Warren's years at the Court—and beyond.

FIFTEEN

The Mirror Cracks

JOHN HARLAN SAT at the conference table thinking about Felix Frankfurter and feeling a "despondency that I no longer have you as an active colleague—this being particularly accented today by the Constitutional Convention into which the Court convened itself at the conference today on the first reapportionment cases."

The Court's conference was examining six state legislative apportionment cases and one congressional district apportionment challenge. *Baker* v. *Carr* had decided that the courts could consider such cases; now, with Warren leading the discussion, the justices were prepared to rule that at least one house of a state legislature must comprise districts of approximately equal population.

Later, the Chief Justice would persuade five of his associates that the equal-population standard should be the rule for both houses of a legislature. Warren would write in *Reynolds* v. *Sims*, "Legislators represent people, not trees or acres. Legislators are elected by voters, not farms or cities or economic interests."

And a majority also voted in *Wesberry* v. *Sanders* that congressional districts could not reflect substantial population disparities. Frankfurter, writing to Philip B. Kurland at the University of Chicago Law School, called the decision "disruptive of the time-honored operations of our government."

Frankfurter was not there, though, and Warren was having his way unimpeded, except for what one journalist called Harlan's "symbolic voice" against activism.

Then there was a knock at the conference room door. A page handed a note to Goldberg, who glanced at it and passed it to the Chief. Warren read it—then wept.

It was November 22, 1963.

That afternoon, Warren drove to Andrews Air Force Base to reassure the new President and console the young widow of the slain one. At Mrs. Kennedy's request, Warren delivered one of three eulogies at the Capitol rotunda memorial service for the murdered President.

A week later, Deputy Attorney General Nicholas Katzenbach and Solicitor General Archibald Cox called on Warren to convey President Johnson's request that he become chairman of a special committee to investigate the Kennedy assassination. Warren declined. It was inappropriate for a sitting justice to serve on a presidential commission. He suggested Stanley Reed for the job.

Within an hour, Joseph Califano, Lyndon Johnson's chief-of-staff, telephoned Warren. The President would like to see the Chief on urgent business, he said.

Warren had no intention of changing his mind. But neither had he any experience with Johnson's storied persuasion. The President told Warren the assassination had triggered "wild" speculation and only the Chief Justice's presence would assure the people of an impartial investigation. The others he intended to appoint, Johnson said, would serve only under Warren's leadership.

"You were a soldier in World War I," Johnson said when Warren restated his reasons for refusing, "but there was nothing you could do in that uniform comparable to what you can do for your country in this hour of trouble."

The President said the crisis was so grave it might lead to war —even nuclear war. "As your Commander-in-Chief, I'm ordering you back into service."

After yielding, Warren, returning to his chambers, was "really shaken," a clerk recalled. "He still thought it was a mistake, but he said, 'When somebody appeals to my patriotism that way, I don't know how I can say no.'"

Among the commission members were John McCloy, Richard Russell, Allen Dulles, John Sherman Cooper, Hale Boggs, and Gerald Ford. Still, Warren took charge of the commission much as he had taken charge as governor and Chief Justice. And many of the commission's decisions bore Warren's special mark.

He decided to suppress the autopsy photographs. "They were so horrible," he said after seeing them, "that I couldn't sleep well for nights." He wanted to keep them from "getting into the hands of sensation-mongers."

He stormed at the staff for asking questions about an affair between a witness and a diplomat. "It's her personal affair," Warren fumed, "and could ruin the diplomat." The testimony was excised from the transcript.

All staff lawyers under the general counsel, no matter how senior, would have the same title—assistant general counsel. Else, Warren feared, some with "higher" titles might later use them for gain—and Warren wanted no one to profit from the commission's work.

In that connection, Warren was infuriated by Representative Ford's reputed "inside story" of the commission published in *Life* only a week after the commission's report was issued. He grew angrier when, two weeks later, Ford signed a book contract.

He and Ford had clashed earlier (Ford wanted a staff member fired as a security risk, but Warren countered by ordering all staff members to undergo security checks). And Senator Russell objected to a categorical conclusion that the President's killer, Lee Harvey Oswald, was not involved in a conspiracy.

In the end, however, Warren persuaded the commission members to support the report unanimously. Russell recalled that Warren rewrote the non-conspiracy finding himself until the senator agreed to the language.

"If I were still a district attorney," the Chief said at a cocktail party, "and the Oswald case came into my jurisdiction, given the same evidence I could have gotten a conviction in two days and never heard about the case again."

Warren continued to hold sway at the Court as well, but trouble was brewing. The issue on which his solid majority was being threatened—and which would create serious schisms on the Court, particularly between Black and Douglas—involved the sit-ins.

They had begun on February 1, 1960, in a Woolworth store in downtown Greensboro, North Carolina. Four students from the all-black North Carolina Agricultural and Technical College sat down at the lunch counter and ordered coffee. They were ignored—but they stayed where they were until closing time. The next day they came back—with five more friends. Again they were ignored—and again they stayed. They came back again and again, maintaining quiet dignity in the face of hoots, threats, and occasional missiles thrown at them by rowdy onlookers.

The movement spread throughout the state and the South. Elsewhere, students and sympathizers picketed Woolworth stores. Then demonstrators turned up at Walgreen, Kress, Grant, Liggett, and other lunch counters. Before long, the effort spread to restaurants, theaters, hotels, parks, and all other segregated public and quasi-public facilities. (The Freedom Riders would challenge public transportation the following year.)

Garner v. *Louisiana* was the first of the sit-in cases to reach the Court. Black college students had been charged with breach of the peace when they refused to leave a Baton Rouge lunch counter. They argued there was no evidence to support their convictions, the statute was improperly vague, and use of the police and courts to enforce segregation was a "state action" violating the Fourteenth Amendment.

At a November 1961 conference, Warren thought the case could be decided on the narrow ground of a year-old decision in *Thompson* v. *Louisville,* involving a petitioner the justices called "Shuffling Sam."

Sam Thompson had been convicted of disorderly conduct and fined twenty dollars for shuffling his feet in time to music for half an hour in a Louisville café. A unanimous Court reversed the decision because there was no evidence that "Shuffling Sam" had been guilty of disorderly conduct.

There was no evidence to support the *Garner* conviction either, most justices agreed. Frankfurter thought, however, that the "inflammable ingredients" in *Garner* made the case different from *Thompson*.

The Chief responded that, if the merits of the case were considered, he would suggest that a sit-in was a form of speech protected by the First Amendment. Douglas and Brennan agreed.

Frankfurter thought the broader view was "ominous." He said he would prefer to "make of this a little case, precisely for the reason that we are all fully conscious of the fact that it is just the beginning of a long story. . . . We are deciding only that these people were convicted in want of evidence, and the closer we stick to the shore of that controlling determination, the less we needlessly borrow trouble of the future—the needless trouble, in emotionally entangled situations, of needless discussion."

All the justices agreed to the decision on the *Thompson* ground. But Frankfurter was right in foreseeing difficulty for the Court. He also sensed Black was troubled by the broad view of sit-ins, too. "No one knows better than you," he wrote the Alabaman, "the view on the Negro question I had—and had translated into action—years before I came on the Court. My convictions regarding Negro constitutional rights have certainly not weakened since I came here. I am sure that you and I are in agreement that it will not advance the cause of constitutional equality for Negroes for the Court to be taking short-cuts—to discriminate as partisans in favor of Negroes, or even appear to do so."

However Warren may have felt about Frankfurter's attitude on the role of the Court in civil rights cases, he nonetheless agreed that the sit-in issue should be kept to narrow legal grounds. The obvious problem was the direct clash of two basic rights—the sanctity of private property against protecting an individual from state-enforced discrimination.

Six cases confronted the Court shortly after Goldberg took his seat in 1962. Four involved arrests in cities with ordinances or policies requiring racial segregation in restaurants, one focused on a black minister for inciting others to conduct sit-ins, and one concerned an attempt to desegregate a privately owned amusement park near Washington, D.C.

At a November 9 conference, Warren advocated deciding all the cases without reaching the constitutional questions. The convictions could be overturned on the basis that ordinances and policies requiring racial segregation could not be used to make arrests for trespass or disorderly conduct.

Black, however, wanted to meet the broader issue. "I'd say we have a system of private ownership of property, and if we're going to trim these down under constitutional provisions, I'd have to look closely to find if there's anything which says the owner can't tell people he doesn't want to get out. I see nothing in the Constitution which says this. Therefore, he can call the police to help protect that right. If that right is in the owner, the law must enforce his right."

Douglas snapped back, "If Black's views of the retail store are adopted, we will have a new *Plessy* v. *Ferguson* regime by private people enforced by the courts. I'd say retail stores can't discriminate and, therefore, state proceedings to help them are unconstitutional." He said he would overrule an 1883 decision of the Court holding that the reach of the Fourteenth Amendment was limited to action by a state—and did not apply to privately enforced discrimination by hotels and restaurants.

Clark, Harlan, and Stewart indicated agreement with Black on the broader issue. But they agreed with Goldberg's view that "it's not necessary to go into the basic questions raised by Black and Douglas." Douglas allowed that "I could probably follow an opinion embodying the Chief's views, though I would prefer to face the issue Hugo proposed—owner's rights."

The substance of the subsequent decisions, issued by Warren, was that the existence of a segregation ordinance or policy preempted "from the sphere of private choice" whether a facility would be operated on an integrated basis.

The case involving the amusement park, Glen Echo, was put over for reargument because several justices believed the owner had instituted segregation in the absence of a state policy.

Delaying the thorny issues posed by the sit-in cases proved

"completely satisfactory to no one except the thirty-one demonstrators whose convictions were reversed," journalist James E. Clayton suggested. Nonetheless, lunch counters, restaurants, motels, parks, and libraries throughout the South had been desegregated since the onset of the sit-in wave in early 1960—including Glen Echo amusement park.

Still, the judicial issue persisted. And on October 18, 1963, Warren and several others thought it was time to meet the basic question posed by the sit-ins. In considering *Bell* v. *Maryland* and *Robinson* v. *Florida,* Warren urged "we should get to the raw of the problem." Convictions of sit-in demonstrators violated the Fourteenth Amendment. "In the field of public accommodations, the owner abandons private choice. If it's a private property, for private use, he can call on the state to throw people off." In public accommodations, however, "as long as they behave themselves, the owner can't have the police to help to throw them out. The state then unconstitutionally enforces discrimination."

Black declared his "pappy," who had run a general store, had the right to decide whom he would or would not serve. "I don't think the Constitution forbids the owner of a store to keep people out."

Douglas circulated a memorandum expressing the view held by the Chief, Brennan, and Goldberg:

> The question in the sit-in cases is not whether there is state action but whether states, acting through their courts, can constitutionally put a racial cordon around businesses serving the public. If they can do it in the restaurant cases, they can do it in drugstores, private hospitals, and common carriers. Property is in one case as sacrosanct as in the other. An affirmance in these cases fastens apartheid tightly onto our society—a result incomprehensible in light of the purposes of the Fourteenth Amendment and the realities of our modern society.

The argument, despite its eloquence, failed to persuade a majority. Clark, Harlan, Stewart, and White voted with Black.

Brennan objected vigorously. He reminded the majority that President Kennedy had sent Congress a bill to prohibit racial discrimination in public accommodations. He and Warren argued that a Court decision upholding the sit-in convictions on the ground of the sanctity of property rights would cripple the bill's prospects for congressional passage. Brennan threatened heatedly to do all he could to delay the Court from handing down its decision—a judicial filibuster of sorts—until he could effect a switch of one vote (converting the minority into a majority) or until Congress enacted a public accommodations proposal.

Black angrily questioned the ethics of such a maneuver—but Warren suggested that, in such an important issue, the Court should delay at least long enough to hear the views of the United States. To Black's dismay, Stewart—one of Black's supporters on the merits of the case—nonetheless agreed with Warren's idea. The justices voted five to four to invite the Solicitor General to file a brief. In the invitation, the majority requested the views of "the United States"—but the churlish minority disputed the necessity of hearing from the "Kennedy administration." Later, the minority modified its haughty tone somewhat by referring instead to the "Department of Justice."

It took the Solicitor General until mid-January of 1964 to file the government's views, and it was March before Black could circulate his draft opinion to Clark, Harlan, Stewart, and White. He wrote that the Fourteenth Amendment does not bar a state "from enforcing its trespass laws so long as it does not do so with an evil eye and a prejudiced heart and hand. We do not believe that the amendment was written or designed to interfere with a property owner's right to choose his social or business associates."

Warren, Douglas, and Goldberg prepared dissents. Warren's argued that the majority "has interposed principles of privacy and the protection of property rights between Negro petitioners and the right to equal treatment in public places. It has elevated to the status of constitutional protection a claimed property right which is, at best, the right to solicit the patronage of Negroes at a lunch counter if they stand up, but to deny it if they sit down."

(Warren's draft was faintly reminiscent of Harry Golden's "vertical integration" plan in which the North Carolina author pointed out that, because elevators and stand-up snack stands in the South were integrated but buses and restaurants were not, schools could be integrated simply by removing desks and chairs.)

The Chief maintained that states were forbidden from denying equal access to public places in the name of private property. The Thirteenth, Fourteenth, and Fifteenth Amendments were designed, he said, "to restore to the Negro that little bit of humanity which he loses each time a state-sanctioned inferior status is publicly thrust upon him."

Despite such importuning, Clark told Goldberg that the five-justice majority in the civil rights cases was "absolutely solid and indestructible"—a claim which, coming from Clark, would ring with irony in a month.

On April 27, 1964, Brennan circulated a dissent on the principal sit-in case—*Bell* v. *Maryland*—pointing out that laws enacted in the state since Bell's conviction prohibited discrimination in public accommodations.

He wrote that common law dictated that repeal or nullification of a criminal statute had the effect of vacating convictions still pending under that statute.

Black replied that was a state question which Maryland's courts could consider; it had no effect, however, on whether the Court ruled on the constitutional issue.

Brennan then determined that the constitutional issue could be avoided altogether. He maintained that *Bell* v. *Maryland* should be decided on the narrow ground of the superseding Maryland laws. To make his point, he notified the justices that he no longer would concur in the dissents drafted by Warren, Douglas, or Goldberg.

"We cannot be blind to the fact," he wrote in a draft dissent, "that the opposing opinions on the constitutional question will inevitably enter into and perhaps confuse the congressional debate. My colleagues thus choose the most unfortunate time to commit the error of reaching out to decide the question. In doing so, they unnecessarily create the risk of dealing the Court a self-inflicted wound, because the issue should not have been decided at all."

Warren and Goldberg quickly joined Brennan in his new quest (although in a new draft Brennan prudently deleted his earlier harsh judgments of the majority). Stewart seriously considered the Brennan option—but when White told him he was firm for the Black opinion, Stewart decided to stay with the majority. Douglas, however, refused to budge. He insisted the Court should reach the constitutional question.

Before the May 15 conference, Black sought to allay the minority's fears by inserting in his draft opinion that "the case does not involve the constitutionality of any existing or proposed state or federal legislation requiring restaurant owners to serve people without regard to color."

Shortly after the justices exchanged their ritual handshakes, Warren prepared to take the final vote on the issue when Clark dropped a bombshell. He asked that *Bell* v. *Maryland* be delayed again; reading Brennan's dissent the night before, Clark had decided he would follow that course. He said he had informed Black of his change of heart just before the conference.

Black glared silently at his fellow Southerner—but, unexpectedly, Douglas burst out angrily. He didn't care what Clark and the others did, he fumed, he would never join Brennan in an effort to evade the issue. With Douglas' refusal to join Brennan's opinion, the Court was divided four to four.

After the conference, Black pursued the Douglas tack in trying to woo Clark back into the majority. When a majority of the justices wanted to reach the merits, he said, it was obligated to do so. Douglas was right about not evading the issue, Black said—and Clark's switch deprived anyone of a majority.

Black pushed too far. Clark snapped that if Black really wanted a decision on the merits, he would give him one. He would join the constitutional view urged by Warren, Douglas, Brennan, and Goldberg—making it five to four declaring that conviction of sit-in demonstrators was unlawful.

Clark then notified Brennan formally he was joining Brennan's approach. Brennan prepared an addendum suggesting that, because Douglas would reverse, if on different grounds, the ruling stood five to four to reverse the conviction.

Douglas remained mulish, however. "I should make it unmistakably clear," he wrote his colleagues, "I would not reverse on any grounds but the ones I have written." He continued that on the issue presented by Brennan, "I join the group headed by my Brother Black which, as I understand it, leaves the majority of the Court against the disposition Brother Brennan has suggested."

Brennan was exasperated at Douglas' quintessential demonstration of having things his way or not at all—with the not so incidental result that, however high-sounding his prose, Douglas' action would uphold the convictions of sit-in demonstrators instead of nullifying the judgments against them.

As the two exchanged increasingly acrimonious memoranda, Goldberg stepped in with a compromise. He proposed that instead of Brennan announcing the Court's judgment, a brief *per curiam* be issued reversing the judgment. It would state that Warren, Clark, and Brennan would reverse because of superseding state laws as discussed in Brennan's opinion, while Douglas and Goldberg would reverse on the constitutional merits which each would delineate in separate opinions.

Douglas agreed to go along—but now Black stiffened his back. He persuaded Harlan, Stewart, and White to join a statement disagreeing that the judgment was, in fact, reversed. "It would be more nearly accurate to characterize the result of the case as an affirmance" because the majority had wished to reach the constitutional merits.

Brennan was shocked. The Black statement, he said, would severely harm the Court's reputation. He drafted an answer in which he, Warren, and Clark declared they "deem too ill-becoming for comment the absurd proposition . . . that [an] expression for a minority of four in support of an affirmance overrides the majority vote of five to reverse the judgment."

At the June 5 conference, Black and his supporters offered a new proposal. Black suggested the Court should grant certiorari to some of the new sit-in cases on the docket and call them up for immediate argument. It was likely, he said, that some of these cases would permit a broader-based result. Douglas indicated his support for the idea. "Five votes can do anything around here," Brennan grumbled.

But Black did not have five. White wanted time to think through the effect a new grant of certiorari might have on the continuing congressional debate.

Two days later, though, Clark reached yet another stance. Although only half serious when he threatened to join Douglas on the constitutional merits of *Bell* v. *Maryland,* Clark now made that decision in earnest—or so it appeared. "It would to us seem strangely inconsistent," Clark wrote in a draft, "to hold that [while] no legislature may authorize a court to prohibit Negroes the use of public restaurants for a moment, the owner, through the use of the state's processes, can prevent their use by Negroes forever."

Warren enthusiastically joined Clark's opinion, which he called "splendid . . . a classic." Despite the ballyhoo, Clark indicated that he remained convinced that Brennan's course was preferable.

If Clark's switch was intended as a shrewd maneuver to break an ideological impasse, it succeeded remarkably. On June 15, the day the reapportionment decisions were announced, Stewart informed Brennan he would join his *Bell* v. *Maryland* opinion, making five to reverse the convictions on the narrow ground of a superseding law.

Stewart's action was founded on the way the Court had expanded reapportionment. His vote in *Baker* v. *Carr* had been crucial, but he strenuously opposed its extension in *Reynolds* v. *Sims* and other decisions mandating reapportionment and equal-population electoral schemes. "When those decisions were being announced," Stewart reportedly said, "I said to myself, 'If I could do anything to keep those cases from being decided that way, I would.' I felt the same way about Clark's opinion in the *Bell* case."

Douglas used unusually sharp language in an opinion denouncing the Court's failure to reach the merits; originally, he even accused the Court of "irresponsible judicial management of the foremost issue of our time" and "abdication of judicial responsibility," but deleted those phrases from his final version.

Black, on the other hand, decided to remove any language from his opinion that might impute discredit to the Court or to members of the majority. He even congratulated Brennan at a cocktail party, expressing admiration and pride at the way he had fought to carry the day for his position.

Douglas harbored enough bitterness, though, to spitefully withdraw his concurrences from several of Brennan's opinions in unrelated cases. And in typical fashion, when the sit-in decisions were announced on June 22, 1964, the last day of the term, Douglas was not on the Bench; he was on one of his regular extrajudicial jaunts elsewhere in the country. Black read Douglas' attack on the Court's failure to reach the merits, and Goldberg read Douglas' view of why sit-ins were unconstitutional.

Ten days later, the Civil Rights Act of 1964—which, among other things, prohibited racial discrimination in restaurants and other public accommodations—became law. The new law made moot the issue that had so sharply divided the justices.

And the justices, once as inseparable as the Musketeers on issues involving race, were coming unstuck as pertinent legal questions and the very nature of the crusade for racial equality became more complex.

A year before, Harlan had puzzled over the historic March on Washington by a quarter million people, and the enormity of the public response to Martin Luther King's "I have a dream . . ." oration at the Lincoln Memorial.

The march, Harlan wrote, "leaves me pretty cold, appearing at this distance more of a Madison Avenue show than what one thinks of as a 'petition for the redress of grievances.' But I must be wrong, for my two law clerks—both sober-minded boys—assure me that it was a very moving affair. I hope it won't lead the Court into doing foolish things."

Clearly, from Harlan's view, it had. In 1964, he, Clark, and White voted against taking a case called *Hamilton* v. *Alabama,* in which Mary Hamilton was found in contempt of court for refusing to answer questions from the witness stand. A black woman, she had been addressed as "Mary"—and she steadfastly declined to answer until she was called "Miss Hamilton."

The Court reversed the conviction, prompting Frankfurter to write Harlan, "I am glad that there were three of you who thought Miss Hamilton's case was a silly case to take on certiorari—but, once it was taken, I think I would have been against you on the merits. That is because I think the American habit of calling people by their first names when you hardly know a person is undignified and indefensible."

Others found some actions of the Court indefensible as well. As 1964 wound to a close, the national political campaigns heated and swelled—and Senator Barry Goldwater, the Republican presidential nominee, determined that the Warren Court was the governmental branch "least faithful to the constitutional tradition of limited government."

J. Edgar Hoover reportedly referred to the justices as "bleeding hearts," the John Birch Society continued selling Warren Impeachment Packets for one dollar, and former Justice Whittaker charged in an address to the American Bar Association that the Court was usurping the right of local self-government by its rulings expanding federal power.

(Warren, hearing Whittaker's criticism, observed, "Charlie never could make up his mind about decisions—until he left the Court." Not all former justices were happy to be gone. Shay Minton, soon after he retired, wrote a former colleague, "When that first Monday in October rolls around, I miss joining the Court. I feel sorta left out.")

In 1964, Goldwater wished that most of the justices would join Minton and Whittaker. He promised that, if elected, he would appoint to the Bench "only seasoned men who will support the Constitution" rather than those who were sacrificing law and order "just to give criminals a sporting chance to go free."

Despite Goldwater's resounding defeat at the polls, his criticisms would live on. Depending on one's view, the best—or worst —of the Court's decisions on criminal justice were yet to come.

SIXTEEN

At the Head of the Table

FOR EARL WARREN, 1965 must have seemed like the best of times.

He controlled a solid majority on the Court and, for the entire judicial term between October 1964 and the summer of 1965, he had not found it necessary to dissent in a single case.

For Warren, the malaise created by the assassination of President Kennedy—and by the Chief's intimacy with its bloody details—was fading. The enactment of major civil rights legislation and the promise of more to come flavored the days with presumptive ratification of the Court's war on racial discrimination.

And he had been "delighted" at the outset of 1965 to swear in Lyndon Johnson as President. Johnson's opponent, Senator Barry Goldwater, had, among some other flights of rhetorical excess, called for replacing most members of the United States Supreme Court.

Like Kennedy, Johnson was an outspoken supporter of the Court and its role as national arbiter and dispenser of final judgments on what was and was not constitutional.

More than Kennedy, however, Johnson went well beyond protocol to solicit the Chief's good will. At a White House reception for the federal judiciary in 1966, Johnson paid Warren the highest compliment when he compared him to his political idol, Speaker Sam Rayburn. When Rayburn ran the House of Representatives, the President recalled, "I considered that wherever Mister Sam sat was the head of the table. Now, wherever Warren sits is the head of the table."

When Warren celebrated his seventy-fifth birthday in 1966, Johnson unexpectedly arrived at the Warrens' home "laden like Santa Claus." Among the gifts the President brought was a photograph inscribed "To the greatest Chief Justice of them all" and a bottle of thirty-year-old scotch. Warren told Johnson the whiskey "will remain untouched until the election night of 1968 when I will drink to your health and continued success."

It was a poignant exchange. When that election night came, it would be tinged with bitterness for both men. That night, the nation—still benumbed by the public murders of two more of its most vigorous leaders, and anguished over a war that many, if not most, judged pointless and horribly wasteful of life and property—would select by the narrowest of margins a new leader determined to undo what Warren and Johnson, each in his own sphere, had created.

Nonetheless, from 1965 until he left the Court, Warren—or, more precisely, Warren's concept of judicial activism in pursuit of human rights—virtually dictated national jurisprudence, though not without challenge and occasional rancor.

In the spring of 1965, the Court faced Connecticut's anti-contraception law which it had deftly sidestepped four years earlier. This time, the head of the state's Planned Parenthood League and the medical director of the League's New Haven center were convicted of violating the law by advising married people on how to avoid conception.

At an April 2 conference on the case, *Griswold* v. *Connecticut*, Warren, as he often did, announced a strong position (he favored reversing the convictions) although still searching for a constitutional justification. "I can't say that the law affects the First Amendment rights of doctors or that the state has no legitimate interest. We can't use equal protection, 'shocking' due process, or privacy."

The Chief thought the Court might strike the law down because of its broad-brush application. "This is the most confidential relationship in our society. It has to be clear-cut—and it isn't."

Clark, who had been eager to avert a head-on clash with the law earlier, now declared, "There's a right to marry, maintain a home, have a family. This is an area where we have the right to be let alone." Goldberg simply maintained that "the state cannot regulate this relationship. There's no compelling state reason justifying the statute."

Douglas argued that the law violated the First Amendment. "We've said that the right to travel is in radiation of the First Amendment, and so is the right of association. There's nothing more personal than this relationship and it's within First Amendment protection, if on the periphery."

"The right of association," Black countered, "is for me a right of assembly—and the right of a husband and wife to assemble in bed is a new right of assembly for me." Stewart supported Black's view that there was nothing in the Constitution prohibiting the state from enacting such a law.

But Brennan persuaded Douglas, who had been assigned by Warren to write for the majority, to abandon the First Amendment approach. Brennan suggested that the First Amendment was meant to protect association where it was essential to fruitful advocacy, not merely the association of one person with another. What Brennan proposed was that "the protection of the Bill of Rights goes beyond the specific guarantees to protect from congressional abridgment those equally fundamental personal rights necessary to make the express guarantees fully meaningful."

Douglas agreed—and wrote an opinion striking the law down as an unwarranted incursion into the right of marital privacy. Harlan and White concurred in the result, but rejected Douglas' broad approach. They urged that the law had violated due process. But Warren, Clark, Brennan, and Goldberg joined Douglas to establish marital privacy as a constitutional right.

The Court continued expanding First Amendment rights respecting religion and freedom of the press. In *United States* v. *Seeger,* the Court considered a law exempting from the draft those opposed to war because of their "religious training and belief" in relation to "a Supreme Being." Opposition to war because of "essentially political, sociological, or philosophical views, or a merely personal code," was insufficient to justify exemption.

Seeger had declared that his "religious" opposition to war was based on his reading of Plato and Spinoza, among others, rather than on a belief in God. At a November 1964 conference, Warren said judges ought not to define "Supreme Being. . . . [Seeger] believes in a guiding spirit and that's enough to give him the exemption."

Black said it was a denial of equal protection "to separate conscientious objectors in the field of morality. If the objection is honest and conscientious, then it's enough." The government, Harlan said, "can't pick and choose between religious beliefs." "Congress must exempt believers and non-believers alike," Stewart said. "What I say," Clark said, "is that any sincere belief which fills, in the life of the objector, the same place as God fills in the life of an orthodox religionist, is entitled to exemption under the statute."

Goldberg added, somewhat obtusely, "The only difference between Seeger and Buddhism is that Seeger isn't a Buddhist." In the end, there were no dissents.

In *Garrison* v. *Louisiana*, the Court held that criminal punishment could not be meted out for statements made against public officials unless they were both false and uttered with actual malice. In this case, the Court threw out a decision by a judge to hold controversial New Orleans District Attorney Jim Garrison in contempt for public criticisms of the court. The ruling extended the 1964 decision in *New York Times* v. *Sullivan*, in which the Montgomery, Alabama, police commissioner had claimed he had been libeled by an advertisement. In that case, the Court first set down the standard that public officials could not recover damages for libel unless they demonstrated actual malice or reckless disregard for the facts. In both cases, Black, Douglas, and Goldberg maintained in conferences that the First Amendment bars *all* libel proceedings, criminal or civil, based on criticisms of official conduct.

While the Court was building a wall of protection around the media, making recovery of damages for libel by public officials (and, later, public figures) extremely unlikely, it took unkindly to the incursion by electronic media into the courtroom.

Time magazine reported that a dozen cameramen, powerful lights, and a tangle of cables "turned the courtroom into a broadcast studio" in the trial of Texas wheeler-dealer Billie Sol Estes. Estes had objected to allowing television coverage of his trial for a multimillion-dollar fraud scheme. He challenged his conviction on the basis of the TV coverage, and the bare minimum of four justices—Warren, Douglas, Harlan, and Brennan—agreed to hear the appeal.

At the conference on April 2, 1965, Warren opened the discussion with a broad condemnation of television coverage of trials.

"I think this violates due process," he said. "To stage a trial this way violates the decorum of the courtroom, and TV is not entitled to special treatment. I see no violation of free speech or press. They may be in the courtroom like the press—only as part of the public. This bears on the question of fair trial. . . . Even with the consent of the accused and his lawyers, I'd be against it."

Douglas, Harlan, and Goldberg strongly supported Warren's view. "A trial is not a spectacle," Douglas declared, "whether [Estes] objected or not. This is the modern farce—putting the courtroom into a modern theatrical production."

Harlan said "the right to a public trial doesn't mean for me that the public has the right to a public performance. This goes more deeply into the judicial process than just the right of the defendant." Goldberg asserted that "the shambles deprived the defendant of a fair trial. In the present state of the art, this was an obtrusive intervention from the outside into this trial."

At the conference, Clark, Stewart, and White opposed a flat constitutional ban on permitting television in the courtroom. Clark agreed with the trial judge's finding that television had not prejudiced the verdict.

Brennan was not ready to make a firm commitment. He wondered whether technological advances could avoid "theater or spectacle" in the future—and whether a ruling here would affect "legislative inquisition." Black said he opposed having television in courts, "but this is a new thing that's working itself out. . . . Someday, the technology may improve so as not to disturb the actual trial."

Black and Brennan joined Clark, Stewart, and White, making it five to four to affirm Estes' conviction. Black assigned Stewart to draft an opinion, which he circulated on May 13. "We are asked to hold that the Constitution absolutely bars television and cameras from every criminal courtroom," Stewart wrote, "even if they have no impact on the jury, no effect upon any witness, and no influence upon the conduct of the judge. However strong our personal views on the subject may be, we cannot find that requirement in the federal Constitution."

The following week, Warren circulated a thirty-four-page draft dissent, which Douglas joined. "Our Constitution insures for every criminal defendant a fair and impartial forum for the determination of the charges against him," Warren wrote. "A decision allowing the courtroom to become a public spectacle and source of entertainment ignores this guarantee. The exclusion of television cameras is not only a reasonable limitation, but it is a necessary requirement for the proper conduct of judicial proceedings."

Goldberg added his own draft dissent because Estes "was denied a fair trial conducted with dignity in a calm and solemn judicial atmosphere."

However, as had become his wont, Clark changed his mind—and that turned the decision around to Estes' favor. Warren had lobbied Clark intensively on the issue during their morning walks together. On May 25, Clark sent a memorandum to his colleagues.

"After circulation of the opinions and dissents, along with my interim study," he wrote, "I became disturbed at what could result from our approval of this emasculation by TV of the trial of a case. My doubts increased as I envisioned use of the unfortunate format followed here in other trials which would not only jeopardize the fairness of them, but would broadcast a bad image to the public of the judicial process. . . . The perils to a

fair trial far outweigh the benefits that might accrue in the tele-
vising of the proceedings."

At Warren's direction, Clark then prepared a sixteen-page
opinion for the majority. Clark intended to banish television
cameras from the courtroom. In his initial draft, he wrote that
"the facts in this case demonstrate clearly the necessity for the
adoption of a *per se* rule. . . . In light of the inherent hazards to
a fair trial that are presented by television in the courtroom, I
would hold that its use violated [the] right to due process."

But Clark deleted that assertion to meet the objections in
Stewart's draft dissent. Nonetheless, White still objected to the
Court's inflexible ban on television without any showing of prejudice. Brennan joined White—but issued his own dissent, pointing out that because of Harlan's concurring opinion, only four
members of the majority really voted for an inflexible ban.

Because Clark's language flatly barring the use of television in
courtrooms had been dropped from his opinion, the dissents
seemed odd. Years later, however, in the 1981 *Chandler* v. *Florida* case, Brennan's prescience paid off for those who supported
his position. In that case, the Court held that a state rule allowing television coverage of a criminal trial did not violate the
Constitution. The majority opinion stressed that Harlan's separate concurrence in *Estes* v. *Texas* meant that a majority there
had not, in fact, voted for a *per se* rule barring broadcast coverage in all circumstances.

By the summer of 1965, the relative calm that had settled over
the nation started to disintegrate. Racial tension had flared anew,
this time in Selma, Alabama. Lyndon Johnson decided to launch
massive bombing raids on North Vietnam and to commit the first
American ground troops to the war—and that opened a "credibility gap" between the people and their President that persisted
through his and subsequent administrations. And because of decisions he made regarding the Court, Johnson would unwittingly
scandalize it, and weaken the confidence that most Americans
had maintained in the institution throughout its most controversial days under Earl Warren's leadership.

It began when Adlai Stevenson died. Johnson was determined

to replace him as ambassador to the United Nations with someone of similar stature. He settled on Arthur Goldberg. Clearly, a
former Supreme Court justice would command instant respect at
the United Nations—and Goldberg's earlier association with John
Kennedy might lessen growing opposition to the President's
Vietnam policies among liberal Democrats and on college campuses.

Goldberg later complained he was dragooned into resigning
from the Court much as Warren was shamed into heading the
commission investigating the assassination of President Kennedy.

"Everyone knows Lyndon Johnson," Goldberg recalled. He
said the President implored him "to join in the greatest adven-
ture of man's history—the effort to bring the rule of law to govern the relations between sovereign states. It is that—or doom."

Later, Goldberg explained, "I have accepted, as one simply
must."

To replace Goldberg, Johnson wanted Abe Fortas, a longtime,
close adviser—and one of the most successful and richest lawyers
in Washington. Fortas did not want the job—and Fortas' wife, a
partner in the law firm, was even more adamantly opposed to it.
"Abe Fortas' wife is very upset over Abe's appointment," Douglas wrote to Black. "It is apparently a very serious crisis."

They weathered it—perhaps because Johnson's methods defied
effective opposition. On July 28, 1965, less than two weeks after
Goldberg resigned from the Court, Johnson summoned Fortas to
the White House. The President asked Fortas to help him draft a
statement for a nationally televised news conference on his decision to raise the number of American troops in Vietnam to fifty
thousand and to double the draft calls to thirty-five thousand a
month. "We did not choose to be the guardians at the gate,"
Fortas helped Johnson write, "but there is no one else."

Minutes before the noon press conference, Johnson took
Fortas aside. "Before announcing this statement," Johnson said,
"I am going to announce your appointment to the Court." Fortas
started to object but Johnson cut him off.

"This Vietnam statement that you approved says fifty thousand more boys are going to Vietnam—perhaps to die. No one is

ever going to shoot at you on the Court. Tell me, how can I send them to battle and not send you to the Court?" To sweeten the pot, Johnson promised to make Fortas Chief Justice if the opportunity arose.

Fortas gave in. He continued the tradition, begun with the appointment of Cardozo in 1932, of occupying the Court's "Jewish seat" (although he was not replaced by a Jew when he resigned in 1969). But in no way was he an ordinary junior justice. The encomiums his appointment generated far surpassed the puffery and political claptrap ordinarily expected in such circumstances. "One of the best minds of anyone ever appointed to the Court" was a line repeated by legal scholars and editorialists across the nation. "The lawyer's lawyer" was a description used by at least a score of lawyers who knew him. One colleague said of Fortas, "He's the brain surgeon—the guy you call in when all else fails."

Harlan, himself regarded as an outstanding legal craftsman, told his law clerks he considered Fortas to be "the most brilliant advocate to appear in my time."

But Fortas' talent was matched by his ego—a belief he was so obviously brilliant, rich, and important that he was beyond taint. In *Who's Who in the South and Southwest,* Fortas' business address was listed as "c/o White House, 1600 Pennsylvania Avenue, Washington, D.C." Author Robert Shogan wrote of Fortas that after his appointment Fortas was "on the Bench—and on call at the White House." Shogan reported that "the first person the President consults on anything is Abe Fortas [and] few important Presidential problems are settled without an opinion from Justice Fortas."

In 1966, when business executive Ralph Lazarus said in a speech that financing the Vietnam War was costing much more than President Johnson's public estimate, Lazarus received a complaining telephone call from Justice Fortas. Fortas told Lazarus his calculations were wrong and his public criticism had upset the President. (In fact, the cost of the war that year was $27 billion, nearly three times the White House estimate.)

And in 1968, when Warren wanted to see Johnson to discuss

resigning from the Bench, the appointment for the Chief Justice to see the President was made by Fortas.

His intimacy with the President gave Fortas added celebrity, which the new justice nurtured. In the end, it contributed to his undoing.

SEVENTEEN

The Bell
Starts to Toll

A FEW CRACKS had marred the solidity of the House That Warren Built when Black split from Warren and Douglas in the *Griswold* case on contraception and in the *Estes* decision on using television in courtrooms.

But the semblance of unanimity and purpose the Court had projected publicly after Frankfurter's departure, and the concomitant diminution of internal waspishness among the justices, started crumbling about the time of Fortas' arrival.

The renewed divisiveness hardly could be blamed on Fortas alone, however. Black seemed to be growing cantankerous. He disapproved of Douglas' divorce and remarriage to a woman young enough to be his granddaughter. He didn't like Fortas— especially because of his newest colleague's tendency to interpret due process as a broad guaranty of fairness. And he was becoming progressively jealous of Warren's expanding fame.

In the fall of 1966, Black delivered a lecture in which he maintained that the Chief Justice had received unwarranted credit for the constitutional revolution the Court had fostered in the previous dozen years. (Black told Warren his statement had been distorted by the press—a claim politicians frequently make after having issued critiques of colleagues. But former Governor Warren wasn't buying the line from former Senator Black. "Look, Hugo," Warren replied, "you can't unring a bell.")

As the Alabaman saw it, the Court under Warren had only written into law the constitutional principles that Black had been advocating since the 1930s. His resentment of Warren's getting the credit sometimes grew excessive and petty. When Warren retired as Chief Justice in 1969, a draft letter of farewell from his colleagues read, "For us it is a source of pride that we have had the opportunity to be members of the Warren Court." Black changed it to "the Court over which you have presided."

Black also seemed convinced that the Court was waging a vendetta against his native South in civil rights cases. To be sure, Black continued playing an important part in some cases, such as *United States* v. *Guest* in 1966. In that case, a majority, with Black assuming a leading role, upset the 1883 *Civil Rights Cases,* which had barred Congress from outlawing wholly private discriminatory actions.

But when five blacks appealed a conviction for breaching the peace when they tried to integrate a public library in Clinton, Louisiana, Black thought the Court was rewriting the facts because the incident occurred in the South.

What had happened was that the five asked for a book. When the librarian said she didn't have it (and, in truth, she did not), she said she would request it from the state's central library. She asked the men to leave, but they refused. They sat in the reading room until the sheriff arrested them for not leaving a public building when directed to do so by a peace officer.

At the December 10, 1965, conference, Warren said there was "no evidence to show breach of peace. Their conduct was not of that kind." The Chief added, "The judge was wrong in saying that this was not a case to prove segregation." He was supported by Douglas, Brennan, White, and Fortas in voting to reverse the convictions.

Harlan contended the Court should examine the case "in the context of a small library, attended by one old woman," before disputing the intent of the authorities. But Black made what one of his colleagues called a "high-pitched dissent on law-and-order." He said, "There is simply no evidence in the record at all that the petitioners were arrested because they were exercising the right to protest. . . . Nevertheless—apparently because the arrests were made in the Deep South—[the majority concluded] that this was the sole reason for the arrests."

Black toned down his views in a dissent joined by Clark, Harlan, and Stewart. But he was disturbed even further by Fortas' opinion, which maintained that the right to use the library was "fundamental" under the First Amendment. Black denounced Fortas' view that a library protest was protected by the First Amendment—and even Brennan and White were not prepared to go that far. Brennan supported reversing the convictions on the ground that the Louisiana statute was too broad. Fortas refused to reconsider his view that the First Amendment protected the actions of the protesters. Warren and Douglas agreed. But to speak for a majority on the issue, Fortas needed both Brennan and White. On the eve of announcing the decision, Fortas tried a time-honored ploy when he told Brennan that if he went along with the Fortas opinion, White would also. Brennan refused, and the Fortas opinion represented only a plurality.

Black's mild paranoia was exacerbated when, in *Greenwood* v. *Peacock,* Douglas challenged southern justice. Black was among five justices who held that civil rights demonstrators in Mississippi, arrested for blocking city streets, could not transfer their cases to federal court on the assumption they could not get a fair trial in the state courts. Douglas circulated a dissent asserting, "We know from the flow of cases coming this way that there are many, many such harassment prosecutions in the South today—not only against Negroes, but against whites as well who take up the cause of civil rights."

Although Warren, Brennan, and Fortas concurred with Douglas' conclusion, they objected to his language. He toned it down and they joined his dissent, which still criticized the majority for leaving the defendants to "local passions and prejudices."

And in 1966, Black succeeded at last in winning over a majority to uphold the convictions of civil rights demonstrators. Clark agreed to join when Black removed from his draft a sentence maintaining that "there is no right to 'demonstrate' which is constitutionally paramount to an owner's right to use his own property."

In this case—*Adderley* v. *Florida*—black college students had been arrested for refusing to leave the grounds of a county jail; they were protesting the arrests of fellow students who had been imprisoned in connection with anti-segregation demonstrations.

Brennan wrote Douglas that "Hugo's opinion will have the most chilling effect on legitimate protests on all forms of public property—parks and malls included." Brennan said the Black opinion would support statutes prohibiting a civil rights march around a statehouse.

Nonetheless, Black held sway in sustaining the convictions of Martin Luther King and other civil rights leaders for leading Easter Sunday protest marches in Birmingham, Alabama. The parade organizers were unable to get a permit, and they proceeded with their demonstration despite an injunction forbidding them to march without a permit. King and the others claimed the injunction and the ordinance prohibiting their march without a permit violated their First Amendment rights.

As expected, Warren urged reversal of the convictions when the Court met in conference on March 17, 1967. "The ordinance is void on its face," Warren claimed, "since it gives unfettered discretion to control First Amendment rights without standards. . . . The injunction was simply a copy of the ordinance and I don't think they can bootstrap it by putting it in the form of an injunction."

Whatever their motives, Black countered, there was no excuse to violate an injunction. Clark, Stewart, and White supported Black immediately; Harlan demurred at first because of the likelihood that the ordinance was applied with discrimination. He made Black's view a majority when he agreed the injunction should not have been ignored, whatever the intent of the ordinance.

Stewart was assigned the opinion by Black, and the tone of it offended the minority. Stewart's draft focused on the theme that people must obey injunctions until they succeed in having them set aside by a higher court. The draft ended by noting, "Patience is a small price for the civilizing hand of the judicial process, which alone can give abiding meaning to constitutional freedom." Stewart changed it to "a modicum of patience" and, finally, to "respect for judicial process."

Brennan's draft dissent lashed out at what he called Stewart's lack of "sensitivity to today's transitory shift in political and social attitudes toward the civil rights movement. For under cover of pious preachments that the Negro exercise a 'modicum of patience,' the Court empties the Supremacy Clause of its primacy." Brennan added that the Birmingham demonstrations were conducted in 1963. "These were the days before 'Black Power' and 'Long Hot Summer' became part of the jargon of the civil rights movement."

Warren agreed to join Brennan if the references to "Black Power" and "Long Hot Summer" were removed. The Chief objected to that kind of language in a judicial opinion. Nonetheless, Warren expressed deep concern over the opinion. He believed the specter of Martin Luther King being jailed for engaging in activities clearly protected by the First Amendment would encourage cynicism about justice and the courts.

Black's absolutist view of the First Amendment inevitably created further dissension between him and some of his colleagues. A major philosophical split developed over obscenity cases involving John Cleland's *Memoirs of a Woman of Pleasure* (popularly known as *Fanny Hill*) and publisher Ralph Ginzburg's promotion of *Eros* magazine and related sex-oriented publications.

It had been a decade since the justices handed down *Roth* v. *United States*, establishing the vague standard that obscene material contained a "dominant theme" appealing to "prurient interest" as "the average person" might determine when "applying contemporary community standards."

But *Roth* had made clear that "obscenity is not within the area of constitutionally protected speech or press."

Nonetheless, when the justices met at their December 10, 1965, conference, Black and Douglas refused to budge from their absolutist view of the First Amendment—and their belief that obscene material was protected by the Constitution.

No one else agreed with that view—but it didn't make it any

easier to reach some accord on defining obscenity and applying that definition. A majority—Warren, Clark, Harlan, Brennan, and White—agreed that *Fanny Hill* was obscene. Brennan was assigned to write that opinion as well as related obscenity cases before the Court.

This time, he expanded his earlier standard. He suggested that to find material obscene, not only should its dominant theme appeal to a prurient interest and be patently offensive to contemporary community standards, but it should be "utterly without redeeming social value."

Brennan included the new definition in his *Ginzburg* draft— and Warren and Fortas joined promptly. But Fortas issued a warning regarding *Fanny Hill*. Finding the book obscene, he said, might lead to a new wave of book-burning. He said he would join Brennan in the *Ginzburg* and related cases only if the *Fanny Hill* convictions were reversed.

Brennan was persuaded. He wrote an opinion declaring *Fanny Hill* was not obscene, because even the court below had found it possessed "a modicum of social value." Based on Brennan's new definition of obscenity, appearing in his *Ginzburg* draft, the *Fanny Hill* convictions must be overturned. Brennan then convinced Warren to change his mind by reminding the Chief of his own dissent in the 1957 case of *Kingsley Books, Inc.,* v. *Brown.* There, Warren wrote that the courts should not judge "the quality of art of literature. To do otherwise . . . savors too much of book-burning. . . . It is the conduct of the individual that should be judged." With Black and Douglas, there was now a Court to reverse *Fanny Hill.*

But White wouldn't go along with Brennan's new definition which gave independent status to the criterion of "redeeming social value." He still held *Fanny Hill* was obscene—and he would not concur in the *Ginzburg* finding as long as Brennan's definition of obscenity remained. So Brennan moved his three-pronged definition to the *Fanny Hill* decision, and White then agreed to sign the *Ginzburg* draft.

Brennan's goal was to get five justices to concur on a definition of obscenity. Now he had three. (The Black and Douglas view of the First Amendment proscribed any limiting definition of speech.) The Chief thought he could get Clark to agree. Stewart then said that to achieve a majority on defining obscenity, he would concur if Brennan would split the definition from the rest of his *Fanny Hill* opinion.

Clark wasn't buying, however. He circulated a dissent which focused on the sexual episodes in *Fanny Hill* to demonstrate its lewdness. Douglas responded with a memorandum to his colleagues that "in view of Brother Clark's passion for detail, why don't we all chip in and buy him a copy of *My Life & Loves* by Frank Harris?"

Clark stood his ground. Requiring a book to be "utterly without redeeming social value" gave "the smut artist free rein to carry on his dirty business." Stewart, seeing that Clark had no intention of joining the *Fanny Hill* decision, withdrew his agreement to join in the Brennan definition of obscenity. When *Fanny Hill* was issued, only three justices—Warren, Brennan, and Fortas—agreed to defining obscenity. Black, Douglas, and Stewart, however, in their separate concurrences to the decision, said they would go at least that far before delimiting First Amendment protection.

After the Brennan definition of obscenity was removed from the *Ginzburg* draft, White and Clark agreed to join it, making four for finding Ginzburg's publications obscene. A fifth was hard to come by. On this issue, Harlan had joined Black, Douglas, and Stewart. And while Fortas thought that one of the Ginzburg publications was obscene (a newsletter on sexual relations called *Liaison*), he thought another one (*The Housewife's Handbook on Selective Promiscuity*) had "therapeutic value." He was less certain about how to vote on the hard-cover magazine *Eros*.

Warren was eager to win a solid majority in *Ginzburg*. In keeping with his view that individual conduct in selling obscene material was within the Court's province, Warren set out to persuade Fortas to make a majority based on what he believed was Ginzburg's "pandering." It had not been discussed at the conference, but Warren made a case to Fortas that by mailing his materials from Intercourse, Pennsylvania, Blue Ball, Pennsylvania, and Middlesex, New Jersey, Ginzburg, displaying the "leer of the sensualist," was representing them as pornographic.

Thus, Ralph Ginzburg stood convicted and subsequently went to jail—not because he published and distributed obscene materials (though a majority of the Court agreed that *some* of his materials were obscene), but because he committed a bad joke.

Ginzburg represented the first full opinion by a majority in an obscenity case since *Roth*. But even its champion, Warren, conceded the decision was less than a textbook example of judicial clarity. As the decision was being announced, Warren passed a note to Brennan observing "the quizzical expression on the faces of some of the Solicitor General's staff. I wonder how happy they are with *Ginzburg*. You know, it will cast quite a work burden on that office and on the U.S. Attorneys."

If the outcome in *Ginzburg* displeased Black, it was nothing compared to his reaction to Fortas' opinion in *Time, Inc.*, v. *Hill*. An article in *Life* magazine purportedly depicted the "real life" people whose experiences inspired the book and play *The Desperate Hours*. Time, Inc., the owner of *Life*, was sued under a New York statute prohibiting invasions of privacy. Time, Inc., was ordered to pay $30,000.

When the conference considered the case on April 29, 1966, Warren maintained that *Life*'s story was "a fictionalization of these people's experience—and false. In this limited application, I see no threat to a free press." (Essentially, that was the position advocated by one of the attorneys arguing before the Court—Richard M. Nixon.) Only Black, Douglas, and White disagreed with the Chief. But when Fortas, who was assigned the opinion by Warren, circulated his draft, tempers began to flare—and votes came unstuck.

Fortas unleashed what one of his colleagues called an "invective" against the press. "The facts of this case are unavoidably distressing," he wrote. "Needless, heedless, wanton injury of the sort inflicted by *Life*'s picture story is not an essential instrument of responsible journalism. Magazine writers and editors are not, by reason of their high office, relieved of the common obligation to avoid inflicting wanton and unnecessary injury. The prerogatives of the press—essential to our liberty—do not preclude reasonable care and thoughtfulness. They do not confer a license for pointless assault."

Fortas decried "the deliberate, callous invasion" of the individual's "right to be let alone. This appropriation of a family's right not to be molested or to have its name exploited and its quiet existence invaded cannot be defended on the ground that it is within the purview of a constitutional guarantee designed to protect the free exchange of ideas and opinions. This is exploitation, undertaken to titillate and excite, for commercial purposes."

Douglas dissented sharply, asserting the First Amendment immunized the press from damage suits. White also dissented, questioning whether the New York law could be applied to true news accounts because they were commercially exploited. The question raised sufficient doubts to set the case for reargument in October 1966.

To Black, Fortas' draft simply was the worst First Amendment opinion he had seen in years. The day before the reargument, Black circulated a sixteen-page memorandum scathingly attacking Fortas' opinion. Black contended that the junior justice reached his conclusion through a "weighing process" in which an individual's right to privacy "under the particular circumstances here, outweighed the public's interest in being informed of the particular subject dealt with in *Life*'s news story."

> The use of the weighing process means simply to me that by legal legerdemain, the First Amendment's promise of unequivocal press freedom . . . has been transmuted into a debased alloy—transmuted into a freedom which will vacillate and grow weaker or stronger as the Court personnel is shifted from time to time. This means that the scope of press freedom is not to be decided by what the Founders wrote, but by what a Court majority thinks they should have written had they been writing now.

Seeming to borrow in tone from his old adversary, Frankfurter, Black condemned the Fortas approach as a blatant usurpation of power by the judiciary. In the view of the majority, Black contended:

> . . . judges are no longer to be limited to their recognized power to make binding *interpretations* of the Constitution. That power,

won after bitter constitutional struggles, has apparently become too prosaic and unexciting. So the judiciary now confers upon the judiciary the more "elastic" and exciting power to decide, under its value-weighing process, just how much freedom the courts will permit the press to have. And in making this decision, the Court is to have important leeway, it seems, in order to make the Constitution the people adopted more adaptable to what the Court deems to be modern needs. We, the judiciary, are no longer to be crippled and hobbled by the old admonition that "We must always remember it is a Constitution we are *expounding*," but we are to work under the exhilarating new slogan that "We must always remember that it is a Constitution we are *rewriting* to fit the times." I cannot join nor can I even acquiesce in this doctrine which I firmly believe to be a violation of the Constitution itself.

With a dash of hyperbole, Black maintained that "after mature reflection, I am unable to recall any prior case in this Court that offers a greater threat to freedom of speech and press than this one does."

Black's denunciation of the Fortas opinion turned the Court around. After the reargument, all the justices except Warren and Fortas switched to Black's view and voted to reverse the finding against *Life*. Ultimately, Clark and Harlan returned to the view that the article had been an invasion of privacy, but the Court ruled five to four to reverse the judgment against the magazine.

Black also engaged in a waspish exchange with Douglas over *Fortson* v. *Morris,* a 1966 challenge to Georgia's law allowing the General Assembly to elect the governor if no nominee received a majority in the general election.

What had complicated the gubernatorial election in Georgia that year was the unexpected victory in the Democratic primary of Lester Maddox, the gnomish owner of an Atlanta restaurant, the Pickrick. His claim to fame had been that he wore a holstered revolver and carried an ax handle to work, publicly threatening to shoot or beat any black who remained in the restaurant after being refused service.

Most Democrats (including Jimmy Carter, who had been among the losers in the primary) supported Maddox. But one prominent Democrat, former Governor Ellis Arnall, decided to enter the general election as an independent. He refused to believe the people would elect a political nonentity merely because he was a harsh racist. In addition, an active, well-financed campaign was undertaken by the Republican nominee, Howard (Bo) Callaway, a wealthy developer and heir to a textile fortune. Callaway actually outpolled Maddox—but the number of votes for Arnall kept either from winning a majority.

With the General Assembly overwhelmingly controlled by Democratic regulars, the selection of the Democrat, Maddox, was a foregone conclusion. But the law was challenged on the ground that allowing the legislature to name the governor deprived Georgia voters of equal protection of the law. A federal district court enjoined the General Assembly from acting, and the case was argued before the Supreme Court on an emergency basis on December 5, 1966. The legislature was required to act a month later, January 9, 1967.

Immediately after the argument, the justices met in conference. The Chief favored upholding the lower court and barring the legislature from naming the governor. "Since Georgia chose an elective system by the people, that must be the way of choice. Here, there is a taking away from the people and vesting it in the legislature."

He maintained, somewhat illogically, that the method of selection "is within the spirit of the unit-rule case." That case was *Gray* v. *Sanders*, in which the Court ruled unconstitutional Georgia's modified federal system of elections—a system which virtually negated the voting strength of the larger cities.

Black responded that *Gray* v. *Sanders* "is inapplicable. That dealt with discrimination between individual voters, which was a denial of equal protection. The unit system operated to effect such a discrimination. But where a wholly proper election fails to produce a majority choice, the question becomes whether the Constitution limited the state's power to choose a governor by a different method. The Constitution doesn't dictate that the governor must be chosen by the people."

Black won the prompt support of five of his colleagues, including Brennan. But Brennan dropped off next day to join Warren, Douglas, and Fortas in dissent.

Black pressed for a speedy decision. He urged that the Court announce its ruling the following Monday, December 12. If it did not, the next decision day was January 9—the very day the Georgia General Assembly was charged by the state constitution to meet and elect a governor. "It would seem to me," Black wrote his colleagues, "that nothing short of an imperative necessity should cause this Court to hold in suspense a decision on the question of the Assembly's power to elect the governor until the very date upon which the Assembly will meet to perform this duty."

He said the decision should be announced even if the opinions would have to be completed and issued later. He wrote Brennan, "I feel that the Court will be negligent in its duty if the case does not go down. A state is entitled to know what it can do and not left suspended in mid-air."

But Douglas objected. He replied, "There is one possible advantage in getting the opinions down quickly in cases like this—it forecloses any possibility of any member of the Court changing his mind. But the issue is a close one in the minds of the Court—a five-to-four vote indicating the narrowest of margins by which we make the decision. And I think that in itself argues for a more deliberate slow speed rather than a deliberate fast one."

Black shot back that "it is impossible for me to believe that it would take any member of this Court a whole month to write out his dissenting views. . . . Georgia should not be put in this unhappy predicament on [this] unsupported and, I believe, unsupportable assumption"—especially "in view of [Douglas'] well-known speed in writing all his opinions."

Black denounced Douglas' tactic—delaying an announcement while hoping to switch a vote that would turn the decision around. "How long should Georgia be kept in ignorance of its constitutional power and have its machinery paralyzed on [this] hope? . . . Members of this Court certainly are sufficiently mature to decide for themselves whether they need more time to announce their votes."

Again, Black's sharp language won the day. The decision was

announced December 12, and a month later Lester Maddox was elected governor of Georgia. (Two years later, Maddox would be publicly embraced by Vice President Hubert Humphrey. And, in 1970, Maddox, prohibited by law from running for re-election, won praise from the man who succeeded him, Jimmy Carter. In both cases, political exigencies appear to have over-whelmed objective judgment.)

But Black stood with Warren and Douglas, along with Bren-nan and Fortas, in deciding *Miranda* v. *Arizona,* a five-to-four ruling that would loose a torrent of protest and make being "soft on crime" as politically unacceptable as being "soft on Commu-nism" had been for the previous two decades.

Ernesto Miranda was arrested and charged with kidnapping and rape. After a two-hour interrogation, he confessed and, sub-sequently, was convicted. At the conference on *Miranda* on March 4, 1966, Warren posited what he viewed as the essential requirements in questioning a suspect. The police, he said, must warn someone like Miranda of his right to silence, that anything he says might be used against him, that he could have a lawyer present, and that a lawyer could be appointed if the suspect could not afford one.

That, Warren said, was the procedure followed by the FBI—and the FBI's record of effective law enforcement indicated that following its procedure would not place a serious burden on the police.

One justice at the conference said, "The statement that the FBI did it was a swing factor. I believe that was a tremendously important factor—perhaps the critical factor—in the *Miranda* vote."

Harlan opposed Warren's view. It represented, he said, an un-warranted extension of the Fifth Amendment. "It is only a testi-monial privilege," Harlan contended. " 'Compelling' means only coerced statements."

Black disagreed. "From the time the government begins to move against a man—when they take him into custody—his rights attach," he argued.

Warren, who assigned the opinion to himself, agreed to stress that the decision was concerned primarily with ensuring Fifth

Amendment guarantees against self-incrimination. Also, at Brennan's suggestion, he removed a passage about authorities in the South using brutal methods to extract confessions from Negroes.

"I wonder," Brennan wrote, "if it is appropriate in this context to turn police brutality into a racial problem? If anything characterizes the group this [*Miranda*] opinion concerns, it is poverty more than race."

The dissents were harsh, charging the new rules would "have a corrosive effect on the criminal laws as an effective device to prevent crime."

Brennan, who had predicted earlier that *Miranda* "will be one of the most important opinions of our time," was dissuaded by Warren from answering these allegations in a short concurrence. The Chief wanted to show unanimity among the bare majority of five justices in the opinion handed down on June 13, 1966.

It was as divisive as it was important. Mayor Sam Yorty of Los Angeles spoke for most local officials when he said the Court's opinion represented "another set of handcuffs on the police department."

Senator Birch Bayh of Indiana, chairman of the Senate's Constitutional Amendments Subcommittee, launched hearings in Washington and across the country to determine the impact of the decision on law enforcement. His witnesses ranged from police chiefs and prosecutors to Truman Capote, who related chilling details of the vicious killers of whom he wrote in his bestselling book *In Cold Blood*.

(In opening those hearings, Senator Bayh first uttered a phrase that was destined to become a campaign cliché for dozens, if not hundreds, of would-be officeholders in the next several years. "A nation that will spend billions to get a man safely to the moon," he said, "must show the same determination to get him safely to the corner drugstore.")

Even some minority justices in *Miranda* retained strong feelings, as they demonstrated in an unrelated case on whether a blood test of a suspected drunk driver constituted self-incrimination. The majority was made up of the four *Miranda* dissenters plus Brennan. In writing the opinion, Brennan included some quotes from *Miranda*. Clark warned Brennan that "some of the boys might bolt" unless the *Miranda* references were removed. He was right. Harlan, Stewart, and White all threatened to leave the opinion unless Brennan pulled out the quotes. Brennan just as stubbornly refused. In the end, the three gave in—but not without some bruised feelings.

Some of Clark's own language in a subsequent case, *Keyishian* v. *Board of Regents,* caused the loss of an erstwhile supporter. The case focused on a New York state law requiring teachers to sign a certificate asserting they were not members of the Communist Party. A state university instructor who refused to sign was not rehired, and he sued. The lower court upheld the state law.

At the November 18, 1966, conference, Warren urged reversing the lower court. "Vague statutes can't be employed this way to do someone out of a job," he said. Black, Douglas, and Brennan agreed. Fortas tentatively joined, but indicated he might change his mind.

One reason was that a 1952 opinion of the Court had upheld the very same law. Nonetheless, Brennan, assigned the opinion by Warren, wrote that subsequent opinions had undermined the previous ruling. In any event, he stayed close to Warren's reasoning that the law was unconstitutionally vague.

While Fortas was mulling the opinion over, Clark distributed his dissent. "The majority," it declared, "has by its broadside swept away one of our most precious rights—namely, the right of self-preservation."

Aware that his language was unusually strong, Clark wrote Brennan, "If you think I am too tough on you, please advise what omissions or changes you would like."

Brennan suggested none, probably aware that its tone would drive Fortas firmly into the majority—which it did. Fortas told Brennan he would join him, calling the Clark diatribe "McCarthyistic."

The announcement of the decision on May 29, 1967, was accompanied by what one person there called "some of the most impassioned oratory which followers of the Court had ever seen." Brennan said that Clark's dissent "indulges in richly colored and impassioned hyperbole in assailing the majority decision." And Clark replied that Brennan's assault showed that the dissent "must have hurt."

Still, when it was over, the even-tempered Texan turned smilingly to Brennan and said, "Well, I guess you got the best of that one."

There was no question as to who came out on top when *Bond* v. *Floyd* was argued at the Court. The case was whether the Georgia House of Representatives had unchallenged authority to determine its membership. Julian Bond, at the time one of the few blacks elected to a southern legislature, had been excluded from the Georgia House because of his "unpatriotic" criticism of the country's Vietnam War policies and the "discriminatory" operation of the draft.

Warren believed the exclusion of Bond had racial overtones, although the state maintained the action resulted from Bond's statements. But the key question was whether the federal courts had jurisdiction. Warren's canny questioning from the Bench at the November 10, 1966, argument put the question to rest.

Georgia's attorney general, Arthur K. Bolton, asserted that the Georgia House, like the Congress, was the sole judge of its members' qualifications. Warren asked what would happen if the House imposed "an unconstitutional qualification."

"Of course, that's not good," Bolton replied.

"Would that give us jurisdiction to determine the propriety of the rejection?" Warren asked.

"Yes," Bolton said.

"Where is the dividing line?" Warren asked.

The Georgia attorney general said, "Whether constitutional rights were violated."

Warren then asked, hypothetically, if Bolton thought there should be judicial relief if the Georgia legislature had excluded Bond because he was black.

Bolton, possibly wishing to please, unhesitatingly conceded that if the expulsion had been racially motivated, the federal court could step in and reverse it.

With that, Warren leaned back in triumph. Having conceded that the courts had jurisdiction over the violation of *any* constitutional right—in this case, racial equality—neither Georgia nor

Bolton could argue logically that the courts had no business protecting *another* constitutional right—in Bond's case, free speech.

Warren wrote the opinion himself, concluding that if Bond had been an ordinary citizen, his statements could not have been the basis for any criminal penalty or state-imposed disadvantage. A representative of the people, he wrote, had at least as broad a right to free expression as an ordinary citizen.

When the decision was handed down on December 5, 1966, all nine justices were united again on an issue involving race, albeit somewhat obliquely.

Unity on any issue was becoming a rare commodity for the Court. But after the Court term ended in June 1967, events restored Warren to his position of leading a solid majority.

Tom Clark decided to resign from the Bench so that his son might become Lyndon Johnson's Attorney General.

Justice Clark's decision to avoid a conflict of interest by making way for Ramsey Clark's advancement was in marked contrast to a similar circumstance thirty-seven years earlier. Then, when Chief Justice William Howard Taft died, President Hoover offered the seat to Charles Evans Hughes. The President reportedly was confident that Hughes would turn down the position because Charles Evans Hughes, Jr., then was Solicitor General of the United States. In that case, however, the son resigned, abandoning his career in government, to make way for the father.

Though Earl Warren and Tom Clark had been close friends, and despite Warren's ability to move Clark to the Chief's position in a number of important cases, Clark remained adamantly independent of Warren's view in most criminal and subversion cases.

When Thurgood Marshall became Clark's successor, however, he became a reliable fifth vote for the Chief when he wanted it and needed it.

Great-grandson of a slave and son of a Pullman steward, Marshall gained national prominence when, as head of the NAACP Legal Defense Fund, he was chief counsel in *Brown* v. *Board of Education.*

President Kennedy had appointed Marshall to the United States Court of Appeals for the Second Circuit in 1961, and

Johnson had appointed him Solicitor General in 1965. When Marshall expressed reluctance at leaving his lifetime appointment to the Bench for the vagaries of the Justice Department position, Johnson is reported to have used his legendary powers of persuasion.

"I want folks to walk down the hall at the Justice Department," Johnson is said to have told Marshall, "and look in the door and see a nigger sitting there."

Johnson had something similar in mind when elevating Marshall to the Court. Justice Douglas wrote, accurately but rather meanly, "Marshall was named simply because he was black." Johnson's own recollection of his motives might have contained a large dollop of self-congratulation, but probably was honest:

> I figured he'd be a great example to younger kids [Johnson told biographer Doris Kearns]. There was probably not a Negro in America who didn't know about Thurgood's appointment. All over America that day Negro parents looked at their children a little differently, thousands of mothers looked across the breakfast table and said, "Now maybe this will happen to my child someday." I bet from one coast to the other there was a rash of new mothers naming their newborn sons Thurgood.

Warren welcomed the appointment—at least outwardly. "All of us know Thurgood," he wrote the President, "and will welcome him to the Court in the belief that he will make a real contribution."

There was serious question about Marshall's judicial capability, however. In January 1962, after Marshall's appointment to the United States Court of Appeals, one of his outstanding colleagues, Judge Henry J. Friendly, assessed Marshall's first months on the Bench.

In a letter to Frankfurter, Friendly wrote that Marshall "seems easily led. I do not have the feeling that he realizes the difficulties of his job and is burning the midnight oil in an effort to conquer them. . . . All this makes life fairly easy for him, save when he is confronted with a difference of opinion, and he tosses a coin." A month later, Friendly wrote in another letter to Frankfurter, "I continue to be alarmed by Marshall's willingness to arrive at quick decisions on issues he does not understand."

Nothing in Marshall's years on the Supreme Court has caused legal scholars to challenge the early views expressed by Friendly. But Marshall did serve as a judicial extension of Warren's views and those usually held by Douglas, Brennan, and Fortas as well.

The availability of Marshall's vote in support of the Chief's usual judicial views nullified Black's growing apostasy during Warren's final two years on the Bench. Before long, however, the Chief would find himself frequently joining Black in trying to slow the onward rush of constitutional revolution for which the two men, more than most justices in history, had been responsible.

EIGHTEEN

The Final Retreat

THE LATTER-DAY MODIFICATION of Warren's judicial activism was represented by his reaction to the issue of draft-card burning. This method of protesting United States involvement in Vietnam had been introduced in October 1965 in New York by a twenty-two-year-old relief-program worker, David J. Miller. Standing on a sound truck from which he planned to proclaim his opposition to the war, he held up his draft registration card and said, "Instead of the speech I prepared, I'll let this action speak for itself." With that, he held a match to his draft card. Miller was arrested the following August; Congress had enacted a law punishing the willful destruction of Selective Service cards with a $10,000 fine or five years in prison.

It was a similar case which reached the Supreme Court for argument on January 24, 1968. A man had burned his draft card on the steps of the Boston courthouse to demonstrate his anti-war beliefs. His conviction in a lower court was reversed by a federal appellate court as an unconstitutional abridgment of free speech. Counsel in the case, *United States* v. *O'Brien,* argued in the Supreme Court that the draft-card burning was "symbolic speech."

Warren asked from the Bench, "What cases do you have that equate the burning of the draft card to symbolic speech? What if a soldier in Vietnam, in a crowd, broke his weapon? Would it be symbolic speech?"

Warren was not alone in his view, however. At a conference two days later, all his colleagues, including Douglas, agreed that the action should not be considered protected by the First Amendment's guarantee of free speech. The virtual unanimity expressed by the law clerks against the Court's position, however, persuaded Warren that his usual constituency would be upset by the decision.

As a result, Warren tried, in his draft opinion, to maintain that O'Brien's action did not qualify for traditional First Amendment protection. Instead, he followed the approach urged by Black in sit-in cases—distinguishing between speech and conduct. He wrote that "an act unrelated to the employment of language or other inherently expressive symbols is not speech within the First Amendment if, as a matter of fact, the act has an immediate harmful impact" related to "the claimed communication itself." Burning a draft card was such an act, Warren contended.

As expected, Black liked it—but the others did not. Brennan contended that the act of burning a draft card was covered by the First Amendment, but he urged Warren to uphold the conviction because there was "a compelling state interest" to justify a limitation on the exercise of First Amendment rights.

Warren revised his draft, embodying much of Brennan's proposed approach. He recognized the communicative elements of O'Brien's conduct. But he maintained the government possessed "a substantial interest" in prohibiting the destruction of draft cards. Everyone now joined—except Douglas, who decided to issue a dissent challenging the constitutionality of a peacetime draft, an issue not raised in the case.

And those who had accused the Supreme Court of handcuffing the police in *Miranda* and related criminal decisions must have been relieved when Warren wrote the majority opinion supporting the authorities in the so-called Stop and Frisk Case—*Terry* v. *Ohio*.

A Cleveland detective, observing two men he suspected were "casing a job, a stickup," stopped the men, identified himself, and "patted down" their clothing. He found a pistol on one man, who subsequently was convicted of carrying a concealed weapon.

At the first conference on the case, Warren maintained that the detective did not require a reason to think a crime had been committed before having the authority to frisk a suspect. The key questions were, he said, "Did a police officer have probable cause to talk to them, and did he have probable cause to believe his life was in danger?" The Court should also weigh the likelihood that "a trained policeman may react differently from an ordinary citizen." Warren also said that "people don't have to answer and may walk away."

Black agreed that the Court should base its decision on "probable cause and not reasonable suspicion. Does an officer have the right to interrogate people doing peculiar things? I don't know that this is forbidden by anything in the Constitution." He added that a policeman also "has the right to defend himself. I don't want anything said that the police can't make a guy stay until he answers or he stubbornly refuses."

The others agreed unanimously, with Brennan suggesting the basis of probable cause be stated in terms of probable cause to investigate suspicious behavior and probable cause to believe a person might be armed and dangerous.

But Warren's draft of February 9, 1968, muddled the issue. In words likely designed to give pause to his severest critics, Warren wrote that the policeman "was entitled to take reasonable measures to protect himself. . . . A police officer is not required to sacrifice his life on the altar of a doctrinaire judicial scholasticism which ignores the deadly realities of criminal investigation and law enforcement."

However, Warren adopted a confusing balancing approach to determining the measure of probable cause. The greater the intrusion by the policeman, the greater the probable cause he would have to show a judge to make the conviction stick. This, Warren thought, encompassed the reality that street encounters were bound to involve a multitude of variables.

Douglas responded to the draft by urging Warren to accept

revisions he thought would make the opinion more explicit and easier to understand. Douglas suggested that Warren write:

> The common sense of the Constitution requires that an officer be able to take reasonable steps to protect himself when his duty to investigate and prevent crimes leads him to confront persons whom he has probable cause to believe are armed and dangerous. In such circumstances a limited search for arms and other weapons is reasonable.

Black took issue with Warren's balancing test, and Harlan urged rejecting probable cause as a standard altogether. Harlan proposed using an American Law Institute formulation that an officer have "reasonable suspicion" of an impending crime.

Finally, Brennan decided to offer Warren a substitute draft which omitted much of the Chief's pro-police rhetoric and abandoned the probable cause approach.

"I've become acutely concerned," Brennan wrote the Chief, "that the mere fact of our [decision] in *Terry* will be taken by the police all over the country as our license to them to carry on —indeed, widely expand—present 'aggressive surveillance' techniques which the press tells us are being deliberately employed in Miami, Chicago, Detroit, and other ghetto cities. This is happening, of course, in response to the 'crime in the streets' alarms being sounded in this election year in the Congress, the White House, and every governor's office."

By basing the decision on reasonableness, Brennan wrote, "it becomes virtually unnecessary for the police to establish 'probable cause to *arrest*' to support weapons charges; an officer can move against anyone he *suspects* has a weapon and get a conviction if he 'frisks' him and finds one."

Except for the introductory pages and a concluding paragraph, Warren adopted the Brennan draft proposal, and all the justices joined—except for Douglas, who surprised his colleagues by issuing a last-minute dissent.

Warren and Black also carried the day against an effort to reverse the conviction of a man for public drunkenness on grounds that chronic alcoholism was not a crime, much as the

Court ruled in the 1962 case of *Robinson* v. *California* that drug addiction was not a crime.

In this case, *Powell* v. *Texas*, five justices decided to reverse the conviction. Warren, Black, Harlan, and Marshall disagreed. Warren argued that it was not chronic alcoholism that was made a crime, but being drunk in public. On April 30, 1968, Black charged in a draft dissent that "the Court relies on its own notions of the wisdom of this Texas law to erect a constitutional barrier, the desirability of which is far from clear." White then wavered from the majority and decided to vote to uphold the conviction. "I have been back and forth for weeks," he wrote Fortas, "but it is more than likely that I am at rest, at least for now . . . the upshot being that I do not join your opinion . . ." That made a new majority, and Warren assigned the opinion to Marshall (directing one of his own clerks to work with Marshall's office so that "the opinion should be done properly").

Warren remained true to his past in two matters—his unbending adherence to promoting racial equality and unyielding opposition to nearly anything smacking of obscenity.

On obscenity, at this time, Warren had Brennan's support, and the Chief assigned Brennan the opinion in *Ginsberg* v. *New York*. A narrow five-to-four majority had voted at conference to uphold a New York law making it a crime to sell material deemed to be obscene to minors under seventeen, whatever the value to adults.

Brennan developed a position which, to his colleague White, suggested he was "riding both horses in this case—that is, this junk is outside the [protection of the] First Amendment but, if it is not, it still may be kept from children because there is a sufficient reason to do so which overrides both the minor's right to read and the right of the publisher to disseminate. This is admirable eclecticism if it gets four other guys."

White decided to become one of those "guys" even though he said he preferred that the conviction be upheld on grounds that obscenity is outside the First Amendment. "Since the more one stirs, the more this pot boils to no good end, I am not moved to write separately," White said.

Brennan decided to incorporate a notion of "variable obscenity" which would reach material aimed at children even if deemed not to be obscene to adults. Warren, White, and Marshall joined while Harlan concurred. Stewart, who at first dissented, decided to concur also.

Warren also relied on Brennan to win a unanimous Court in *Green* v. *County School Board,* a case testing "freedom of choice" plans for integration. In the case, New Kent County, Virginia, had allowed students of both races to decide which of its two previously segregated schools they preferred to attend. In the three years since "freedom of choice" had been adopted, no whites opted for the school previously designated for blacks, and 85 percent of the black students attended their old school.

"The purpose of *Brown* was to break down segregation," Warren declared at an April 5, 1968, conference, "and the school district must have procedures to do that. So this is a problem of remedy, nothing more. There are alternatives that will do it—and they can't ignore them." Warren said the Court could avoid making a *per se* rule on freedom of choice, however.

Only Black disagreed, maintaining that free choice was the governing principle in school assignments throughout the country. It was not merely a southern plan to comply with desegregation orders.

Warren hoped that Brennan would win Black over and make a unanimous Court. However, Brennan ran into unexpected trouble. His opinion, based on the famous *Brown* decision fourteen years earlier, stressed that "the stigma of inferiority which attaches to Negro children in a dual system originates with the state that creates and maintains such a system. So long as the racial identity ingrained . . . by years of discrimination remains in the system, the stigma of inferiority likewise remains."

Brennan's draft won a quick majority—Warren, Douglas, Stewart, and Fortas throwing in with him. But Harlan and White held back at the May 17 conference on the issue. They objected to the *Brown*-like references to "inferiority," fearing they might unnecessarily anger opponents of integration, making compliance more difficult to obtain.

White also said that modern sociological and psychological

data did not support the "stigma" notion relied upon in the first *Brown* decision. Had he been on the Court in 1954, he said, he would have disagreed with the footnote referring to Gunnar Myrdal's famous work on discrimination in America.

Warren was leery of anyone "fooling around" with the *Brown* decision. But he said he would agree to reasonable modifications if they produced a unanimous Court. Meanwhile, Black suggested some changes in Brennan's draft that would enable him to go along with a decision finding this manifestation of "freedom of choice" unconstitutional. An elated Brennan quickly adopted Black's changes, and deleted the passages that had offended White and, to a lesser extent, Harlan. Although Harlan still expressed dissatisfaction with the "tone" of Brennan's opinion, he agreed that unanimity was essential—and he went along. So did Warren, who preferred stronger references to *Brown* but who knew, more than anyone, the value of a unanimous Court on sensitive issues.

When he joined the opinion in *Green,* Warren wrote Brennan, "When this opinion is handed down, the traffic light will have changed from *Brown* to *Green.* Amen!" The Chief may have been too optimistic (as well as a trifle color-blind), but the decision's impact was reflected in Georgia when Governor Maddox ordered state flags to be flown at half-staff.

As the judicial term was ending, Warren viewed the political scene with some hope.

Lunching with one of his law clerks near the Supreme Court on Saturday, June 1, 1968, the Chief predicted that Senator Robert Kennedy would win the California primary three days later.

Warren was impressed with the size of the crowds that Kennedy had attracted along his route from the Los Angeles airport. "You know," he said, "I'm now persuaded that Bobby Kennedy's going to be elected President."

A few days after Kennedy was shot to death on the night of his primary victory, a glum Earl Warren decided to quit the Court. To be sure, retirement was not a new idea to Warren. He had advocated privately that justices should retire at seventy— until he reached that age himself. Then he said it ought to be seventy-five. Now he was seventy-seven.

But Kennedy's death, in addition to adding weight to the sense of sorrow that had been enveloping Warren since the first Kennedy assassination, the recent murder of Martin Luther King, and the growing national disaffection over the Vietnam War, persuaded him that his old enemy, Richard Nixon, would become President of the United States.

And however deep his consternation at the excesses his own judicial revolution had wrought, Warren shrank from the idea that Nixon would be able to name the new Chief Justice.

On June 11, a week after Kennedy's death, Fortas arranged an appointment for Warren with the President. On June 13, Warren met with Johnson for twenty minutes. Presidential assistant James R. Jones wrote in a memorandum that Warren "came down to say that, because of age, he felt he should retire from the Court, and he said he wanted President Johnson to appoint his successor—someone who felt as Justice Warren did."

Warren told the President his resignation was "effective at your pleasure." The President instructed Attorney General Clark to draft a reply explicitly acknowledging that Johnson "will accept [Warren's] decision to retire effective at such time as a successor is qualified."

On June 17, Warren presided over the last session of the Court term. He expected it would be his last, because Johnson was about to announce his nomination of Fortas to become Chief Justice after Warren's retirement.

As it turned out, however, it would be a long, hot summer for Fortas—and the Chief would not be spared the ignominy of swearing in as President a man he thoroughly despised.

When Johnson announced the nomination of Fortas to be Chief Justice and that of his longtime friend former Congressman Homer Thornberry of Texas to take Fortas' seat as an Associate Justice, an ambitious young Michigan Republican, Robert Griffin, immediately challenged the appointments as "cronyism" by a "lame duck" President.

Griffin, of course, was correct. Thornberry had been nominated to the federal bench by President Kennedy at Vice President Johnson's urging. He was confirmed in July 1963. But he remained in Washington at Johnson's behest well into 1964 because Johnson, then President, told him he needed Thornberry's vote on critical issues before the House Rules Committee.

Griffin insisted that because Johnson had withdrawn from the 1968 campaign for re-election, Warren's replacement should be named by the new President. Even Griffin's leader in the Senate, the venerable Everett McKinley Dirksen, harrumphed at Griffin's intemperate invective. He called Griffin's allegations "frivolous, diaphanous . . . [an] argument that just does not hold water."

"You do not go out looking for an enemy to put him on the Court," Dirksen said. "It's about time we be a little more circumspect about the kind of language we use."

The Senate Judiciary Committee invited Fortas to testify at its confirmation hearings and, to Warren's chagrin, Fortas accepted the invitation—the first nominee for Chief Justice ever to do so.

Fortas was at a double disadvantage. Not only did he decline to answer questions about the judicial process, but he begged to be excused from answering questions about his White House ties on the ground of the executive's need for confidential communications.

For four days, he was the subject of intensive grilling by those who opposed both Johnson and a "liberal" judiciary. Fortas handled himself with supreme confidence and skill, but hardly could conceal his privileged White House status.

Worse, Fortas spoke of his connections to the President in terms bordering on self-aggrandizement. He conceded he attended White House conferences—but on "matters that are very perplexing and that are of critical importance to the President," including "fantastically difficult decisions about the war in Vietnam." In addition, he said he had provided assistance "in that critical and desperate situation" when Detroit was under siege by racial riots.

In the latter case, Fortas admitted seeing Johnson's message ordering federal troops to Detroit, but he did not "approve. . . . The President does not ask my approval."

For hours, Senator Sam J. Ervin of North Carolina and Senator Strom Thurmond of South Carolina berated decisions of the Supreme Court not to their liking.

Thurmond harped on *Mallory* v. *United States,* in which the

Court (in a unanimous 1957 opinion read by Frankfurter) reversed a rape conviction because the accused had not been arraigned promptly as required by the Constitution. That was about eight years before Fortas had joined the Court. But Thurmond, in increasingly disrespectful terms, demanded an answer from Fortas on the justice's opinion of the case.

"With the greatest regret," Fortas said, "I cannot respond to that, because of the constitutional limitation."

"Mallory," Thurmond repeated. "I want that name to ring in your ears. Mallory—a man who raped a woman, admitted his guilt, and the Supreme Court turned him loose on a technicality. . . . Is not that the type of decision calculated to encourage more people to commit rapes and serious crimes? Can you as a justice of the Supreme Court condone such a decision as that?"

Fortas paused, then replied quietly, "Senator, because of my respect for you and my respect for this body, and because of my respect for the Constitution of the United States, and my position as an Associate Justice of the Supreme Court of the United States, I will adhere to the limitation that I believe the Constitution of the United States places upon me—and will not reply to your question as you phrased it."

Fortas' composure and polish in the face of vituperative attacks from segregationists and "hard-liners" on the crime issue should have won him the unbending support of the Senate's liberal wing.

Yet Fortas' openly hawkish positions on Vietnam, and his near braggadocio in describing his apparent sense of indispensability to the President (and, by implication, to the good of the nation), seemed to sap his supporters' will. Before Congress recessed for the national political conventions in August, the pro-Fortas majority of the Senate Judiciary Committee failed to assemble a quorum. The Fortas nomination had to wait.

When the Senate met again after Labor Day, Fortas' opponents had fresh ammunition. There was a report that Johnson had entrusted the rewriting of his 1966 State of the Union message to Fortas and Clark Clifford. A Republican senator, Gordon Allott of Colorado, produced evidence that Fortas had helped draft a bill providing Secret Service protection for presidential candidates. And it was disclosed that Fortas had led an advanced seminar on law at American University for which he was paid fifteen thousand dollars—funds which were raised by private donors described by one senator as representing "a complex of business and financial holdings that scarcely could be extricated from anything touching upon the Court."

When the nomination at last reached the Senate floor in September, Fortas' onetime backer, Dirksen, abandoned him. The mounting unsavory disclosures—plus Fortas' vote in a case which might require setting aside the death penalty in the case of Chicago mass murderer Richard Speck—resulted in the defection of the Illinois senator, who was up for re-election.

When the Senate failed by a fourteen-vote margin to cut off a lackluster filibuster, Fortas asked Johnson to withdraw his name from nomination. The President was furious at the turn of events —but he complied. Warren's resignation would be delayed for a year—and the Court's reputation, which Warren had guarded jealously and held intact throughout the years in which the Court had come under brutal attack, now had been severely damaged.

Although Fortas had asserted in the midst of his crisis that "I cannot and will not be an instrument by which the separation of powers specified in the Constitution is called into question," the truth was, as writer John P. MacKenzie observed, "the principle itself was discredited and diminished by his conduct."

Even two years later, MacKenzie reported, Fortas perceived no conflict in his simultaneous role as justice and presidential adviser:

> In my view [Fortas said], if the President of the United States asks a justice of the Supreme Court or a barber or a priest for advice, he should give it to him. With one exception, which is, of course, you don't discuss anything with the President of the Court's business.
>
> If I had to do it all over again, I'd do it the same way. In the first place, you *can* tell if it's going to come to the Supreme Court. Issues come to the Court refined, polished, and sharpened. But suppose you are wrong. You can disqualify yourself.

Fortas' difficulties, then, had been exacerbated not simply by his close involvement with a President (Vinson and Frankfurter had been the most recent examples of that well-established, if not universally admired, precedent), nor even by financial interests raising conflict-of-interest questions.

What appeared to weaken the resolve of his putative defenders was Fortas' adamant refusal to acknowledge the differences among the roles of justice, barber, or priest in the context of the separation of powers. And that same ethical myopia would result in subsequent, more serious allegations against him—allegations that would force his resignation only a few months later.

Fortas' indiscretions subjected the entire Court to the sort of close scrutiny of private ethical behavior previously reserved for key political figures in the legislative and executive branches—a development which, though not wholly undesirable in a democracy, seriously dimmed the aura of dignity the Court had enjoyed since Reconstruction, even among many of its harshest critics.

Warren remained in the center chair as the Court began its deliberations in October 1968. Johnson made it plain he would not submit another Chief Justice nominee during his "lame duck" period. And despite Vice President Humphrey's incredible late-campaign surge in his campaign for the presidency, the White House expected a Republican victory. A memorandum for the President of October 3 read: "Nixon's views—albeit exaggerated by campaign oratory and compromise—make it highly unlikely that he would pick a successor in the Warren tradition."

But well before the election, Warren himself retreated from "the Warren tradition" when he opposed what may have been one of the Warren Court's most important contributions to the longevity of judicial activism—*Shapiro* v. *Thompson*.

The case grew from the denial of a mother's application for assistance from the government's program of aid to families with dependent children. At the time she applied, she had not resided in her home state for a year—a requirement for all applicants. Congress, in establishing the aid, permitted the states to establish residency requirements which did not exceed a year.

The case first was discussed in conference on May 3, 1968. Warren maintained that "Congress allowed the one-year requirement. . . . I can't see how I can say that the federal statute is unconstitutional." Warren's view was joined by Black, Harlan, Brennan, Stewart, and White.

The Chief's view was challenged on the basis of the constitutional right to travel among states. Warren rejected that notion. People "are still free to move from state to state and to establish residence wherever they please," he argued in his draft opinion of the Court. "There is nothing inherently suspect, arbitrary, or invidious about the durational residency requirements challenged in these cases. . . . The question, stated quite simply, is whether the congressional authorization for durational residence requirements is rationally related to a legitimate legislative purpose. . . . We cannot say that the congressional judgment was unreasonable."

Fortas, writing for the dissenters, maintained simply that the residence requirement was unconstitutional "as an impermissible and unjustified burden on the right to travel."

By the June 13 conference, Brennan switched to Fortas' position while Stewart backed away from supporting Warren. That changed the six-to-three vote in support of the residency requirement to a four-to-four split with Stewart unsure. So the justices decided to order that the issue be reargued in the fall.

In late October 1968, Warren found himself in the minority, supported by Black and Harlan with White passing. Douglas assigned the opinion to Brennan, who decided to use the case to expand the concept of judicial review in equal protection cases.

Brennan introduced the concept he had tried unsuccessfully to expound through Warren in the *O'Brien* case—the concept of "compelling interest." Simply put, the Brennan thesis was that if a state were to limit a "fundamental right," such as the right to travel, it must have a "compelling interest"—rather than merely a "rational interest"—in doing so.

Before long, Brennan won a majority to his "compelling interest" view with Douglas, Stewart, White, Fortas, and Marshall joining him. Stewart had vacillated at first. Later, when Harlan's dissent had included critical comments about two of Stewart's earlier opinions, Stewart decided to write a separate concurrence criticizing the Harlan opinion. Black, meanwhile, decided that he would join Brennan because of an earlier Black opinion supporting the right to reside where one wished; later, Black apparently forgot about that commitment and noted his dissent.

Warren tried to compromise. He said if Brennan removed language categorically forbidding Congress from authorizing state residency requirements, he would go along. Brennan was willing —but the others were not. To skirt the question of congressional power on the issue, Fortas wrote, created "the department of utter confusion." Douglas said he would write separately and the others indicated they would join.

Warren was angry with those who insisted on holding that Congress did not have the authority to establish state residency requirements for aid to dependent children. The holding, he said, was "gratuitous."

He contrasted it with *Street* v. *New York*, where the Court's majority avoided the constitutional issue. Street was convicted of burning an American flag on a street corner. He had heard a news report about the shooting of civil rights activist James Meredith and had rushed outdoors. "We don't need no damn flag," he shouted as the emblem burned. "If they let that happen to Meredith, we don't need an American flag."

"The only question is whether New York can punish public burning of the flag," Warren said at an October 25, 1968, conference. "I think the state can do so to prevent riots and the like. It's conduct—and not speech, or symbolic speech." Black agreed with making the distinction between "speech" and "conduct"— but Harlan led the majority away from the notion that the New York law on flag desecration was at issue. Harlan contended that Street's verbal expression led to his conviction and, therefore, his right to free expression had been abridged.

Black contended that the majority had engaged in "an extraordinary, gymnastic feat. It has struck down a law . . . as a denial of the right of freedom of speech guaranteed by the Constitution of the United States without ever once mentioning the First Amendment." Fortas and White also dissented, making the vote five to four to undo Street's conviction.

The *Shapiro* case would have impact well after Warren left the Court. When the Burger Court decided the landmark abortion case of *Roe* v. *Wade,* for example, it permitted medically supervised abortions because the states did not have a "compelling interest" in prohibiting them.

Both Warren and Black objected to the majority's view in *Shapiro* on grounds that Brennan's "compelling interest" test was an unwarranted expansion of the Court's review power; and they questioned whether the Court was not going too far in *Street* by expanding individual rights at the expense of societal interests. Perhaps the revolutionaries found themselves overwhelmed by their revolution.

If Warren was shrinking from the judicial transilience he had wrought, however, he defended the Court's supremacy to decide any and all questions of jurisdiction and review authority. And although it was abundantly clear that Warren would be unlikely to champion causes favored by the new President, Nixon nonetheless asked Warren to remain on the Bench through June 1969 and to preside at the inauguration.

Despite Warren's outward grace in swearing in Nixon as President on January 20, 1969, the Chief murmured to Herbert Klein immediately after the inaugural ceremony that, but for Nixon, Earl Warren would have been sworn in as President sixteen years earlier.

So it was no surprise when, two months later, Warren was outraged when a Nixon administration emissary privately advocated a judicial outcome compatible with government interests—the same sort of pressure that seemingly had troubled him less when applied by Solicitor General Lee Rankin during the Eisenhower administration.

This time, the action arose from cases involving convicted Soviet agents who claimed they had been subjected to unlawful government wiretapping. The Court refused to accept the government's unsupported assertion that the overheard conversations were irrelevant to the prosecutions; further, the Court rejected the government's motion that the transcripts of conversations be turned over *in camera* to the trial judge, who would release to the defendants only relevant material.

In an opinion by White on March 10, 1969, the Court ordered
the government to turn over all conversations in which the accused was involved or which occurred on the premises of the accused.

In addition to the espionage cases, the ruling affected about
twenty pending cases, including prosecutions of Teamsters'
Union president James R. Hoffa and heavyweight champion Mu-
hammad Ali. (It was through the prosecution of Ali, then known
as Cassius Clay, that the public learned the FBI had been tapping the telephone of civil rights leader Martin Luther King.)

On March 12, Brennan received a telephone call from the Justice Department's new public information officer, Jack Landau, a
former legal affairs correspondent for the Newhouse News Service in Washington. Brennan's daughter-in-law had also been a
Newhouse columnist, and the justice had once agreed to recom-
mend Landau for a journalism fellowship to Harvard University.

Landau, recently employed by the new Attorney General,
John Mitchell, asked to see Brennan on an urgent matter. Lan-
dau, appearing very nervous, paced the room as he spoke to
Brennan.

Mitchell had dispatched him, Landau said, because the March
10 decision requiring disclosure of the tapped conversations
posed "a real crisis" for United States relations with foreign governments. The reason, he said, was that one of the transcripts
which the government was required to yield to Ali's defense lawyers included a conversation between the boxer and a Latin
American embassy. Through that, Landau said the government
feared, it would be disclosed that the FBI had tapped the tele-
phones of numerous foreign embassies in Washington—forty-six
in all, he said the Attorney General had told him.

Could Brennan do anything to limit the obvious consequences
such disclosures would have on United States diplomatic relations?

"Well, now," Brennan said, "I'm not the one who can answer
that. I'll call the Chief Justice." When the two entered Warren's
chambers, Landau had become so nervous he started stuttering.
Warren heard the story out, and replied that the Court might ad-

dress such a request if the government filed a petition for re-hearing.

Landau said that he carried a message from the Attorney General that he would do anything in his power to limit congressional action that might curtail the Court's jurisdiction. Warren later described the incident as an "outrageous . . . deliberate attempt to surreptitiously influence . . . a Court action." Warren called the justices together, reported the incident, asked Brennan to confirm his report, and adjourned the brief conference.

The government filed a petition for rehearing—and the Court rejected it on March 24.

If Warren would brook no interference from the executive, neither would he accept congressional assertions limiting the Court's review authority. Warren might have grown wary of the activist instinct on the Court to extend its powers beyond what he deemed to be acceptable bounds—but he believed strongly that it was for the Court and no one else to decide what those bounds were.

In his final assertion of authority as Chief Justice, Warren took on the Congress, which, after the 1968 election, had voted overwhelmingly to exclude from membership Adam Clayton Powell, the dashing, flamboyant black congressman from Harlem.

Powell's apparent misappropriations of public funds were extraordinary less for the amounts involved than for their nature and for his cavalier attitude toward the allegations. Already a fugitive from his own state (to avoid paying damages awarded a plaintiff he had publicly slandered as "a bag woman"), Powell had spent funds of the House Education and Labor Committee to take a lingering vacation on a Caribbean island with a beautiful woman on the committee payroll. Powell's defense was limited to brash statements suggesting his constituents experienced vicarious pleasures through his exploits—a kind of high living few blacks were able to enjoy.

As if to ratify Powell's bravado, his congressional district, in a special election, returned him to the seat from which he had been excluded. This time, the House said he could reclaim his seat—but on condition of paying a fine of twenty-five thousand dollars.

Before the special election, however, Powell sued to regain his seat, and the suit had been dismissed on the ground that the House of Representatives could determine its own membership. Powell appealed, and Judge Warren E. Burger wrote the opinion of the United States Court of Appeals affirming the trial court's decision. Burger agreed that the courts had no business challenging Congress's decision on the makeup of its own membership.

Warren didn't see it that way. The Chief maintained that Congress had no business asserting an unreviewable power to deny an elected congressman his seat, even though he met all the qualifications for membership enumerated in the Constitution.

"I would render a declaratory judgment that they must seat an elected congressman who meets those qualifications," Warren said at the conference. Stewart said the issue was moot because Powell had since been re-elected and the House had agreed to seat him. Warren disagreed because the House was wrong in trying to assess a portion of Powell's salary.

Even Harlan, who might have been expected to demur on a separation-of-powers issue, found that the House's "basic argument is simply untenable." At Black's suggestion, Warren, who wrote the opinion for the majority (only Stewart dissented, on the question of mootness), added a citation of *Marbury* v. *Madison*—maintaining in his final important opinion that the Supreme Court and no one else will issue the final judgments in constitutional matters.

Warren announced the decision in the Powell case on June 16, 1969. A week later, he swore in his successor—the man whose decision involving congressional versus judicial authority he had just overturned.

It was not a happy day for Warren—nor a happy time. A month earlier, Fortas had been forced to resign over disclosures that in January 1966 he had accepted a "consulting" fee of twenty thousand dollars from a foundation created by financier Louis E. Wolfson. At the time, Wolfson was being investigated by the Securities and Exchange Commission for fraud. When indictments were returned against Wolfson in December 1966, Fortas returned the money.

The public disclosures in *Life* magazine, however, were only a part of Fortas' dealings with the foundation. Attorney General Mitchell met privately with Warren to show him a contract between Fortas and the foundation.

When Mitchell left, Warren called a conference. With Fortas present, Warren told the justices what he had seen—a contract providing for an annual, lifetime fee to Fortas of twenty thousand dollars; after the justice's death, the foundation would continue paying the fee to his widow.

Fortas explained he had paid back the money he had received. One justice asked why Warren had called the conference. "I thought that you should know all that I know about the matter," he replied. He then adjourned the meeting.

In private discussions later, Douglas urged Fortas to fight it out. Fortas' close friend Clark Clifford persuaded him to step down—a result quietly but strongly endorsed by Warren.

Ironically, Douglas would find himself the target of an impeachment effort a year later. The effort was led by House Republican leader Gerald R. Ford (with whom Warren had clashed during the investigation of President Kennedy's murder). A Ford-inspired congressional inquiry examined Douglas' association with the Parvin Foundation. The House committee found that the justice received a fee of twelve thousand dollars a year for his participation in the foundation's concededly creditable endeavors. The problem was that much of the foundation's income came from hotel gambling casinos in which Albert Parvin, a longtime Douglas admirer who had established the foundation, held financial interests.

Stung by the Fortas revelations (and, perhaps, mildly suspicious of Douglas' outside interests), Warren, shortly before his retirement, pressed the federal judiciary to adopt stringent rules of judicial conduct—including a code of ethics, broad financial disclosure, and restraints on off-the-bench income. The rules applied to federal judges below the Supreme Court. But when, on June 13, 1969, Warren tried to get his colleagues to adopt the rules for themselves, they turned him down. A majority voted to delay any action until the following Court term starting in October—when there would be a new Chief Justice.

No action was taken, however—and the new rules for lower court judges were also suspended as too strict.

As he yielded the gavel to his successor, looking down on Richard Nixon dressed in striped trousers and morning coat, Warren must have reflected on what he later termed Nixon's 1968 campaign "exercise in the rhetoric of accusation and recrimination which just increased divisiveness throughout the nation."

But he confided to a law clerk that whomever Nixon might appoint to the Court in the years ahead, "the pendulum swings back and forth" in the Court's response to the public and legal issues confronting it.

In the five years from his retirement until his death, Warren wrote, lectured, raged against the proposal to create a National Court of Appeals, lived to see his bête noire, Nixon, brought low by a Court led by Nixon's own appointee, and enjoyed (or, perhaps, endured) innumerable public tributes to the social and political revolution founded on the Warren Court's innumerable landmark decisions.

One tribute that must have remained as a warm memory, however, occurred in the basement lounge of the law school at Notre Dame University. Hundreds of students had packed the room to hear Warren's lecture. When he concluded to thunderous applause, several students started calling out questions. As the former Chief Justice paused to answer, one student near the back shouted, "Some people have suggested that you'll go down in history with Marshall as one of the two greatest Chief Justices. Do you think . . . ?"

Warren interrupted in a booming voice.

"Could you say that again—a little louder please?" the former Chief called out, breaking into a broad grin. "I'm having a little trouble hearing."

BIBLIOGRAPHY

Acheson, Dean. *Present at the Creation: My Years at the State Department.* New York: Norton, 1969.

Alsop, Stewart. *The Center: People and Power in Political Washington.* New York, Evanston, London: Harper & Row, 1968.

Brinkley, Alan. "A Justice in the Making," New York *Times Book Review,* 1 Aug. 1982, pp. 10, 21.

Brodie, Fawn M. *Thomas Jefferson: An Intimate History.* New York: Norton, 1974.

Chambers, Whittaker. *Witness.* New York: Random House, 1952.

Clayton, James E. *The Making of Justice: The Supreme Court in Action.* New York: Dutton, 1964.

Clendinen, Dudley. "Rulings on School Segregation Key Target for Conservatives," New York *Times,* 17 May 1982, pp. A1, D14.

Cooke, Alistair. *Alistair Cooke's America.* New York: Knopf, 1974.

Cushman, Robert E., and Robert F. Cushman. *Cases in Constitutional Law.* New York: Appleton-Century-Crofts, 1958.

Donovan, Robert J. *Eisenhower: The Inside Story.* New York: Harper, 1956.

———. *Tumultuous Years: The Presidency of Harry S. Truman, 1949–1953.* New York: Norton, 1982.

Douglas, William O. *The Court Years 1939–1975: The Autobiography of William O. Douglas.* New York: Random House, 1980.

Dunne, Gerald. *Hugo Black and the Judicial Revolution.* New York: Simon & Schuster, 1977.

Faulk, John Henry. *Fear on Trial.* New York: Simon & Schuster, 1964.

FitzGerald, Frances. *Fire in the Lake: The Vietnamese and the Americans in Vietnam.* Boston: Little, Brown, 1972.

Frankfurter, Felix. *Felix Frankfurter Reminisces.* Garden City, N.Y.: Doubleday, 1962.

Gailey, Phil, and Linda Greenhouse. "Ehrlichman Disputed on Nixon-Burger Talks," New York *Times,* 11 December 1981, pp. A1, A32.

Garreau, Joel. *The Nine Nations of America.* Boston: Houghton Mifflin, 1981.

Goulden, Joseph C. *The Benchwarmers: The Private World of the*

Powerful Federal Judges. New York: Weybright and Talley, 1974.

Green, Mark J. The Other Government: The Unseen Power of Washington Lawyers. New York: Grossman, 1975.

Greenhouse, Linda. "Even the High Court Discovers That Not All the Facts Are in the Record," New York Times, 21 Feb. 1982, p. E5.

——. "Ex-Justice Abe Fortas . . . Shaped Historic Rulings on Rights," New York Times, 7 April 1982, pp. A1, A15.

——. "The Fall and Rise of the Tenth Amendment," New York Times, 17 Jan. 1982.

——. "Justices Rule States Must Pay to Teach Illegal Alien Pupils," New York Times, 16 June 1982, pp. A1, D22.

Harrell, Mary Ann. Equal Justice Under Law: The Supreme Court in American Life. Washington, D.C.: Federal Bar Association Foundation/National Geographic, 1975.

Hirsch, H. N. The Enigma of Felix Frankfurter. New York: Basic Books, 1981.

Huston, Luther. Pathway to Judgment: A Study of Earl Warren. Philadelphia: Chilton Books, 1966.

Jensen, D. Lowell, vs. Stephen H. Sachs. "A Debate: Pro and Con More Leeway for the Police," New York Times, 28 Feb. 1982, p. E20.

"Judges Judged, by History." Editorial, New York Times, 28 Aug. 1982, p. 22.

Kamisar, Yale. "Yet Again, School Prayer," New York Times, 17 May 1982.

Katcher, Leo. Earl Warren: A Political Autobiography. New York: McGraw-Hill, 1967.

Kaufman, Irving R. "Judges Must Speak Out," New York Times, 30 Jan. 1982, p. A19.

Kearns, Doris. Lyndon Johnson and the American Dream. New York, Hagerstown, San Francisco, London: Harper & Row, 1976.

Kluger, Richard. "He Had a Dream," New York Times Book Review, 1 Aug. 1982, pp. 10–11, 21.

——. Simple Justice: The History of Brown v. Board of Education and Black America's Struggle for Equality. New York: Knopf, 1975.

Lane, Mark. Rush to Judgment: A Critique of the Warren Commission's Inquiry . . . New York, Chicago, San Francisco: Holt, Rinehart & Winston, 1966.

Levy, Leonard W., ed. The Supreme Court Under Earl Warren. New York: Quadrangle Books, 1972.

Lewis, Anthony. Gideon's Trumpet. New York: Random House, 1964.

——. "A Rage to Judge," New York Times, 18 Jan. 1982, p. A19.

————. "Revolutionary Justice," New York *Times Book Review*, 4 July 1982, pp. 1, 17–18.

Lipsen, Charles B., and Stephan Lesher. *Vested Interest: A Lobbyist's Account of Washington Power* . . . Garden City, N.Y.: Doubleday, 1977.

McDowell, Gary L. "Earl Warren's Good Intentions Weren't Enough," *The Wall Street Journal*, 26 Aug. 1982.

MacKenzie, John P. *The Appearance of Justice*. New York: Scribner's, 1974.

Manchester, William. *The Glory and the Dream: A Narrative History of America, 1932–1972.* Boston, Toronto: Little, Brown, 1974.

Margolick, David. "Brandeis Paid Frankfurter to Push His Political Ideas," New York *Times*, 14 Feb. 1982, pp. 1, 58.

————. "When Judges Take a Role in Politics, Secret or Not," New York *Times*, 16 Feb. 1982, p. A16.

Mazo, Earl. *Richard Nixon: A Political and Personal Portrait*. New York: Harper, 1959.

Miller, Merle. *Plain Speaking: An Oral Biography of Harry S. Truman*. New York: Berkeley, 1974.

Morgan, Charles, Jr. *One Man, One Voice*. New York: Holt, Rinehart & Winston, 1979.

Murphy, Bruce Allen. *The Brandeis/Frankfurter Connection*. New York: Oxford, 1982.

Parrish, Michael E. *Felix Frankfurter and His Times: The Reform Years*. New York: Free Press, 1982.

Pollock, Jack Harrison. *Earl Warren: The Judge Who Changed America*. Englewood Cliffs, N.J.: Prentice-Hall, 1979.

Rawls, Wendell, Jr. "Judges' Authority in Prison Reform Attacked," New York *Times*, 18 May 1982, pp. A1, A21.

Schlesinger, Arthur M., Jr. "An Ideological Retainer," New York *Times Book Review*, 21 March 1982, pp. 5, 22–23.

————. *The Imperial Presidency*. Boston: Houghton Mifflin, 1973.

————. *Robert Kennedy and His Times*. Boston: Houghton Mifflin, 1978.

Schwartz, Bernard. *The Law in America: A History*. New York: McGraw-Hill, 1974.

Shogan, Robert. *A Question of Judgment: The Fortas Case and the Struggle for the Supreme Court*. Indianapolis: Bobbs-Merrill, 1972.

Simon, James. *Independent Journey: The Life of William O. Douglas*. New York: Harper & Row, 1980.

Smith, Page. *The Shaping of America: A People's History of the Young Republic*. New York, St. Louis, San Francisco, Düsseldorf, Toronto: McGraw-Hill, 1980.

Taylor, Stuart, Jr. "Attacks on Federal Courts Could Shift Historic Roles," New York *Times*, 16 May 1982, pp. 1, 58.

———. "Hinckley Case and Suspects' Rights," New York *Times*, 25 Feb. 1982, p. A24.

Tocqueville, Alexis de. *Democracy in America*, ed. Phillips Bradley. New York: Vintage, 1945.

Tuchman, Barbara. *Practicing History*. New York: Knopf, 1981.

Warren, Earl. *The Memoirs of Earl Warren*. Garden City, N.Y.: Doubleday, 1977.

Weaver, John D. *Warren: The Man, the Court, the Era*. Boston: Little, Brown, 1967.

Weinreb, Lloyd L. "Judicial Activism," New York *Times*, 3 Feb. 1982, p. A27.

White, G. Edmund. *Earl Warren: A Public Life*. New York: Oxford, 1982.

White, Theodore H. *The Making of the President 1960*. New York: Atheneum, 1961.

———. *The Making of the President 1964*. New York: Atheneum, 1965.

———. *The Making of the President 1968*. New York: Atheneum, 1969.

Wilkins, Roy, with Tom Mathews. *Standing Fast: The Autobiography of Roy Wilkins*. New York: Viking, 1982.

INDEX

Barth, Alan, 130
Bartkus v. *Illinois*, 166–68
Bates, Ruby, 176, 177. *See also Pow-
ell* v. *Alabama*
Bayh, Birch, 251
Beaches, public, integration of, 99
"Beat generation," 141
Bell v. *Maryland*, 220–26
Bentham, Jeremy (Benthamites), 58
Berkeley, University of California at,
9
Betts v. *Brady*, 177–80
Bible reading in public schools, 183
Bickel, Alexander, 26, 37, 91, 208
Biddle, Francis, 138–39
Bill of Rights, 10, 111, 133–34, 145,
200, 230. *See also* specific amend-
ments, aspects, cases
Birch, John. *See* John Birch Soci-
ety
Birmingham, Ala., civil rights movement in, 159, 241–42
Birth control. *See* Contraception
Bismarck, Otto von, 8
Black, Hugo L., 23, 25, 26–27,
30–31, 33, 49, 50–62 *passim*, 69,
77, 82, 99, 100, 122–24, 125, 127,
128, 129, 132, 135, 137, 138,
182–83, 209–10, 230, 231, 233,
235, 245, 246–50, 269, 270, 271;
absolutist view of First Amendment rights, 59–60, 242–43; and
Communist (subversion) cases,
105, 106, 110, 111, 112, 134, 252;
and criminal cases, 122–23, 129,
168, 174–75, 178, 179, 180, 250,
259, 260–61 (*see also* specific
cases); described, 25, 50–56, 58,
59, 61–63, 125, 165, 166, 238;
and Douglas, 61–63, 238, 247,
249–50; and Frankfurter, 5, 31,
52–56, 58–62, 77–78, 123, 124,
128, 130, 138, 199; and Harlan,
125; and Jackson, 5, 51–56, 61;
and judicial activism, 49, 50–62
passim, 128, 165 (*see also* specific
aspects, cases); as judicial alter
ego to Douglas, 61–63; and military jurisdiction cases, 144, 145,

146, 147, 148; and pornography
(obscenity) cases, 174–75,
242–44; "preferred position"
theory of, 111–12; and school
prayer issue, 182–83; and segregation (civil rights) cases, 23, 25,
26–27, 46, 60, 80, 82, 83, 85–86,
89, 97, 98, 163–64, 210, 217, 218,
219, 220–21, 223–26, 239–42,
262–63; and sit-in cases, 217, 218,
219, 220–21, 223–26; and voter
reapportionment cases, 186,
187–88, 190, 191, 192, 193; and
Warren, 5, 31, 238–44, 256
Blacks (Black Americans, Negroes),
3–6, 209–11, 213, 217–27,
239–42, 273–74; first justice appointed to U.S. Supreme Court,
69; first law clerk to Supreme
Court named by Frankfurter, 69;
and franchise, 4, 8, 12 (*see also*
Voter reapportionment); as justices on Supreme Court bench,
69, 201–2, 254–56; and rights of
defendants in criminal trials,
176–80; and segregation (civil
rights) cases, 4–6, 21–27, 41,
45–47, 79–102, 103–4, 155–64,
175–77, 202–5, 209–11, 213,
217–27, 239–42, 253–56, 262–63
(*see also* specific aspects, cases);
and sit-in demonstrations, 4, 60,
213, 217–26; voter reapportionment (*see* Voter reapportionment) Warren Court and, 3–6,
79–102 (*see also* specific aspects,
cases, developments, individuals)
Blood test for drunkenness, 128–29,
173, 251
Blue Laws. *See* Sunday Blue
Laws
Boggs, Hale, 216
Bolling v. *Sharpe*, 87–88
Bolton, Arthur K., 253–54
Bond, Julian, 253–54
Bond v. *Floyd*, 253–54
Bookmaking, 76. *See also* Gam-
bling
Bouvier, *Law Dictionary* of, 50
Bowron, Fletcher, 11

Douglas, William O.); enunciates essence of his political philosophy, 186; and failing health, stroke, 179, 197, 200, 206, 210; and Harlan (*see under* Harlan, John Marshall); and incest case, 178–79; and interest and involvement in politics, 55, 268; on judicial nullification of legislation as undemocratic, 57–58; and law clerks, 37–38, 47, 69; and Learned Hand, 138–39 (*see also under* Hand, Learned); and military jurisdiction cases, 144–47, 149; and pornography cases, 142–43, 172–73, 175; and political activists, 126–27, 130–39; reverence for Fourth Amendment, 200–1; and segregation (civil rights) cases and issues, 4–5, 23–27, 60, 80–82, 83, 84–85, 86, 87, 88, 91, 97, 98, 104, 128, 159, 161–62, 163–64, 210–11, 218; and voter reapportionment, 186, 187, 188–96, 197, 201; and Warren, 5, 30–31, 43–44, 57, 114, 119–20, 123, 124, 127, 128–29, 130–35, 138, 199, 207

Freedom of speech, press, religion, and assembly, 4, 51, 59–60, 105, 142–44, 171–76, 258, 270. *See also* First Amendment; specific cases

Freedom Riders, 202–5, 217
Freund, Paul, 201–2
Friendly, Henry J., 169, 255–56

Gaines case (1938), 21–22
Gambling, 9, 10, 172; bookmaking, 76; wiretapping and, 76–77
Garner v. *Louisiana*, 217–18
Garrison, Jim, 231
Garrison v. *Louisiana*, 231
General Motors Corporation, 135–36
Georgetown University Hospital, 1
Georgia, 70, 92, 120–21, 247–50, 253–54, 263; county unit electoral system struck down, 192; discriminatory electoral system in,

186–87, 192, 248–50. *See also* specific cases, places

Gerry, Elbridge, 184–85; and gerrymandering, 185
Gibson v. *Florida Legislative Investigation Committee*, 210
Gideon, Clarence Earl, 39, 179–80
Gideon's Trumpet (Lewis), 39
Gideon v. *Wainwright*, 39, 179–80
Ginsberg, Allen, 141
Ginsberg v. *New York*, 261–62
Ginzburg, Ralph, 143, 242–45
Girard case, 149–50
Glen Echo amusement park case, 219, 220
Goldberg, Arthur J., 166, 207–9, 211–12, 215, 230, 231, 232, 233; background, described, appointed to Supreme Court, 207–9; and departure from Court for United Nations, 235; and sit-in cases, 218, 220, 221–24, 226; and Warren, 207–9, 211
Golden, Harry, "vertical integration" plan of, 221–22
Goldwater, Barry, 227, 228
Golf course, municipal (Atlanta, Ga.), integration of, 99, 101
Gomillion v. *Lightfoot*, 190–91
Governor's Conference (1943), 12
Graham, Frank Porter, 22
Grant, Ulysses S., 73
Graves, John Temple, 52
Gray v. *Sanders*, 184, 192, 248–50
Great Britain, 70
Great Depression, 3, 106, 141
Greensboro, N. Car., 217
Green v. *County School Board*, 262–63
Greenwood v. *Peacock*, 240
Griffin, Robert, 264–65
Griffin v. *Illinois*, 130–31
Griswold v. *Connecticut*, 229–30, 238
Guest case. *See United States* v. *Guest*
Guilt "beyond a reasonable doubt" requirement, 51
Gunther, John, description of Warren in *Inside U.S.A.* by, 19